Immaterial

Immaterial

Rules in Contemporary Art

SHERRI IRVIN

OXFORD

UNIVERSITY PRESS

OXFORD
UNIVERSITY PRESS

Great Clarendon Street, Oxford, OX2 6DP,
United Kingdom

Oxford University Press is a department of the University of Oxford.
It furthers the University's objective of excellence in research, scholarship,
and education by publishing worldwide. Oxford is a registered trade mark of
Oxford University Press in the UK and in certain other countries

First Edition published in 2022

Impression: 1

Published in the United States of America by Oxford University Press
198 Madison Avenue, New York, NY 10016, United States of America

British Library Cataloguing in Publication Data
Data available

Library of Congress Control Number: 2021941290

ISBN 978–0–19–968821–0

Printed and bound by
CPI Group (UK) Ltd, Croydon, CR0 4YY

To Zed

Contents

Acknowledgments

This book has taken a long time to complete, and some of the ideas have been percolating for over twenty years. I'm grateful to many people for supporting the project, and me, in ways both concrete and intangible.

My doctoral students Stephanie Holt, Zachary Jurgensen, and Madeline Martin-Seaver supported this project as research assistants, and my intellectual life has been greatly enriched by my work with them as well as with Atabak Akhlaghi, Cheryl Frazier, Jeremy Fried, Babak Mohammadizadeh Khoshroo, Angela Black, and Ruth Tallman. I received valuable research assistance from undergraduate students Kelly Koupash, Hannah Neher, and Kiersten Strachan.

Peter Momtchiloff of Oxford University Press has offered helpful guidance and shown admirable patience, while also securing comments from reviewers both early in the project and on the completed draft. I am grateful to the reviewers for their helpful feedback and suggestions.

Shelley Konieczny and Gabe Serrano in the University of Oklahoma Department of Philosophy have provided outstanding administrative support and unfailing kindness. The owners and staff of Gray Owl Coffee and Lazy Circles Brewing in Norman, Oklahoma, and Elemental Coffee in Oklahoma City provided essential refreshments and a welcoming atmosphere.

I'm grateful for the writing time and research opportunities afforded by a National Endowment for the Humanities Summer Stipend, a Franklin Research Grant from the American Philosophical Society, a University of Oklahoma Arts and Humanities Faculty Fellowship, and a University of Oklahoma Humanities Forum Fellowship.

Artists Janine Antoni and Jill Sigman engaged in extensive discussions of their work and provided me with opportunities to learn about many aspects of their creative practice. Sanneke Stigter and Vivian van Saaze were generous in sharing drafts of their work in progress as I was thinking through related issues. In addition to providing feedback and encouragement, Anne Eaton and Ivan Gaskell have invited me to participate in exciting cross-disciplinary research symposia, including repeated opportunities for discussion with Glenn Wharton. I've received valuable feedback on my work at various points from Kathryn Brown, David Davies, Stephen Davies, Dom Lopes, Bob Stecker, and Amie Thomasson. A discussion with Renee van de Vall's interdisciplinary research group, including Deborah Cherry, Hanna Hölling, IJsbrand Hummelen, Tatja Scholte, Sanneke Stigter, and Vivian van Saaze, played an important role in shaping the project. I have been grateful for the friendship, encouragement, and professional collaboration of heather ahtone, Eleen Deprez, Darren Hudson Hick, Karlos Hill, Sheila Lintott, and Paul C. Taylor. Alexander Nehamas agreed many years ago to supervise my dissertation from afar, though I had never studied aesthetics; without his generosity and guidance this project could never have gotten off the ground.

Without having Martin Montminy to talk my ideas through with early on, I would never have earned a PhD or conceived this project. He is a wonderful friend and co-parent. Zed Montminy Irvin has kept me going with delicious cakes and cookies and stimulating conversation, and has been patient with me when I'm sleepy from early morning writing and when I've needed a minute to finish a paragraph.

List of Figures

Introduction

In this book, I focus on a cluster of developments in contemporary art. They have to do with *material* and *what to do with it*. Developments having to do with *material* have been widely recognized: many contemporary artworks are made of materials that are weird or have been put through a weird process on their way to arthood. The material of some artworks is an event instead of an object. For many artworks in new media, it is hard to pin down what the material is at all: neither the "thing" label nor the "event" label works very well. As the material has gotten weirder, the boundaries between (what used to be) different art forms have broken down.

One development about *what do with the material* has been widely noticed: *interactivity*. These days we may be able to walk around in an artwork, eat a piece of it, change its appearance, play with it, or take part of it away with us. A couple of other developments, though, have gotten less mainstream attention. First, the issue of *how to display the material* has gotten vastly more complicated. Some artists spend as much time telling museums how to display things as they spent making the things in the first place. Some artists don't make any things at all! They just tell museums to get some things and display them. Second, there are new questions about *how to take care of the material*, even when it isn't on display. These matters of display and conservation might seem like technical issues that only a museum professional could love. In this book, though, I'll argue that getting a handle on them is crucial to understanding much art these days. They affect what artworks *are* and what they can *mean*. Here is a quick taste of where we're headed.

Pranking Painting

Consider the art of painting up until, say, the late nineteenth century. Paintings were made on (approximately) flat supports. A painting was a picture of something. Displaying the painting was straightforward: the painted surface should face away from the wall, and the picture should be right side up. Conserving the painting was always a complicated business, but it had a central goal: preserving the look and substance of the painted surface.

Now let's think about some twentieth- and twenty-first-century interventions in painting.

Intervention #1: Georg Baselitz (1978)

Georg Baselitz made pictures to be displayed upside down. *The Gleaner* is bending down to glean, but her feet and head are at the top of the painting rather than the bottom (Figure 0.1). Somebody who found *The Gleaner* in an attic (okay, unlikely), and didn't know the figure is supposed to be upside down, would seriously misunderstand it.

Intervention #2: Fiona Banner (2007)

Fiona Banner made a text-based drawing in graphite and framed it (Figure 0.2). She flipped it around and applied the words "Shy Nude" on the back. Then she gave instructions to show it leaning into a corner with the back side, rather than the drawing, facing the audience.

Figure 0.1 Georg Baselitz, *Die Ährenleserin* (The Gleaner), 1978. Oil and egg tempera on canvas, 129⅞ × 98⅜ in. (330.1 × 249.9 cm). Solomon R. Guggenheim Museum, New York. Purchased with funds contributed by Robert and Meryl Meltzer, 1987.
© Georg Baselitz 2022
Artwork photo: Friedrich Rosenstiel, Cologne
Courtesy Archiv Georg Baselitz

Figure 0.2 Fiona Banner, *Shy Nude*, 2007. Graphite on paper with spray paint and aluminum frame. Frame: 50½ × 34¾ in. (128.3 × 88.3 cm).
Richard Brown Baker Fund for Contemporary British Art, 2009.11
© Fiona Banner. Courtesy of the artist and the RISD Museum, Providence, RI

Intervention #3: Saburo Murakami (1957)

Saburo Murakami made a series of *Peeling Pictures* (Figure 0.3). Historically, breaches of the painted surface had been a crisis—something to be stopped, fixed, hidden. Murakami made paintings that are designed to erode via peeling paint, and embraced this erosion as part of the work. (See discussion in Schimmel 1999.)

Intervention #4: Gerald Ferguson (1979–82)

Gerald Ferguson made a series of *Maintenance Paintings*. Each carries a label saying that the "end user" is allowed to repaint it (Figure 0.4). He said, "If someone bought a green painting, for example and felt it would look better white, they could repaint it. That would be aesthetic maintenance."[1]

---

[1] Gerald Ferguson, "Notes on Work: 1970–1989." Undated document supplied by Curator of Collections Shannon Parker at the Art Gallery of Nova Scotia. Punctuation as in original.

Figure 0.3 Saburo Murakami, *Peeling Picture*, 1957. Oil on canvas, 20⅞ × 17¹⁵/₁₆ in. (53 × 45.5 cm).
Collection Axel & May Vervoordt Foundation, Belgium

These interventions changed how we have to understand painting as an art form. They destabilized the connection between the *object* and the *artwork*: if all you have is the object without further information, you don't yet quite know what the artwork is. They also highlighted something that was true all along, though not obvious: works of painting aren't just physical objects, but physical objects governed by rules. These rules were once fixed by social conventions that were so reliably in force that they were invisible: no one would have had to tell you that you should hang Artemisia Gentileschi's early seventeenth-century *Judith Slaying Holofernes* with the picture right side up, facing away from the wall so that it is visible to the viewer, or that preserving the painted surface is essential to avoiding the work's destruction. These rules were obvious enough to go unmentioned—but they were still rules. But one by one, our interventionists (those I've listed, as well as many others) challenged these conventions. Baselitz challenged the idea that the picture must be right side up. Banner challenged the idea that the principal marked surface must be presented to the viewer. Murakami made the work's surface an essentially evolving thing, transforming painting into a time-based

Figure 0.4 Gerald Ferguson, labels on the reverse of *Maintenance Painting No. 30*, 1980–94. Latex on canvas, 12 × 10 in. (30.3 × 25.4 cm).
Collection Art Gallery of Nova Scotia, 2005.801
Gift of Bruce Campbell, Antigonish, Nova Scotia, 2005
Courtesy of the Art Gallery of Nova Scotia. Photograph by RAW Photography

medium. And Ferguson challenged the idea that the viewer must leave the painting alone. These challenges operate by violating conventions that had at previous points applied to all paintings. The violations do two things: they force us to notice the conventions, and they weaken their force.

So: painting involves not just physical things but rules, and we have entered an era in which these rules are not fixed by rote application of convention. Artists can fashion *custom rules* for their work. This means we can no longer walk up to a painting and be sure we know what the rules are. If we see that a painting is hung at different orientations on two different days, does this mean someone hung it wrong at least one of those times? Or does it mean that the artist gave permission to hang it however you like? Or did the artist supply a strict schedule for changing the orientation? All of these possibilities, and others, are open. The artist gets to write the rules. This is what makes the situation I'm describing unique: it's not just that artists are breaking earlier rules—which has surely characterized artistic innovation in many contexts and historical periods—but that they are creating specific, custom rules that partly constitute works in art forms like painting that are often defined in terms of physical media.

The interventions I've listed feel like pranks, and they are. Instead of just making paintings, these artists are remaking painting. Some people find this annoying or boring: annoying because now you need background information just to know what the work is, and boring because all this attention to rules can undermine the attention to creating a surface that is visually satisfying. Why create a really stunning surface if you're just going to give people permission to paint over it or turn it away from the viewer? Neither Ferguson nor Banner has prioritized a visually lush surface.

I'm not here to tell you whether or not these pranks are annoying or boring. But I will say that writing custom rules for the artwork has become a big part of the job for some artists, and the rules themselves have become part of the *medium* that artists are working in. Painting used to mainly involve manipulating *paint*. Now artists can choose to manipulate *paint + rules* to make their work. This point about rules extends well beyond painting and has helped to break down the boundaries of medium in contemporary art. These rules are part of the medium because they help to generate the work's meanings. If it were turned so that the inscribed surface faced the viewer, Fiona Banner's *Shy Nude* couldn't lead us to question, in the same way, the tradition of presenting nude bodies, especially nude female bodies, in art while treating their display as lewd and shameful in other contexts. The rule that thwarts our vision is essential to the way the work makes its point.

Feeling impatient? Here are some FAQs:

Q. Is it good for artists to have the power to write these rules?
A. Sometimes.
Q. What if we lose track of the rules over time?
A. What if we lose a physical chunk of an artwork? Depends how big the chunk is. Same story for rules.
Q. What if the rules aren't followed?
A. Depends how badly they are violated. The work might be destroyed, it might fail to be on display, or things might be mostly fine.
Q. What if audience members don't know (or care) about the rules?
A. Depends how significant the rules are. The audience might miss the work's point entirely, or it might be a minor issue.
Q. Where do the curators, conservators, and other folks who have to follow the rules fit in?
A. Everywhere.
Q. Is this story relevant to contemporary art that doesn't involve the artist devising custom rules?
A. Yes.

These questions are why I've written a whole book. I'll elaborate on the answers in subsequent chapters.

Disclaimers

Philosophy of "contemporary" art

What do I mean by "contemporary"? I don't care very much about the specific details of the definition. There is some art that I want to talk about, and I'm going to slap the label "contemporary art" on it because that's a label other people tend to slap on it.

If you like time periods: most of my examples are from the 1980s and forward, though at some points we will stretch back to 1960. So long ago, right?! Some of my claims about contemporary art apply to works created even earlier in the twentieth century. Is this my fault, or is it because the word "contemporary" is used in a strange way when it comes to art? Or both? You be the judge.

I include works that are obviously "visual" and works that are conceptual or performative but clearly connected to visual art traditions. Many of my examples are of what is often called "conceptual art" when that term is used broadly.[2] This is not because I think all contemporary art is conceptual, or only conceptual art is interesting. But conceptual art is the locus of key developments that affect how we should think even about contemporary artworks that aren't conceptual.

Philosophy of contemporary "art"

I'm not talking about all art made these days. How could I? I focus on art that is linked to the international network of contemporary art galleries, museums, and biennials: art that is shown there, aspires to be shown there, or responds to work shown there. Artists, galleries, museums, and art communities all over the world participate. I like and value many other kinds of art that don't fit this description—art that emerges from local communities or cultural traditions that either aren't in touch with the international gallery scene or just aren't engaging with it—where by "not engaging" I *don't* mean actively rejecting or disdaining, which are ways of

---

[2] Narrowly speaking, conceptual art belongs to a movement mainly of the 1960s and 1970s—though, for some, it stretches as far back as the works of Marcel Duchamp in the early twentieth century—in which, as Sol LeWitt put it, "The idea itself, even if it is not made visual, is as much of a work of art as any finished product" (LeWitt 1967). However, the label 'conceptual' is frequently applied to works of later decades that do not seem to exist as ideas independent of material realizations—and, indeed, where fabricated objects can play quite an important role—if these works also involve questioning of the nature of art, challenge to traditional boundaries among mediums, or reference back to the intention of the artist.

responding that do fall within my purview. But these forms of art won't make much of an appearance here.

"Philosophy" of contemporary art

I am a philosopher, so this is a philosophy of contemporary art, not a history. I won't be examining specific artistic movements and how they influenced one another. I won't be looking much at the historical progression of the developments I discuss, or offering a sociological perspective on the reasons why they came about. Even the interventions in painting I discussed weren't in chronological order—did you notice? I will pay more attention to showing *that* these developments have occurred and are pretty widespread, and showing *why* and *how* this is important: because they affect what artworks can mean and what we need to know about them.

Some of the artworks I'll discuss are important and well known; others are obscure, perhaps rightly so. I chose some because they illustrate a point especially cleanly, some because I happened upon compelling documentation or intriguing details, and still others because they function jointly to show the very different ways that structurally similar rules can shape aesthetic experience and meaning in different contexts. Not all of the works I discuss are of deep art historical significance, but this is, in my view, as it should be. The developments I track are relevant to works both central and marginal; they are not restricted to a remote segment of the contemporary art world.

"Immaterial"??

Lucy Lippard wrote a famous book in which she spoke about the "dematerialization" of art in the late 1960s and early 1970s (Lippard 1973). Martha Buskirk (2003) writes of "the contingent object of contemporary art," also beginning in the 1960s. Art around that time was sometimes sold in the form of unrealized plans, and artists were given to saying things like this:

> The idea becomes a machine that makes the art. (LeWitt 1967)
> The art is formless and sizeless; however the presentation has specific characteristics. (Joseph Kosuth, quoted in Lippard 1973, 72)
> 1. The artist may construct the piece.
> 2. The piece may be fabricated.
> 3. The piece may not be built.
> Each being equal and consistent with the intent of the artist...(Lawrence Weiner, quoted in Lippard 1973, 73–4)

Such declarations by artists, along with the dematerialized structure of many conceptual works, has led some theorists, such as Goldie and Schellekens (2009), to suggest that ideas are the very substance or medium of conceptual art. I will argue, to the contrary, that conceptual artworks are continuous with prior materialized works in that they consist of structures that *express* ideas. The dematerialization of art consists not in a shift from objects to ideas, but in a shift from object-based works with implicit, conventional rules defining a fixed form to works that consist wholly or partly of explicit, custom rules for constituting a display, with rules functioning as a medium that is especially apt for expressing certain kinds of ideas.

Since the "high conceptual" period, art has been substantially rematerialized, but the relation of the artwork to its material has shifted. Whereas a specific fabricated object was once an unquestioned necessity, now the relation between the artwork and the material on display is far more variable. Some artworks have no necessary material: displays are newly constituted for each exhibition and then destroyed, leaving nothing in storage except documents (and, occasionally, not even those). Some artworks have materials that are necessary, but can or must be displayed in different ways on different occasions. Some have a combination of necessary objects and replaceable parts. And even for those with only necessary objects, what can or must be done with these objects varies: some must be carefully preserved in an ideal original state, while others may or must be interacted with or permitted to decay.

How does it happen that this relation varies from work to work? And what are the implications of this variable relation for audience members, for museum practitioners, and for the very nature of the artwork itself? This renegotiation of the relation between the artwork and the material of its display is what this book is about. I won't ignore the artwork's material elements, but I will argue that immaterial elements—like rules—have an equally critical role to play.

1

Rules in Art?

Eat the Candy

Felix Gonzalez-Torres gave us something to eat.

"Untitled" (Portrait of Ross in L.A.),[1] created in 1991, involves a pile of hard candy in colorful wrappers, displayed on the floor of a gallery (Figure 1.1). We are allowed to eat the candy, and the pile is periodically replenished at the institution's discretion, as per Gonzalez-Torres's instructions. *"Untitled" (Portrait of Ross in L.A.)* relates to the death from AIDS of Gonzalez-Torres's lover, Ross Laycock, and the "ideal weight" of the pile, 175 pounds, is often associated with Ross's ideal body weight[2] (Sautman 2003, 8). So the work, while appearing fun-loving and light-hearted, explores issues of mortality and of the squeamishness and fear surrounding AIDS: since this is a portrait of Ross, we are symbolically consuming him, although many would have been reluctant even to touch him during his illness.

"Untitled" (Portrait of Ross in L.A.) and other consumable candy works by Gonzalez-Torres are also compelling in an art context, even for those who know nothing about Ross and his death from AIDS: it can be wonderful, after spending a day in a museum looking at beautiful, remote, perplexing things, to be able to pick up a piece of an artwork and lay claim to it, or, better yet, to be able to eat it and appreciate its sweetness. There is something generous about these works (and something interesting about the way they enlist the museum, usually a great protector of artworks from audiences, in this generosity). These works—often known as candy spills—also raise questions about the nature of the experience we expect and receive from art. We tend to treat artworks as great cultural treasures, but is the enrichment we receive from them, especially after museum fatigue has set in, really greater than the fleeting but real and immediate enjoyment of a piece of candy? To what extent should artists play to the viewer's desire for a reward?

It should be immediately clear that this work is not like a traditional sculpture: the stuff we see was not fabricated by the artist and isn't essential to the work.

---

[1] This discussion of *"Untitled" (Portrait of Ross in L.A.)* is revised from Irvin 2008. I follow the artist's preference, confirmed by the Felix Gonzalez-Torres Foundation, for the word "untitled" to appear in quotation marks.

[2] While the interpretation associating the ideal weight of the pile with Ross's ideal body weight is widespread, the Felix Gonzalez-Torres Foundation suggests that the artist did not wish to restrict the work to this interpretation (correspondence with Caitlin Burkhart, October 12, 2018).

Figure 1.1 Felix Gonzalez-Torres, *"Untitled" (Portrait of Ross in L.A.)*, 1991. Candies in variously colored wrappers, endless supply. Overall dimensions vary with installation. Ideal weight: 175 lb. Installation view: Objects of Wonder: From Pedestal to Interaction, ARoS Aarhus Kunstmuseum, Aarhus, Denmark, October 12, 2019– March 1, 2020. Cur. Pernille Taagard Dinesen.
Photographer: Lise Balsby
© Felix Gonzalez-Torres
Courtesy of The Felix Gonzalez-Torres Foundation

Indeed, the work can survive 100 percent replacement of the stuff. So what kind of thing is Gonzalez-Torres's work? It is not identical to the particular candies that are dumped on the floor the first day of the exhibition. Is it a *pile* of candy, where a pile is a physical entity that can survive the gradual replacement of all the particular items it contained when it was first constituted? This possibility is interpretatively attractive, in that a pile of candy is similar to a human body in this respect: human bodies are physical objects that survive the gradual replacement of their physical components. In this way, then, the construal of the work as a pile of candy would connect it to the body of Ross.[3]

   If the work were a pile of candies, however, the work would cease to exist whenever the pile ceases to exist. Were the curators negligent in restocking the candies on a busy weekend, the work might accidentally be destroyed. And were the museum to discard the remaining candies between exhibitions, they would have destroyed the work. But in fact, there is nothing in critical or institutional

---

[3] I am grateful to Jason Southworth for this point.

practice to support the idea that the work can be destroyed in this way, or that it is an entity with discontinuous existence. Works of this type, which involve the assembly of new materials for each display, continue to belong to museum collections, and are spoken of by critics in the present tense, even when years elapse between exhibitions. Moreover, regarding the work as existing discontinuously would make it out to be a very odd sort of thing indeed: a non-contiguous entity in four-dimensional space-time, made up of a series of piles.

Gonzalez-Torres's work thus has a complex relationship to any particular pile of candies through which it is presented: it clearly is not identical to the pile, and it is constituted by some pile or other at most partially and intermittently. To see why the nature of the work matters, let us consider some hypothetical scenarios where things go a bit differently than they have gone in the real world.

Static Pile: In selling the work to the museum, the artist delivers a particular 175-pound batch of candy, with instructions that, for display, the candy is to be placed in a pile in the corner of the room and should not be touched by viewers.

Vanishing Pile: The work resembles the actual case in all respects except that the artist's instructions specify that when all the candies have been eaten, they are not to be replenished.

Stingy Curator: The instructions are the same as in the actual case (the candies may be eaten and periodically replenished), but the museum curator decides that visitors should not be allowed to eat the candies. Thus, the presentation ends up being the same as that specified in *Static Pile*.[4]

How should we understand the work in these cases? It seems that in the *Static Pile* scenario, the work functions like a traditional sculpture. The artist is presenting the pile of candies as an artifact to be put on display, stored between exhibitions, and so forth. In the absence of any indication to the contrary, the candies will be treated by the institution as essential to the work and will thus be subjected to careful storage and conservation procedures. This is because preservation of objects supplied by the artist remains the default procedure: this default can be overturned, but something has to be done to overturn it. The stuff is essential to this work.

The work in *Static Pile* has to be understood differently than the real *"Untitled" (Portrait of Ross in L.A.)*. It does not offer the same sense of generosity; it does not challenge the taboos associated with AIDS in the same way; and rather than

---

[4] Ann Temkin (1999, 48) mentions that, once the candies originally used to realize Gonzalez-Torres's work become unavailable, "[t]he museum might stop allowing people to take the candies (explaining in a label that they would once have been allowed to do so)." However, the Felix Gonzalez-Torres Foundation clarifies that substitution of other candies would be permissible (correspondence with Caitlin Burkhart, October 12, 2018).

poking fun at the distance that institutions often impose between artworks and viewers by subverting it and allowing the candy to be consumed, it pokes fun at this distance by preserving it and directing it at an object with respect to which such distance seems completely ridiculous. The work still comments on many of the same issues, but coldly and sarcastically rather than in a playful and inviting way: since Ross has AIDS, we cannot physically engage even with his symbolic stand-in; since artworks are precious objects with which we are not permitted to engage, we cannot eat even a simple, easily replaceable piece of candy on the floor of a gallery, as long as it is part of an artwork. This version of the work takes the institutional imposition of distance as an unfortunate given, a lamentable convention that we're stuck with, whereas Gonzalez-Torres's actual work, rather than adopting such a defeatist mode, proposes that this distance is something art can lightheartedly traverse. The nature of the commentary that the work of *Static Pile* would make on matters of institutional distance depends upon its essential connection to a particular physical object that will be protected and conserved by the museum.

The work in *Vanishing Pile* is different, in important ways, both from the actual work and from the work in *Static Pile*. Because eating the candies is allowed in *Vanishing Pile*, this work doesn't maintain the sense of institutional distance present in *Static Pile*. But whereas the actual work is characterized by inexhaustibility and generosity, and gives us a tribute in which the artist's love for Ross is immortalized, the work in *Vanishing Pile* confronts us very firmly with the finiteness of things. Each time we take a piece of candy, we must recognize that we are hastening the work's demise, just as Ross's demise was hastened by his disease. Should we eat a piece and thus enjoy the full experience of the work, or should we be frugal, simply imagining what it would be like to eat one of the candies, so that the work can last longer? Who will eat the last candy, and thus consign the work to oblivion? Seeing the work as essentially connected to a particular physical object allows us to understand it as making a particularly poignant commentary on mortality. However, as we see by comparing *Static Pile* with *Vanishing Pile*, the close connection of the work to a particular pile is only one factor among others: works that are closely connected to the same kind of object can have quite different meanings.

Now consider *Stingy Curator*, in which the artist's instructions are exactly as in the actual case: the pile is ideally 175 pounds, but it is permissible for audience members to eat the candies, and the pile may be replenished indefinitely. However, a curator decides, for some reason, that audience members are not to be allowed to eat the candies; or perhaps museum guards are unaware of the instruction that the candies may be eaten, and they thus prevent audience members from approaching them.

Notice that what the audience will experience, in *Stingy Curator*, is just what they would have experienced in *Static Pile*. And the evolution (or lack thereof) of the pile of candies will also be the same as in *Static Pile*. That is, the display will be precisely the same in both cases. But should we therefore interpret *the work* as being different than it is in the actual case? No: the curator's choice doesn't change the work's meanings. It might make it harder for audience members to *grasp* the work, just as hanging a painting upside down might make it more difficult for the audience to grasp the work. But it does not change what it is appropriate to say in interpretation or evaluation of the work. For this reason, the work in *Stingy Curator* is the same as in the actual case, despite the fact that the presentation differs.

What lessons can we draw from this discussion? First, the artist's artmaking role is not exhausted by the creation of a physical object. Gonzalez-Torres's artmaking activity didn't involve making stuff. Instead, he determined the features of his work by communicating instructions to the museum, giving the work a title, and so forth. Through these activities, he made it the case that *"Untitled" (Portrait of Ross in L.A.)* involves the presentation and, at the gallery's discretion, periodic replenishment of a (roughly) 175-pound pile of candies that can be eaten by viewers. And by these same activities, he made it the case that the artwork is not identical to or essentially connected to any particular stuff. Through a different set of decisions, however, he *could* have made a work that was essentially constituted by a particular pile of candies.

Second, there is a fit between the *nature* of the work and the *meanings* it can have. This is not to say that there is a single right answer to questions about what the work means. But finding meaning in an artwork is a matter of making sense of what is presented, and there are some prominent features of the work that can't be ignored. When the artist makes a work that requires the display of a particular physical object, this makes available different kinds of meaning than if the artist had stipulated that an array of objects with varying features can be presented. Artworks can have different kinds of connection to physical objects, and specifying the connection is part of the artist's creative activity in making the work. Acknowledging differences in the works' natures allows us to acknowledge important differences in their meanings as well.

Third, there is the gap: simply by seeing a particular display we don't know which work we are encountering, and so aren't in a position to recognize the relevant meanings. This means that we will often need at least a bit of background information to understand what the work is.

Crucial takeaways:

(1) The fact that the work is made from non-standard stuff, candy, is essential to its ability to express the meanings it does in the ways that it does: it enables a particular kind of sensory experience and connects the concept of sweetness very directly to Ross.

(2) The specific rules that *we are permitted to eat the candies* and *the museum may replenish them* are essential to the way the work comments on AIDS and on the typical relationship of museum, artwork, and audience member.

(3) To grasp this work fully, we need to know those rules. If you just see an inert pile of candy on the floor, and you don't know you're allowed to take a candy and eat it, you're missing something really important.

Falling Salt

In 2007, Israeli artist Sigalit Landau made a collection of lamps with intricate shades that hang from the ceiling and cast elaborate shadows (Figure 1.2). The shades seem to be made of a white, crystalline material adhering to a metal frame. Their uneven texture and irregular shapes give these objects an appealing idiosyncrasy: if they were installed in a domestic interior they would provide considerable visual interest, but without overwhelming their surrounds. I find these objects easy to enjoy based on their sheer visual appeal. But simply to enjoy them visually would not be to engage with them as artworks; or, at least, it would not be to engage with them as the artworks they are. The title, *Barbed Salt Lamps*, helps

Figure 1.2 Sigalit Landau, *Barbed Salt Lamps*, 2007. Barbed wire and Dead Sea salt. Studio installation view.

Photo by Yotam From
© Sigalit Landau
Courtesy of the artist

us to understand what we are seeing. The white coating is salt, and it covers a framework made of barbed wire. What does it mean to make an artwork out of salt and barbed wire? Barbed wire wounds; salt can be rubbed into a wound. Landau clearly wishes us to be mindful of these connotations: she has sometimes shown the lamps in conjunction with a video of her performance *Barbed Hula* (2000), which shows welts and puncture wounds appearing on her bare skin as she uses a length of barbed wire as a hula hoop.

Landau is Israeli, and to create the lamps she immersed the barbed wire structures in the Dead Sea, allowing salt to crystallize around the structure until the barbed wire was no longer visible. The medium of the work is listed as "barbed wire and Dead Sea salt." Now we have a more specific context for understanding the significance of barbed wire and salt. Barbed wire: a powerful and ubiquitous symbol of oppression, both of Jews by the Nazis in World War II and of Palestinians under Israeli occupation. Salt from the Dead Sea: a tourist attraction; a tonic (unless, of course, it is being rubbed into your wounds); a substance that flows freely between Palestinian and Israeli territory, uncontainable by the barbed wire fences that have been erected to separate the two. This salt is being used to hide the barbed wire, to cover it over with a decorative, innocuous-seeming surface. These genteel objects, whose muted palettes and handmade qualities give them the stamp of luxury, are constructed out of the harshest of materials.

Now let us turn to an aspect of the works that isn't as easy to learn about through the usual channels (titles, wall labels, etc.). The salt coating of the lamps is fragile. As they are exhibited, stored, and relocated, the salt begins to chip away. Most sculptures would be sent for restoration if parts of the material began to fall off. When Rachel Whiteread's plaster sculptures are chipped, there is a very specific procedure: the plaster chips are to be collected, ground down, and mixed with water to form a paste, which is used to fill in the gaps. It is important that the original plaster be used because plaster tends to discolor, and the whiteness of new plaster would stand out against the gray patina the work has acquired over time.[5] But when it comes to the *Barbed Salt Lamps*, Landau specifies that they are not to be restored: the gradual revelation of the barbed wire as the salt is lost is part of the work.[6] Does this matter? How?

Through the use of barbed wire and Dead Sea salt, the works allude to the political context of conflict between Israelis and Palestinians: the salt locates us geographically, and the barbed wire has connotations of separation and confinement. The knowledge that the salt is not to be repaired when it chips off adds a crucial element of meaning to the work: it suggests the cracking over time of a fragile, decorative façade to reveal a brutal underlying structure. Now, consider a

---

[5] Interview with Miami Art Museum Senior Curator Peter Boswell, July 2010.
[6] Interview with Miami Art Museum Senior Curator Peter Boswell, July 2010; Miami Art Museum Conservation Record for *Barbed Salt Lamp 16*.

series of works that look just like these *Barbed Salt Lamps* and were made in the same way and of the same materials. But suppose that the artist has given instructions like the ones Whiteread gave for her plaster table, specifying that the salt is to be painstakingly reattached to the surface every time a piece chips off. Would these works have the same meaning? No: they would not allude in the same way to the notion of a fragile political situation that is destined to crumble. To make fragile objects but cling to the idea that they can be maintained in their original form has different expressive import than to make fragile objects and allow the consequences of their fragility to play out unhindered.

Like Gonzalez-Torres's *"Untitled" (Portrait of Ross in L.A.)*, the lamps are not made of standard artmaking stuff. The nature of the materials matters deeply, not just because they deliver a certain kind of appearance, but also because they contribute crucial meaning elements to the work. In addition, Landau has created a rule governing the works: not a rule permitting interaction, as in *"Untitled" (Portrait of Ross in L.A.)*, but a rule that embraces change over time. The traditional emphasis on conservation and restoration, on maintaining the objects in a pristine state, has yielded to a welcoming of change as an element of the work. This rule converts the medium into a time-based one, even though the pace of change over time is likely to be slow.

Both of these aspects of the work—the significance of the materials used and the embracing of change over time—stem from choices the artist has made in creating and presenting the objects. She made the lamps from barbed wire and Dead Sea salt and also chose to announce that they were made in this way. She highlighted the salience of barbed wire by presenting the lamps in conjunction with another work in which injuries from barbed wire were made manifest. And she specified that the salt is not to be reattached if it drops off. When we encounter the *Barbed Salt Lamps*, we are able to appreciate them more fully by attending to these choices made by the artist and considering how they contribute to the work's meaning. As with *"Untitled" (Portrait of Ross in L.A.)*, to appreciate the *Barbed Salt Lamps* fully we need specific background knowledge. We need to know that the lamps are made from barbed wire and Dead Sea salt. And, ideally, we need to know about the rule that the lamps are not to be restored when salt chips off, since this aspect of the work, too, is laden with meaning.

However, the rule about conservation is not as central to the *Barbed Salt Lamps* as the rule that one may eat the candy is to *"Untitled" (Portrait of Ross in L.A.)*. Landau has gone to great pains in the fabrication of specific objects, and respond-ing to these objects in their materiality is our main task in appreciation. Knowledge of the rule supplies nuance in our thinking about the work's meaning—it is available and may prove fruitful for our interpretative efforts—but this is not to say that a viewer lacking knowledge of the rule will seriously misunderstand the work.

The Artist's Sanction

As our examples show, seeing the physical stuff doesn't fully inform us about which work we are faced with: more than one work is compatible with a particular physical display. To fully appreciate the meanings that are available to us, we need to know the nature of the work the artist created. But what is meant by talk of the work's "nature"? Where does this "nature" come from? A straightforward answer is that the work becomes the kind of thing that it is through a process of making. Artworks are made by artists, and artists are responsible for determining the nature and features of their works. So let's explore this process of artmaking.

The making of a visual artwork is often thought of as a process of fabricating a physical object; and, indeed, such fabrication is often central, as when Sigalit Landau shaped her barbed wire lampshades and immersed them in the Dead Sea. But contemporary art often involves processes of making that are distinct from—and even occasionally exclude—fabrication. In addition to making or selecting some physical object, structure, event, process, or state of affairs, the artist often specifies rules for display, which may include acceptable venues and physical configurations: recall Georg Baselitz's upside-down pictures. I describe this determination of the work's properties through the artist's acts of artmaking as the artist's *sanctioning* of certain features of the work (Irvin 2005b). The artist sanctions physical features by fabricating or selecting a physical object, but may also sanction rules by communicating about how the object should be displayed or treated. The artist's creative activity of sanctioning can place greater emphasis on physical stuff, can focus on rules, or can involve a balance of the two. Gonzalez-Torres and Landau offered sanctions related to both material and rules for its treatment. However, their methods and emphases in doing so were different. In making *"Untitled" (Portrait of Ross in L.A.)*, Felix Gonzalez-Torres didn't fabricate anything at all; he told the museum what kind of material to get and supplied rules for the audience and museum to follow in dealing with it. In making the *Barbed Salt Lamps* (2007), Sigalit Landau fabricated particular objects, but she also sanctioned a rule for their conservation. We will see further examples at many points on the spectrum between material-focused and rule-focused artistic creation.

Not all sanctioning of artwork features is done explicitly. When a set of powerful conventions is in place (painted surface facing the viewer, picture right side up), the artist activates the associated rules just by presenting an object. Artemisia Gentileschi never had to tell anyone how to hang *Self-Portrait as the Allegory of Painting*; we can tell by looking (given a context of knowledge that is so far in the background we don't even realize we're drawing on it). By presenting a particular object, she sanctions the fact that that object is essential to her work, and she also implicitly sanctions rules for displaying it. From our current vantage point, we can even say that she sanctions a rule of non-participation: viewers don't get to come along and repaint the artwork. She sanctions this rule *implicitly* by presenting the object in a context where a non-participation convention is strongly in force—indeed, so strongly in force that no one might ever notice it as a convention at all. The artist need not ever think about or notice the rule to implicitly sanction it.

Longstanding conventions for display, non-participation, and conservation have been destabilized by the interventions we saw in the introduction and by many other contemporary artworks, as we will see in the following chapters. However, they have not been entirely eliminated. There are still *default* rules: when a painting is a picture of something, that picture is hung right side up unless otherwise specified. Audience members are not permitted to alter, rearrange, or remove physical components of the display unless otherwise specified. And so forth. It is now possible for artists to devise custom rules that go against these defaults, but an artist who does not say anything about the rules has not thereby failed to sanction rules. Instead, the default rules are sanctioned, well, by default.

Even today, then, artistic conventions eliminate the need for the artist to explicitly sanction every one of a work's features either by giving the object certain characteristics or by saying something about whether the work has this or that feature. If an artist had to directly specify every possible feature and rule, then no work would ever be completed, because an infinite number of possibilities would have to be ruled out. The artist's sanction determines the artwork's features in the context of conventions that specify default artwork boundaries.

I use the word "sanction" to signify that the artist is not just *making* something, but *presenting and endorsing* it as her work in a given context. When the work is still in the studio and has not yet been exhibited or sold, it may be unclear just what the work is (or will become), since the artist's outward expression of aspects of the work may be incomplete. As we will see, even after the work is first exhibited, there may be continued evolution as the artist communicates—and sometimes makes—decisions about how the objects are to be displayed and treated in the future.

Not every statement by the artist serves to sanction features of the artwork. Sometimes artists make interpretative statements about their work: Sigalit Landau might, for instance, tell us what comment the *Barbed Salt Lamps* are meant to make about the Israeli occupation of Palestine. This sort of interpretative statement might suggest some directions for us to pursue in our interpretative thinking, but it does not constitute a sanction: sanctioning, as part of the creative activity of making the work, operates at the level of determining the work's *features*. The meanings a work can have are constrained, but not wholly determined, by its features. My view, then, doesn't imply that the artist can fix the work's meaning by fiat.

When we try to make sense of a work by attributing themes and meanings to it, we should pay attention to its features. Both the physical features of the presented object and the rules the artist devises are features of the work that we should consider. The artist's sanction constrains interpretation only indirectly, by determining the work's features. The sanction does not establish the ultimate meaning of those features or of the work itself. And when artists make statements about the themes or meanings of their work, we are not bound to accept them; we can assess whether those statements make sense in light of the work's actual features. (See Gover 2012b for a similar point in relation to a work by Benedetto Pietromarchi.)

The sanction is closely related to the artist's intention: artists engage in acts of making, including object fabrication and communication about rules, on the basis of their artistic intentions, and our interest in the artwork is often guided by concern for what the artist intended. However, the sanction may not always correspond to the artist's intention. Artists take great care in the fabrication of their works, and typically the final structure of a work will closely track what the artist intended. However, the structure that is sanctioned can diverge from the artist's intention if the artist's communication is unclear or internally contradictory, includes mistakes, or omits important information. An institution that acquires a contemporary work by a living artist will typically aim to resolve such issues and bring the work into line with the intention where possible; revisions to the work can happen as new information, including new communications from the artist and others who were in dialogue with the artist, come to light. But if no such process of clarification occurs, it may occasionally happen that the work as sanctioned diverges permanently from some aspects of the artist's settled intentions.

Kinds of Rules

We will examine three kinds of rules that contemporary artists tend to customize as part of their artmaking process. First, we have rules for *display*, as when Felix Gonzalez-Torres specifies that the museum should install a 175-pound pile of wrapped hard candy. As conservator Gwynne Ryan (2011, 108) describes, a substantial proportion of contemporary art in museum collections "requires some form of installation and assembly to be accessible to its audience. Unlike a traditional painting or sculpture that exists as an artwork even when it is not on display, these works exist as disassembled parts." The amount of variability that is permitted by rules for display can vary dramatically: some sets of objects must be configured exactly the same way for every display, while in other cases dramatically different arrangements may be permitted or even required.

Second, we have rules for *conservation*, as when Sigalit Landau specifies that the salt of her *Barbed Salt Lamps* is not to be reattached, whereas Rachel Whiteread supplies detailed instructions for repairing damage to her plaster objects. Such rules have increasing prominence in contemporary art, partly due to the use of non-standard materials that degrade more rapidly than traditional artistic materials. Rules for conservation also play a prominent role in works with technological components: since these components are destined for obsolescence, and replacement or repair will eventually become impossible, decisions must be made about whether and how the works will weather such changes. Does a work cease to exist when a particular component ceases to function and replacements are no longer available? Or is it permissible to migrate the work to another sort of technology, preserving the qualities of the display to the extent possible?

Third, we have rules for *participation*, as when Felix Gonzalez-Torres specifies that we may eat the candies, and when Gerald Ferguson specifies that the "end user" may paint over his *Maintenance Paintings* (as described in the introduction). Once we have examined how these three kinds of rules function in a variety of actual works, we will be in a position to step back and examine rules and the artist's sanction from a theoretical perspective.

There are not always hard and fast distinctions among these three kinds of rules. In fact, they are sometimes intertranslatable. We see this in the case of Ferguson's *Maintenance Paintings*. His rule permitting repainting of the surface can be expressed in any of the following ways:

Rule for display: "Displays of this physical object are acceptable, even if its surface has been repainted by its owner."

Rule for conservation: "It is not necessary to protect this painting against repainting of its surface by its owner."

Rule for participation: "It is permissible for the owner of the painting to repaint its surface."

Clearly, display, conservation, and audience participation are not separate issues. I separate the rules into three broad clusters because each kind tends to operate most strongly at particular moments for particular agents who are engaging with the work. Rules for display have particular relevance to the team involved in installing and maintaining a display; rules for conservation guide the work of conservators even when the work is not on display; and rules for participation have special relevance for audience members. Thus, while I separate the rules into three broad categories, we'll see plenty of contact among them.

Methodological Reflections

The aim of this book is to analyze a practice that has become widespread in contemporary art: the practice of artists articulating custom rules that are partly or wholly constitutive of their work. In the following three chapters, we will look in detail at examples of artworks for which the artist has articulated custom rules for display, conservation, and participation. These examples will position us to draw conclusions about the nature of contemporary artworks. Before proceeding to the examples, I'd like to reflect a bit on the method that guides this inquiry.

My ontological theorizing about contemporary art is an exercise in social metaphysics: offering an account of a kind of thing that is constructed by people and plays a role in the social practices of a community (cf. Rohrbaugh 2012, 29–30). This is why I restrict my inquiry to the artworks that have been generated within the visual arts tradition associated with a particular—albeit rather diffuse—community, namely the international gallery and museum system since about 1960. This community's practices have evolved significantly over the past several decades, with implications for the ontology of art. Artworks emerging from a different community with a distinct set of practices would require a different account. For instance, street art, which typically operates outside of institutional spaces and practices, cannot be assimilated to the account I offer here, even as many works of street art are informed by and responsive to some of the phenomena I discuss.[7]

The basic idea is that through its practices, a community can construct things that meet its needs and perform functions for it. As John Searle discusses in *The Construction of Social Reality* (1995), someone may build a wall in order to keep out intruders, but over time a community may come to accept the wall not just as providing a physical barrier but as defining who has *rights* to occupy and use the space. The resulting political boundary, which is a socially defined object, may continue to be respected even once the wall has largely eroded (Searle 1995, 40). The wall thus has not just a physical function as a barrier but, to use Searle's term, a *status function* as a boundary defining rights to the space.

Communities, then, can imbue objects with status functions. A status function is not something an individual can assign by fiat; it is the product of community conventions, practices, or agreement. A status function may be assigned to an individual object through community consensus, or the community may set up institutions that allow for status functions to be assigned through a series of prescribed actions. Once the institution of marriage is established, two people can come to have the status of spouses by engaging in a prescribed ritual (perhaps

---

[7] For discussion of street art, including the inherently rule-defying nature of many street art works, see Bacharach 2015, Chackal 2016, and Riggle 2010.

METHODOLOGICAL REFLECTIONS 23

involving official paperwork), without the need for specific community agreement (Searle 1995, 82).

Searle's original formulation requires that there be some physical object to bear the assigned status function. As Barry Smith (2003), Amie Thomasson (2003), and others have pointed out, however, status functions can arise without being attached to physical objects. When a government makes a law, a bank offers a mortgage, or a new corporation is established, the entity that bears the relevant status function is not a physical object. There may be a physical copy of the bill that was signed into law, but the law itself would survive the destruction of that sheaf of papers and is thus not identical to it. Searle's subsequent formulation of the position in *Making the Social World* (2010) acknowledges that sometimes a status function comes to exist without there being an existing physical object to which the function is assigned.

Searle associates status functions with *institutional facts*, which have a normative character (Searle 2010, 23). If there is a mortgage, it is an institutional fact that one party owes money to another party, and that the creditor has the right to repossess the property designated as collateral in the event of non-payment. If there is a law, it is an institutional fact that relevant individuals or corporations have an obligation to comply and, typically, that some entity is empowered to enforce compliance through a system of penalties or rewards. Searle refers to the normative character of these institutional facts and their corresponding status functions as "deontic powers," including rights and duties, that "provide us with reasons for acting that are independent of our inclinations and desires" (Searle 2010, 9).

Our first task in identifying the nature of the artwork is to figure out which status functions and which institutional facts are associated with it. We'll attempt to ascertain what *functional role* the artwork plays for the relevant community. (The community may be diverse and fragmented in many respects—it may be better understood as a set of overlapping sub-communities—but I will use the singular "community" for terminological simplicity.) What does the artwork do for its community? How does the community understand the work and its functioning? What are the rights and obligations associated with the artwork, and who bears them? Once we have figured out what functional role the artwork plays, we can work on ascertaining what kind of thing it must be in order to play that role.

How can reflecting on the functional artwork-role shed light on the ontological nature of the entity that satisfies that role? Consider again the example of the wall that is imbued with the status of a political boundary. If we reflect on this example (and some actual historical instances), we find that the political boundary can endure even after the wall and all its traces have vanished; and in other cases, a political boundary may come to be through a process that never involved any physical barrier (cf. B. Smith 2003, 290–1). The political boundary, then, is not identical to or essentially constituted by a physical barrier, though it may be connected to one by a genealogical process. This is a negative rather than a positive ontological conclusion: it tells us what the political boundary is not, without telling us what it is. But we'll aim to form a positive ontological view that informs us about what the artwork *is* rather than simply telling us what it is not.

I rely here on an approach much like the "pragmatic constraint" articulated by David Davies:

> Artworks must be entities that can bear the sorts of properties rightly ascribed to what are termed 'works' in our reflective critical and appreciative practice; that are individuated, and that have the modal properties that are reasonably ascribed to 'works', in that practice.   (D. Davies 2004, 18)

While Davies focuses on "critical and appreciative practice," I privilege the practices of art creation, conservation, and curation that are centrally concerned with the artwork's identity and persistence conditions. (The *modal properties* Davies speaks of have to do with the work's being susceptible to change over time or susceptible of having been different under different circumstances. If Felix Gonzalez-Torres had sanctioned a 180-pound pile of candy rather than a 175-pound pile, his work *"Untitled" (Portrait of Ross in L.A.)* would have been a bit different. In our normal practices of identifying artworks, we say that *that same work* could have been different had the circumstances been different.)

A view about the nature of the contemporary artwork, then, is a view about the kind of thing that fills the functional artwork-role for the relevant community. My suggestion is that we begin by paying special attention to the practices in which artists and museum professionals, who are central members of this community, understand themselves to be fixing the nature of the artwork and the conditions for saying the same artwork persists over time; and we then attempt to locate an entity that can play the right role in these practices. Our understanding of the artwork-role must rely on fairly robust aspects of the practices of this community, not on matters that are massively in flux or in dispute. At the same time, perfect consensus is not required: a law or political boundary can exist even though some people choose to violate it, others do not recognize its legitimacy or its very existence, and still others reject the very notion of law or political boundary.

In speaking of a contemporary art community and its practices, I do not assume or imply that this community is extremely tightly knit or its practices homogeneous. Practices of collection, display, and interpretation are divergent, contested, and in flux. However, some aspects of these practices are sufficiently robust to allow us to define the functional role of the contemporary artwork.

What Is the Functional Role of the Artwork?

To identify the functional role of the artwork, we have to look at the practices of the community. This is an empirical project, not something that can be completed from the philosophical armchair. My analysis relies on a number of primary and secondary sources:

(1) documents artists supply to institutions that acquire or display their work
(2) records of correspondence between artists and institutions regarding the conditions of display and conservation
(3) records and recommendations generated by conservators
(4) interviews with and writings by artists about the display and conservation of their works
(5) interviews with conservators and curators about works they have collected and/or displayed
(6) theoretical articles grounded in the above sources
(7) critical discussions of artworks.

Projects in philosophical metaphysics don't usually rely heavily on such data, but in my view, they are essential to our understanding of the relevant practices.

Some broad dimensions of artworld practices are widely shared. Over the last several decades, a now widespread practice has emerged of institutions' accepting and soliciting information from artists about how their works are to be displayed and preserved. A parallel practice has emerged among artists of supplying such information, sometimes proactively and sometimes in response to institutional requests. Every collecting institution I have studied, large or small, encyclopedic or focused on contemporary art, regional or of international prominence, collects such information from the artist, maintains it in a file associated with the artwork, and treats it as authoritative (though not always completely definitive, with implications we will explore later) in decisions regarding the display and conservation of the artwork. There are research groups dedicated to best practices for collecting information upon artwork acquisition, as well as repositories of artist interviews focusing on how specific works should be displayed and conserved.[8]

Researchers working on this topic tie the information collected from the artist to such concepts as the integrity and authenticity of the artwork, which are intimately connected to its identity. As conservator Pip Laurenson of Tate says, "Any discussion of damage or loss quickly moves into the realm of ontology in the

---

[8] These include Artists Documentation Program (http://adp.menil.org/), DOCAM (http://www.docam.ca/), Forging the Future (http://forging-the-future.net/), INCCA (https://www.incca.org/), Inside Installations (https://www.incca.org/articles/project-inside-installations-2004-2007), Matters in Media Art (http://www.tate.org.uk/about/projects/matters-media-art/acquisitions), and the Variable Media Network (http://www.variablemedia.net/).

need to define change against something perceived as the identity of the work" (Laurenson 2006, n.p.). Artists, too, speak of instructions about display and conservation as integral to determining whether and under what circumstances their work persists. When Nam June Paik specifies the replaceability of some components of his work, he explicitly addresses artwork persistence: "If TV sets get old, throw away and buy a new set. *It is still the authentic original.*"[9]

Institutions follow artists' instructions, up to the point of ceasing to display the work or declaring it destroyed if the artist concludes that acceptable displays of the work are no longer possible. Real-world examples include Liz Magor's *Time and Mrs. Tiber*, which Magor has agreed should be moved to the study collection of the National Gallery of Canada when no longer suitable for display (Irvin 2005b, also discussed in Chapter 7), and James Turrell's *Tending, (Blue)*, at the Nasher Sculpture Center, which was declared destroyed by the artist (see Chapter 3 for discussion).

However, there is a strong tendency to continue displaying the work if at all possible, even if the display is not considered ideal; both institutions and artists wish to keep works available and thus often accept imperfect displays, which will be discussed at length in Chapter 9.

These aspects of current practice surrounding contemporary art are sufficiently robust that, in my view, they should be incorporated within an account of the functional role of the artwork. The consideration of a wide variety of examples helps to substantiate this claim.

Of course, practices are not homogeneous. Some institutions have a system for collecting extensive information about the work upon acquisition; others do this information gathering in a more informal and ad hoc way. Some artists are meticulous about supplying additional information whenever it is requested; others eventually move on, leaving the institution to handle any difficulties on its own. (For an example of the latter situation, see van Saaze 2013, 169–72.) Some institutions allow the artist to make rather extensive changes to the rules, even well after the work is acquired; others resist such changes (Irvin 2006; Wharton 2016). The ontological account I offer here does not hinge on attributing agreement in these practices where none exists. However, it can, by offering a systematization of widespread practices, provide guidance for extending central tendencies of those practices to further cases. What should we do when a new situation arises on which the artist's stated rules are silent, if the artist is unavailable or unwilling to engage? What should we do if the artist initiates substantial changes in the rules after acquisition? An understanding of the nature of the artwork can offer insight into such cases by helping us to see in what the work's identity consists and what degree of change it can tolerate while still maintaining that identity.

---

[9] Undated Artist Questionnaire filled out by Nam June Paik for *TV Cello*, Walker Art Center, unpublished. Emphasis added.

The analysis offered here cannot be readily extended to other artistic communities and art forms, because the practices of those communities may be very different from those documented here. There is overlap between contemporary dance practices and contemporary performance art in the visual arts tradition: both dance and performance art practitioners may explore quotidian movement or create sculptural constructions as part of their movement practices, for instance. However, to the extent that they are responding to different histories and traditions, and presenting their works in different contexts where distinct conventions and expectations are operative, it may not be possible to offer an account of the nature of the work of performance art that also applies to the work of dance, however similar some of the performances of these works may appear.[10] Similarly, artistic practices of communities that work largely outside the international contemporary art gallery and museum scene are likely to be far less oriented toward instructions that will be carefully consulted to govern future displays: that is to say, such artistic practices are less likely to be centered on and to support the expression of elaborate rules that are integral to the artwork, because this practice requires the existence of some institution that is receptive to and capable of implementing the rules. The sort of ontological position I will defend here, according to which rules are central to the ontology of the artwork, thus cannot be extended to those works: the functional artwork-role will be different for a community with different practices, and the entity that fulfills that role will be correspondingly different.

Here are the most basic and fundamental aspects of the functional artwork-role. The work is created by one or more artists. It is presented for audience members to encounter, perhaps on multiple distinct occasions; these audience members, including critics and members of the public, experience it and respond to it. Frequently, it is the object of restoration and conservation efforts. Frequently, it is the sort of thing that a museum may collect.

The artwork, then, is a thing that is displayed, that audience members respond to, that may be restored and conserved, and that may be collected. When we identify the artwork, we are identifying the entity that is the target of these practices; and when we make ontological claims about the artwork, we must be sure that we have identified a kind of entity that can play the appropriate role in such practices, as Davies notes with his pragmatic constraint.

There may be no one entity that satisfies all aspects of the artwork-role perfectly. This is because the practices of different constituencies in the community may focus on somewhat different aspects of things. Conservators are essential members of the contemporary art community, and some aspects of conservation practice require a focus on the specifics of material objects: the size of objects for

---

[10] I am grateful to Jill Sigman for discussions on this point.

crating, the chemical composition of materials for restoration purposes, and so forth. Some of these details may be of less interest from a curator's, audience member's, or artist's perspective. The artwork-role from the conservator's perspective, then, may not perfectly match the artwork-role from a different perspective.

Nonetheless, these practices all centrally involve an entity referred to as the artwork. Artworks are what artists take themselves (and are taken by others) to make, what institutions take themselves to acquire and display, and what critics and other audience members take themselves to be appreciating, assessing, and interpreting. And the overlapping sub-communities engaged in each of these activities take themselves to be addressing the same entity: the conservator who collects information about the guidelines for displaying a work, the installers and curators who make decisions about a specific display, the artist, and the audience member who reflects on the work all think of their activities as addressed to the same entity.

When I speak of "the artwork," I'm referring to the entity that occupies the artwork-role. And when I offer an account of the ontological nature of the artwork, I'm answering the question: What sort of thing plays the artwork-role for these various constituencies?

Locating the entity that we should identify with the artwork depends on looking at the specifics of community practices. When an artist and an institution work together to display a work or transfer it into the institution's collection, what is the target of their activities? Careful investigation of examples will help us to answer these questions. We will find that for many contemporary artworks, the artwork-role is played by a structure that involves both fabricated objects and rules for what to do with those objects: how to display them, whether and how to preserve them, and how the audience may engage with them. To set the stage for the consideration of examples, let's look a bit at the notion of rules.

Rules in Games, Music, and Art

I will argue that for many contemporary artworks, the artwork-role is played by a structure that is partly or wholly constituted by *rules*. Some contemporary works are hybrids of rules and fabricated objects, while others are constituted entirely by rules. The following three chapters are dedicated, respectively, to discussion of rules for *display*, which govern how displays of the work should be mounted; rules for *conservation*, which govern treatment of the objects used in displays; and rules for *participation*, which govern whether and how the audience may participate in the display. Here we will examine some fundamentals about rules by considering how they function in games and in musical works.

The rules constituting a contemporary artwork, as I conceive them, are similar to the rules of a game.[11] Game rules consist of instructions that specify a set of required and permitted actions, along with consequences of taking those actions. The normative force of a game's rules is grounded in the project of playing the game: the requirement to dribble the ball rather than simply carrying it in my arms has no force outside of my engagement with the game of basketball.

The rules constituting a game do not sharply define the boundaries of what counts as playing the game: compliance with the rules, narrowly understood, is neither necessary nor sufficient. If we diverge too far from following a game's rules, eventually our activity will cease to count as playing it, but a rule violation, even if intentional, does not immediately disqualify an event as a playing of the game, and some games with clearly defined penalties even incorporate strategic rule-breaking (Fraleigh 2003). Moreover, a form of activity that complies with all requirements and prohibitions but does not engage with permissions may not count as a playing of the game: while a hockey player is never required to shoot the puck during regular play, an event in which players simply pass the puck and refrain from shooting even when the opportunity is clearly available may not count as a playing of hockey (Maitra 2011, 278).

The formal rules underdetermine the game: there is, in addition, an *ethos* consisting of "conventions determining how the formal rules of that game are applied in concrete circumstances" (D'Agostino 1981, 7). For instance, the amount of force required to designate physical contact in basketball as a foul rather than non-foul, or as a flagrant rather than standard foul, may be a matter of ethos rather than formal rules and may vary with the context of play. Ethos also includes normative expectations that are not codified in the formal rules, such as rules of good sportsmanship (Nguyen 2017, 11). The rules of the game can evolve to encompass things that were initially matters of ethos: the governing organizations for professional sports typically aim to codify rules to maximize consistency in officiating and minimize disputed outcomes. But informal play of the same game often returns to ethos some matters that are settled in the formal rules used by professionals. As we will see, contemporary art likewise involves a combination of clearly articulated rules and normative background understandings constituting an ethos.

The rules constituting a contemporary artwork are also similar, in some ways, to a musical score, and some artists and theorists speak of scores for contemporary artworks.[12] A musical score might be understood as a structure of requirements and permissions: to perform a musical work, one is required to produce a sound

---

[11] See Suits 2014 for an influential account of games and constitutive rules. Reiland 2020 surveys views about rule following and offers a detailed account of constitutive rules and rule-governed activity.

[12] E.g., Laurenson 2006, Rinehart 2007. Sol LeWitt said of his wall drawings, "I think of them like a musical score that can be redone by any or some people" (Roberts 2012, 193).

structure that complies with certain constraints while admitting certain types and degrees of variability. As Stephen Davies puts it, "Scores have the function of specifying works by instructing performers on how to produce a performance or on what to produce" (2001, 21). As Davies indicates, the notated score (where one exists) may overdetermine the work in some ways and underdetermine it in others.

> Typically, not everything indicated in the notation has the status of a work-determinative instruction, and not everything work determinative is notated. The player can perform the work on the basis of a score only in the light of a clear understanding of the appropriate notational conventions and of the performance practices assumed by its composer. (S. Davies 2001, 21)

Because of the complicated relationship between the score and the work-determinative instructions, Davies notes (2001, 21), interpreting the score "is not a straightforward matter." The conventions and practices Davies describes play a role comparable to that of the ethos for games: they concern matters not codified in the score that nonetheless have normative force for performers and that help us to grasp how the score should be interpreted. This includes how to interpret concepts deployed in the score (what range of tempos counts as *adagio*?) and how strictly performers are expected to adhere to various indications in the score. As we will see, analogous points apply to the rules constituting contemporary artworks, with the important difference that the lack of notation system and variability of practices surrounding the specification of rules make for an even more fluid interpretative situation in contemporary art.

As Davies indicates, musical works for performance may be thickly or thinly specified.

> If it is thin, the work's determinative properties are comparatively few in number and most of the qualities of a performance are aspects of the performer's interpretation, not of the work as such. The thinner they are, the freer is the performer to control aspects of the performance... By contrast, if the work is thick, a great many of the properties heard in a performance are crucial to its identity and must be reproduced in a fully faithful rendition of the work. The thicker the work, the more the composer controls the sonic detail of its accurate instances. (S. Davies 2001, 20–1)

Some musical works may require the use of specific instruments (Levinson 1980), while others do not. The rules of contemporary art are analogous in both respects: some works require very precise adherence to a detailed set of rules, while others leave a great deal of latitude; and some works require the presentation of a specific fabricated object or a specific type of object, while others are more open as regards the material elements of the display.

In both games and music, the normative force of the rules is grounded in engagement with the activity; if one does not intend to play chess or to perform Tania Léon's *Stride*, then the associated rules do not bind one. Something similar is true in contemporary art: if one does not intend to display or appreciate Felix Gonzalez-Torres's *"Untitled" (Portrait of Ross in L.A.)*, one has no reason to follow or attend to his rules for display and participation. Of course, even if one does not intend to perform a musical work, there may be independent considerations that require or prohibit certain forms of engagement with the work: publicly creating a sound event that recognizably appropriates parts of the structure prescribed by Léon for *Stride*, especially without attribution, may violate both ethical and legal requirements. Likewise, there may be constraints on who can perform *Stride* or display *"Untitled" (Portrait of Ross in L.A.)*. If I pile some wrapped hard candies in the corner of my living room, allow people to take them, and periodically replenish the supply, this is not a display of *"Untitled" (Portrait of Ross in L.A.)*. However, it is possible for such constraints to be suspended: an artist can declare that anyone who intentionally adheres to the rules can create an authentic display. Constraints on appropriation and other forms of unauthorized engagement may be less applicable to games and to musical works passed down informally through a long tradition, especially when they do not have an identifiable creator or author.

In the first instance, the rules of games and musical works govern the activities of players and performers. But they are also relevant to audiences in at least two ways. First, they regulate how audience members may or should engage with the game or performance. The ethos of musical performances may, depending on the performance tradition, specify that the audience should be quiet, engage in call and response, sing along, or applaud at some moments and not others. In contemporary art, some aspects of how audience members may or should participate have been made explicit in the rules associated with the work, as when Felix Gonzalez-Torres specifies that audience members may take the candies.

Second, and crucially, rules are relevant to appreciation. To appreciate an event in basketball, it is important to know what constraints the players are operating within, because these constraints motivate their choices and structure their activity. To appreciate the achievement constituted by a musical performance, it is relevant to know how the performance relates to the score: for instance, which aspects of the performance are improvisatory (reflecting a compositional or quasi-compositional achievement on the part of the performer) and which are interpretations of a sound structure prescribed by the composer.[13] Moreover, as Andrei Marmor discusses, the rules that constitute a game or artistic genre help to

---

[13] For discussion of the view that art appreciation requires attention to the achievement of the artist, see David Davies 2004, especially chapter 4.

structure "the values we associate with the game [or genre] and a whole range of evaluative discourse that appropriately applies to it" (2009, 36). The rules of chess, for example, constitute a form of activity with specific values embedded within it, including "intellectual skills of strategic computation [and] memory" (2009, 36). Awareness of rules is necessary for appropriate evaluative judgments about "what counts as an elegant move or sloppy one, a brilliant strategy as opposed to a reckless one, and so on" (2009, 37). Something similar is true of contemporary artworks: when artists devise specific rules to govern matters that might previously have been left to the ethos of artistic practice—for instance, when they articulate specific rules about whether and how the objects they fabricate should be subjected to conservation treatment—they thereby both constitute and signal the importance of specific kinds of values that appreciators should attend to.

What makes it the case that a game or musical work exists and is constituted by these rules rather than those? Games and musical works are created, and the rules constituting them are established, in the context of social institutions or practices that treat certain forms of activity (notation in a score, authorization by the National Basketball Association, transmission and uptake through longstanding tradition) as rule-determinative. A rule is in effect if it has been articulated through such a form of activity. Where there is a very clear process for establishing rules, a rule can be in effect even if there is resistance: a governing body may make a rule change against which players, teams, or referees push back. Where the practices surrounding the articulation of rules are less clearly defined, for instance in games that are transmitted through person-to-person teaching without formal notation, uptake by participants may be a key condition that determines whether a rule has been established.[14]

To say that a game or artwork is constituted by rules is not to say that its structure cannot change over time. As Timothy Williamson notes, "in the ordinary sense of 'game', games such as tennis gradually change their rules over time without losing their identity; the constitutive role of the rules is qualified by that of causal continuity" (Williamson 1996, 490). Indrek Reiland proposes accordingly that we "think of games as evolving entities that are at each moment fully constituted" by a set of rules, "but that could at the next moment be fully constituted by a different one" (Reiland 2020, 151). I will outline a related

---

[14] As Cristina Bicchieri (2005, especially chapter 1) discusses, the existence of a social norm need not depend on its being followed. I suggest that something similar is true of rules: a community may accept that a rule exists and belongs to the constitutive structure of a game, musical work, or artwork, but have pragmatic or ethical reasons not to follow it: for instance, if a song lyric comes to be understood as offensive or a sports rule is known to create danger of injury to the players. Such situations may lead to explicit rule changes or to evolution in the rules, but in my view the mere fact that a rule is not generally followed does not immediately undermine its status as a rule: it may still have recognized normative force that is overridden by other considerations. Related cases will be discussed in Chapter 9.

understanding of contemporary artworks, noting that both essential material elements and constitutive rules may be subject to evolution.

I should address two distinctions commonly deployed in philosophical discussions: the distinction between *rules* and *conventions*, and that between *constitutive* and *regulative* rules. A convention, as I use the term, is a widespread practice within a community that guides activity in a particular domain. Conventions are part of shared background understanding and may not be expressly articulated. So, for instance, a longstanding convention of painting is to display works so that their pictorial content appears right side up. This convention creates a shared set of expectations between artists and audience members. It is possible for an artist to make a specific rule that contravenes such a convention, as Georg Baselitz did with works like *The Gleaner*, which are to be hung such that their represented subjects are upside down.[15]

Searle (1969) introduces a distinction between *constitutive* rules, which constitute a form of activity, and *regulative* rules, which merely govern a pre-existing form of activity. The rule that you should drive on the right-hand side of the road does not constitute the activity of driving or of driving on the right-hand side of the road; the activity could be fully described in the absence of the rule. But the rules of chess *constitute* the game of chess: the descriptions we could offer without appealing to the rules, such as a description of moving such-and-such a piece here or there on a checkered board, are not descriptions of the activity of playing chess (Searle 2010, 96). My analysis focuses on constitutive rules which, as Marmor describes, "always have a dual function: the rules both constitute the practice, and, at the same time, they regulate conduct within it" (2009, 36). The rules of contemporary art constitute artworks and the practices of displaying them; they also regulate how installers, curators, conservators, and audience members should engage with the works.

I will argue, then, that many contemporary artworks, like games and (on some construals) musical works, have rules as part of their constituting material. These rules serve to determine what counts as a display of the work, to structure forms of activity for museum professionals and audience members, and to constitute the work's expressive content.

---

[15] I use what I take to be the broader colloquial sense of *convention* rather than restricting my use of the term, along the lines of the account offered by David Lewis (1969), to norms or practices that are arbitrary solutions to coordination problems. Presenting paintings with their represented content right side up is far from arbitrary, given how both our necks and our apparatus for processing visual information are structured. But it is nonetheless a widespread practice that structures mutual expectations and can be suspended by an expressed rule to the contrary.

Who Makes the Rules?

My account recognizes significant authority for artists to sanction custom rules for display, conservation, and participation. This authority is not sui generis, but a function of the evolution of art community practices. Artists' interventions to establish new conditions for display, conservation, and participation have gradually received uptake by art institutions, leading to the emergence of new social practices such as the now widespread practice of gathering explicit information about the rules for displaying and conserving newly acquired works. Through these social practices, sanctioning rules has become an established aspect of contemporary artmaking. It is now possible for artists to do things they could not have done, and to make works they could not have made, a hundred years ago.

There are constraints on how far rule-making can go: if artists want their works to be collected, to be displayed and treated in accordance with their sanction, and to be taken seriously, they must restrict their rules so as not to endanger audiences, museum staff, architectural structures, or other artworks; and—especially if they are not already well established—they must create works that do not excessively tax institutional resources. Institutions sometimes decline to meet artists' demands. But the level of commitment institutions are willing to make has increased: there is now an expectation that when a museum acquires a complex work of contemporary art, it may need to establish special measures to manage both the physical objects and the information about the rules.

The artist's authority to sanction rules does not extend indefinitely after the creation of the work. The work's authenticity is generally understood to reside in an initial creative act, and when artists attempt to make changes to the rules much later a collecting institution may legitimately choose to maintain the version of the work they acquired rather than to accept the artist's proposed changes.[16] For similar reasons, if unanticipated conservation issues arise long after the work was initially created, the institution may rely on an understanding of the work's authenticity that derives from the artist's original creative act in determining whether and how to conserve or replace specific objects, rather than deferring to the artist's current judgment.

The fact that artists can sanction custom rules means that artwork creation does not stop at object fabrication and that some works have an essential component of information about the artist's creative activity that must be maintained in order for the work to persist fully intact. Nothing about this situation implies an absurd or tyrannical level of artistic control; indeed, we will see in Chapter 2 that an artist may use rules to relinquish control over matters that are usually handled through deference to the artist. Because complex rules can be realized only in the context of

---

[16] See Irvin 2006 for discussion of related issues surrounding Jana Sterbak's 1984–5 *I Want You to Feel the Way I Do . . . (The Dress).*

supportive institutional structures, the process of articulating rules is often a deeply collaborative one involving both practical and theoretical discussions that deepen the artist's thinking about their own creative practice. We will see instances in which artists change rules during extended processes of discussion and sometimes negotiation with museum professionals. In my view, there is nothing anomalous about this situation: artists have always made creative decisions for a wide variety of artistic and pragmatic reasons, and sometimes in a context of extensive consultation with or pressure from others.

The possibility for artists to sanction custom rules in making their works is thus a historically specific phenomenon that emerges out of, and is in some ways continuous with, developments in earlier historical moments. What stands out is that for works deploying custom rules, new kinds of information must accompany the fabricated object in order for the work to be understood and, in many cases, to persist at all. This is because information is required to identify the work's very structure, which is not fixed by the conventions of artistic medium.

But even here, it has long been true that to understand an artwork fully, one needs access to information that is not embedded in the fabricated object, such as information about what is depicted, what site and purpose the object was created for, and what surrounding artistic or historical events the artist was responding to. The full significance of the artwork has never been contained within a decontextualized fabricated object, and our ability to apprehend many works has no doubt been compromised by the loss of historical context that is essential to grasping the artist's project.

Works involving custom rules create a risk of new kinds of artwork erosion: if museums do not maintain their systems for collecting and preserving work-specific information, works that are governed by custom rules will eventually be reduced to fabricated objects, and some aspects of their specific nature as artworks will be lost. In some instances, the work may be destroyed by loss of information, even if future audiences are not aware that what they are encountering is a relic and not the artwork the artist originally created. Of course, loss of information about the historical context in which a work was created has always created a risk of misunderstanding. The difference is that for contemporary artworks with custom rules, loss of information functions more like the loss of a physical piece of the fabricated object: if we lose the rules we are directly losing parts of the work's very structure.

Artists can, of course, be frivolous, grandiose, or unreasonable in sanctioning custom rules, and the whole situation of artists being able to carve out custom boundaries for their work, pushing back against a longstanding ethos of artworks with fixed form, is a curious one. But when used well, custom rules can eventuate in artworks that have distinctive expressive potential, critique social and institutional power structures, invite us to engage our agency, and foster the formation of community. Custom rules are a powerful addition to the arsenal of creative resources that artists can draw on to pursue their projects.

Rule-Making or Rule-Breaking?

Contemporary art is often chaotic, so it might seem surprising to suggest that rules are at issue. We might walk into a museum and find a bunch of tiny sculptures made out of toilet paper squares, or a ritual carried out in a hut made of used water bottles or defunct electronic components. The same work might look completely different on different viewings. The artist may not have made, or ever seen or touched, any of what we see. The objects may decay over time, or they may be accidentally tossed out with the trash. These developments might be chalked up to rapid innovation in the form of rule-breaking: artists are throwing out old conventions and art forms and operating in a new landscape where anything goes. This makes it hard for audience members to know what to focus on or how to appreciate it, because the standards of artistic value have been thrown out along with the rules and conventions that were previously operative.[17]

It is true that art for well over a century has been characterized by a turn to rule-breaking and rapid innovation. And characterizing artistic innovation in terms of the development of new rules is not new: even in the late eighteenth century, Kant spoke of the production of a great artist in terms of nature giving a "new rule" to art.[18] Thus, as with most artistic movements, the groundwork for the developments I'm focusing on in contemporary art has been in process for some time. But these developments are not simply an extension of a more general atmosphere of breaking rules, dismantling conventions, or replacing old values and practices with new ones. Though the art forms, materials, and structures that have emerged in contemporary art are extremely diverse, they have been achieved through a specific type of creative activity: the articulation of *custom rules* that govern matters of display, conservation, and participation that were previously fixed by convention. These custom rules are often extremely fine-grained, though occasionally they govern multiple works in an artist's oeuvre.

The emergence of custom rules for display has made it possible for artists to conceive large, complex, multi-object works that may be disassembled between displays and may be subject to variable configurations. The emergence of custom rules for conservation, especially in combination with the use of non-standard

---

[17] Rosalind Krauss tells a story like this about the decline of artistic media, to be discussed in Chapter 6.

[18] Kant 1790/1987, 186. While I don't want to delve into interpretation of Kant, it is clear that he meant something quite different than I do in speaking of new rules: he focused on unarticulated rules that emerged from the artist's body of work and was not speaking of work-specific rules governing matters of conservation or display.

materials, has made it possible for artists to shape the evolution over time of objects, incorporating an explicitly time-based element into visual art forms that have historically been characterized by an attempt to restrict the evolution of art objects to only a narrow range of changes, such as craquelure, associated with the respectable patina of age. The emergence of custom rules for participation has allowed audience members to be actively involved in the constitution of displays, from which they had previously been excluded.

My claim is not that phenomena such as complex configurations, evolving objects, and audience participation are historically unprecedented, but that despite their diversity and the diversity of form and content of the resulting works, they can be accounted for through a common mechanism, the articulation of custom rules. Identifying an entrenched convention, such as *preserve the painted surface*, and articulating a contrary rule governing the specific work, such as *allow the painted surface to deteriorate* or *repaint the surface at will*, is a specific form of artistic practice that has become widespread over the last several decades and has led museums to alter their practices of acquisition, conservation, and display. The practice of articulating custom rules is the common scaffolding for a variety of art forms and artistic developments that may seem remarkably heterogeneous on their face.

Is this a good thing? As with many artistic resources, custom rules can be used well or poorly. The resulting works can seem gimmicky and may frustrate our expectations, especially if we arrive expecting the work's value to be accessible in direct encounter but come to realize that critical information is not available just by contemplating the display and applying background knowledge that would have sufficed for works of an earlier historical moment. Some works involving custom rules create tremendous challenges for museums: they can be extremely demanding to acquire, store, conserve, and display. But such works can also make available new kinds of sensory, intellectual, participatory, and immersive experiences. My aim here is not to defend the value of these developments, but simply to identify the common structure underlying a diverse array of artistic developments and trace its implications for the nature, understanding, interpretation, and appreciation of contemporary art. Along the way, we will take a careful look at a variety of works, and hopefully this will foster both an honest assessment of the ways this strategy can go wrong and an appreciation for the value it yields when it goes right.

2

Rules for Display

Generally speaking, there is a right way to display an artwork. Almost every painting has a right side up. Traditionally, the painting was right side up when the picture on the painted surface was right side up; but there is nothing essential about that rule, as Georg Baselitz showed us. Sculptures, too, typically have a top and a bottom. When there is a correct orientation for the objects making up an artwork, this is a *rule for display*.

Zhan Wang's (2006) *Urban Landscape: Beijing* involves hundreds of stainless-steel kitchen implements (Figure 2.1). Zhan did not fabricate these implements; his artmaking activity involved selecting them and devising an arrangement that cleverly represents Beijing. Clearly, correct configuration is crucial to the work, which otherwise would be just a collection of pots and pans. If a museum receives all the kitchen implements that are needed to construct a display of *Urban Landscape: Beijing* but lacks rules about how to arrange the implements, they don't yet "have" the work.

In addition, many artworks of the last several decades involve multiple objects that are subject to *variable display*: they can or must be configured differently depending on the space in which they are installed and other factors. There are limits on the nature and scope of variability, and these limits vary from work to work; the variability among displays may be subtle or dramatic.

Sometimes the artist's principal activity is object fabrication, with rules for display playing a subordinate role, and sometimes the rules are much more central. In addition, there is a spectrum from very precise rules, which specify the arrangement of elements in excruciating detail, to loose rules that permit or even require autonomous decision-making on the part of the people constructing the display. In examining some contrasting cases, we can see how the rules sanctioned by the artist, like fabricated objects, serve as resources for the construction of experiences and meanings.

Precision vs. Openness

Artists' choices about how precisely to constrain displays of their work contribute to how the work functions expressively. To see this, we'll compare a precisely specified work by María Fernanda Cardoso, with rules designed to rein in variability, with a work by Ann Hamilton that embraces variability.

Figure 2.1 Zhan Wang, *Urban Landscape—Beijing*, 2006. Stainless steel tableware. Dimensions variable.

© Zhan Wang
Courtesy of the artist

Colombian artist María Fernanda Cardoso's 1992/1999 *Cemetery—Vertical Garden/Cementerio—jardín vertical* is a complex wall drawing and sculpture that must be reconstituted each time it is exhibited (Figure 2.2). One edition of the work is in the collection of the Pérez Art Museum Miami (PAMM), and the acquisition process involved securing a set of rules that would allow the museum to install the work without the artist's involvement. The work involves an array of crypt shapes that are drawn onto the wall in pencil. Once the drawing is complete, holes are drilled into the wall, and a stem of white artificial flowers is inserted into each hole, creating large clumps of flowers that cross over the boundaries between crypts.

Cardoso supplied extensive handwritten instructions and diagrams, along with a set of full-size templates that the installers lay on the wall to trace the crypt shapes and another set of templates supplying the location of every single hole into which the thousands of stems of white artificial flowers are to be inserted. She gave detailed descriptions of how each stem is to be positioned once inserted in its respective hole (Figure 2.3). For a viewer of the work, it might not be evident that the instructions are so detailed: one might think that the artist (as installation artists sometimes do) had left a great deal of leeway to the museum in deciding just how to install the work. In fact, though, as little as possible is left to chance or to the judgment of the installation team.

Figure 2.2 Maria Fernanda Cardoso, *Cemetery—Vertical Garden/Cementerio—jardín vertical*, 1992/1999. Artificial flowers and pencil on wall. Dimensions variable.
Collection Museum of Contemporary Art San Diego
Museum purchase with funds from Charles C. and Sue K. Edwards, 2000
© Maria Fernanda Cardoso 1992
Photo: Pablo Mason

Ann Hamilton's (1988/1996) *(the capacity of absorption)*, a version of which is also in the PAMM collection, consists of a set of "vortex units" and an old-fashioned telephone mouthpiece that is installed a few feet from them (Figure 2.4). Each vortex unit consists of a wall-mounted glass of water beneath which is a concealed motor that causes a magnet in the water glass to spin, creating a vortex. When no one is speaking into the mouthpiece, the motors operate at maximum speed. But when an audience member speaks into the mouthpiece, the motors slow or stop, depending on the amount of sound produced.

While the work involves detailed instructions about how to install and power the vortex units, significant variability is permitted. A diagram shows how to wire five groups of vortex units in parallel. The importance of parallel wiring, which is required to ensure that each unit receives a uniform amount of power from the common power source, is emphasized in capital letters: "DO NOT LAY OUT THE CIRCUITS IN A CONNECT-THE-DOT FASHION." However, the diagram is only an illustration of the wiring pattern: it does not offer a prescribed configuration of the units. The artist's intention is that the configuration look random, but it is up to the installation team to come up with a configuration that

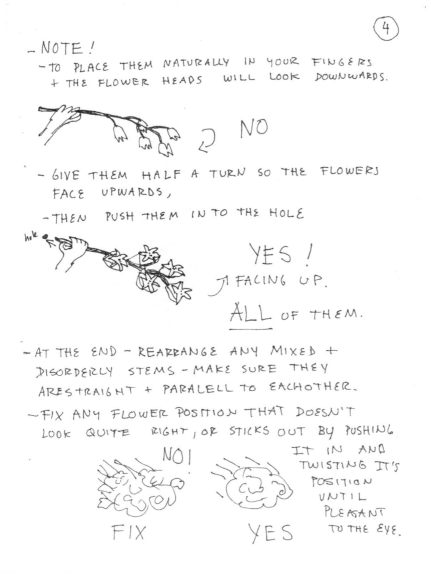

_ NOTE !

   - TO PLACE THEM NATURALLY IN YOUR FINGERS
    + THE FLOWER HEADS WILL LOOK DOWNWARDS.

NO

   - GIVE THEM HALF A TURN SO THE FLOWERS
   FACE UPWARDS,

   - THEN PUSH THEM INTO THE HOLE

hole

YES !
FACING UP.
ALL OF THEM.

_ AT THE END - REARRANGE ANY MIXED +
DISORDERLY STEMS - MAKE SURE THEY
ARE STRAIGHT + PARALELL TO EACHOTHER.

_ FIX ANY FLOWER POSITION THAT DOESN'T
LOOK QUITE RIGHT, OR STICKS OUT BY PUSHING
                  NO !   IT IN AND
                              TWISTING IT'S
                              POSITION
                              UNTIL
                              PLEASANT
     FIX   YES   TO THE EYE.

Figure 2.3 Maria Fernanda Cardoso, instructions for installing *Cemetery—Vertical Garden/Cementerio—jardín vertical*, 1992/1999.
© Maria Fernanda Cardoso. Courtesy of the artist

has the desired look of randomness.[1] Hamilton also does not prescribe the settings for the controller box that determines the precise effect of a given level of noise on the activity of the motors: her instructions say, "Setting the controls really requires

---

[1] Interview of senior curator Peter Boswell by the author, July 2010.

Figure 2.4 Ann Hamilton, *(the capacity of absorption—vortex 30)*, 1988/1996. Thirty glasses, water, magnets, copper pipes, old-style handheld telephone receiver, electronic controller. Dimensions variable.
© Ann Hamilton
Courtesy of Ann Hamilton Studio

just playing around to see what happens...Start with the controls set to the recommended positions...Then start experimenting with the settings." Finally, the scale of the installation can vary: the number of vortex units installed can range from thirty to one hundred.

Both Cardoso and Hamilton supplied extensive installation instructions, but one specified the precise configuration of the work while the other did not. This affects the works' expressive import. Cardoso's *Cemetery—Vertical Garden* uses a combination of drawing and artifact to invite us to consider rituals of mourning. To care for and decorate a gravesite is to express care for the person whose grave it is—unless the decoration is done in a perfunctory fashion, by someone who is going through the motions out of a shallow sense of duty or because they have been commissioned to do so by someone else. To attend to how the flowers are positioned is to manifest one's love and respect for the dead; an act of arranging them any old way, or asking that someone else do so, would fail to express such care.

A gardener typically helps to set in motion processes whose unfolding depends on environmental conditions substantially out of the gardener's control. The wildness of the garden, only partially constrained, constitutes much of the appeal both of gardening and of gardens themselves. Cardoso's work resists these connotations of gardening through the artificiality of the materials and the exertion of extreme control over their configuration. And it makes sense to consider this resistance in relation to grief and mourning. The death of a person one loves is profoundly out of one's control; this work stubbornly refuses to acquiesce in this loss of control, and perhaps in mortality itself, through the very obsessiveness of the installation process.

Returning to Hamilton's (*the capacity of absorption*), the configuration of the vortex units is not prescribed; the aim is for an appearance of randomness. Insofar as randomness is relevant to the work, it seems important that there *not* be a prescription for the work to be installed the same way every time. Even if the prescribed configuration were initially generated by some sort of random procedure, repeating it over and over again would undermine the force of the randomness—in part because an attentive viewer, seeing the work installed on two distinct occasions, would notice that the configuration was the same.

Of course, having the installation team choose a random-looking configuration is not the same as having a truly random configuration. But this sort of human-determined quasi-randomness is in keeping with the work's spirit. Even though the work is a machine, it's a quirky, human sort of machine that invites viewers to control its functioning by speaking to it. There is nothing cold and algorithmic about it; like all of Hamilton's work, it invites us to reflect on aspects of the human condition. A companion piece, *untitled (the capacity of absorption)*, is a video showing water pouring into an ear. It is natural, considering these works together, to see them as having to do with communication and with the ways that we overwhelm and silence each other. The artist's relinquishing of control to the will of the installation team, rather than involving some sort of truly random process free of human judgment, is in keeping with the work's engagement of us, as humans, in response to a creation that is itself entirely a human production.

Variability and Its Uses

We've seen that a contemporary artwork may have very precise rules for display, like Cardoso's, or rules that tolerate some degree of variability, like Hamilton's. Now we'll delve further into variability, examining some of the reasons that artists sanction variable display. We'll also examine one instance of variability of display that was introduced by a museum's rule violation.

Variability as practical and expressive: El Anatsui's wall-hung sculptures

El Anatsui, a Ghanaian artist who has long lived and worked in Nigeria, has created a remarkable body of wall-hung sculptures consisting mainly of caps from liquor bottles connected with copper wire.[2] These works look like large tapestries, and they are often installed with dramatic folds that make a striking contribution to the display.

The artist is usually responsible for the main visual elements of displays of an artwork, so it would be natural to assume that Anatsui has made the choices about orientation and draping. In fact, though, these works include no installation instructions, except the express instruction that installers are free to choose how to hang them: which side is up, whether and how to fold and drape, whether to let part of the object spill onto the floor, and so forth. (See Binder 2010, McCrickard 2006, and Vogel 2012 for discussion.) Some works have multiple panels or detachable parts, and the installation team decides where and how to attach them.

The absence of instructions is not simply an omission on Anatsui's part: it is the result of conscious practical, aesthetic, and conceptual choices. From his base in Nsukka, Nigeria, Anatsui needed to be able to travel with or ship his works to gain access to the international contemporary art market. It must be possible to fold the works and put them in manageable crates. He notes, "I think the nomadic aesthetic developed as a result of the need to address a certain problem; to create works that are packing, storage and transportation efficient or friendly" (McCrickard 2006, n.p.). Anatsui also wants his works to be exhibitable in a wide variety of spaces, whether modest or grand: allowing the installers to make decisions about folds allows them to condense the work to fit a smaller space if necessary.[3] *Sasa*, for instance, which is 28 feet long, can be crimped or simply draped onto the floor if, as is typical, the wall is not tall enough to accommodate it (Vogel 2012, 59).

Some might object to the idea that a rule initially made for such a mundane practical reason could have aesthetic import or, as I will argue later, be work-constituting. But artists make all manner of creative decisions based on practical considerations, including cost of materials and feasibility of display. Such practical constraints on artistic creation set up a problem for the artist to solve as part of the activity of artmaking. If the solution is successful, it will constitute part of the work's merit; if it is not entirely successful, the effects of the practical constraint (e.g., the choice to use a suboptimal material) may constitute an

---

[2] An abbreviated version of this discussion is found in Irvin 2019.

[3] Anatsui discusses this element of the work in an undated interview with Chris Noey of the Metropolitan Museum of Art, found in the object file for *Dusasa II* (2007): "[A]part from the fact that you can crease it, you have this idea of...changing the size, as well. [You can] make it smaller by putting in more creases..."

aesthetic flaw. In the most successful works, such a practical decision is typically integrated into the broader artistic project such that it does not appear to be merely ad hoc. However, even in a less successful work that does not achieve such integration, an ad hoc decision still affects the work's features. In this respect, artists' choices in relation to rules are analogous to their choices in physical fabrication: a rule made for a practical reason may be more or less successfully integrated into the broader artistic project, and the work can be criticized in relation to its rules just as in relation to its other features. As we will see, Anatsui integrates the rule sanctioning variability with the other features of his works in a way that is conceptually satisfying while affording a rich experience to the audience.

Anatsui's welcoming of display decisions by the installation team is an extension of the involvement of others in the production of his works. His large-scale hangings are extremely labor-intensive to fabricate and are produced in a highly collaborative workshop situation with thirty to forty assistants (Vogel 2012, 68). Curator Susan Vogel, who has interviewed Anatsui extensively for a book and documentary about his work, estimates that a square foot of each work takes more than one person-day to complete, though for some particularly elaborate techniques it might be considerably longer.[4] In addition, for a large work like *Dusasa II* (2007), assembly of all the blocks into the sculpture might take two to three months, over and above the time it took to fabricate the blocks themselves, when undertaken by a team of five or six people (Vogel 2012, 68).

The assistants make autonomous aesthetic contributions to the objects they are helping to construct. While Anatsui sometimes requests a specific color combination or technique, at other times he leaves the instructions more open. He says,

> Certainly the alternating freedom and restriction means that there are inputs from the workshop. So work develops organically and in most cases in unpredictable ways. [The assistants] are more a part of the process; they are not all the time just hands. Working this way, I have got to understand both the material and the different touches or styles of each assistant. It is like conducting an orchestra of musicians each with particular performing skill.
>
> (McCrickard 2006, n.p.)

Given the active involvement of his studio assistants in the construction of the sculptures, it is perhaps natural that the constitution of displays should be seen as a collaborative project as well. He wishes for installers to experiment and engage their own creativity, not simply to follow a set of instructions or attempt to replicate what they have seen in a photograph of an earlier display. Anatsui

---

[4] For a fascinating illustrated taxonomy of the various techniques, see Vogel 2012, 74–5.

connects this idea to broader concepts of human relationships and the artist's role. "[H]uman relations are not fixed, you know. They change from time to time, they are dynamic."[5] He wishes for his work to invite and express this same dynamism. This combination of interests and concerns led Anatsui to embrace the idea of *nonfixed form* in his works, which he connects very directly to the nature of the artist's role and relationships. "I don't believe in artworks being things that are fixed. You know, the artist is not a dictator" (Vogel 2012, 104).

This process sometimes results in dramatic variability among displays of the same work. When *Drifting Continents* (2009), a work consisting of multiple detachable panels, was installed in the exhibition A Fateful Journey, which opened in Osaka in 2010, the display was dramatically different from one documented by the artist outside his studio.[6] Whereas Anatsui's hang aligned the tops of all panels (perhaps simply for practical purposes, given the available structure on which the panels were hung), the Japanese installation allowed panels to reach up to different heights on the wall, attached them together in a different order, and even rotated some panels so that what had been the top became the bottom. When the same work was installed at the Brooklyn Museum as part of a traveling exhibition, Gravity and Grace: Monumental Works by El Anatsui, in 2013, the panels were again reordered; the work was allowed to turn a corner in the gallery, occupying two walls; and one panel was rotated 90 degrees, from vertical to horizontal.[7] Figures 2.5 and 2.6 show still other configurations of the work when it traveled to the Museum of Contemporary Art San Diego and the Akron Art Museum as part of the same exhibition. According to Vogel, "Anatsui encourages and enjoys such drastic recasting of his works" (Vogel 2012, 99).

Christopher Spring observes that when Anatsui's *Woman's Cloth* (2001) was installed in 2002 at October Gallery, a center for international contemporary art in London, "it fairly flounced into the room, all its paillettes aflutter—in contrast to the more static hang published by the British Museum, where the piece has been straightened to the horizontal" (Spring 2009, 21).[8] The work may, then, have the ability to reveal tendencies of the institutions it passes through: a willingness to be bold and experimental, or an inclination to treat objects in a conventional fashion.[9] Anatsui is well aware that his invitation for the installation team to

---

[5] "El Anatsui Installing 'Between Earth and Heaven,'" video, Metropolitan Museum of Art, January 7, 2008, https://www.youtube.com/watch?v=G7UBvknG8c4.

[6] See Kawaguchi 2011 for discussion of the Osaka exhibition and Vogel 2012, 94 and 96 for images.

[7] An image of the Brooklyn Museum display of *Drifting Continents* is available here: http://www.artsobserver.com/2013/04/17/at-the-brooklyn-museum-the-wonderful-world-of-el-anatsui/.

[8] An image of the October Gallery display is available here: https://octobergallery.co.uk/artists/anatsui.

[9] The British Museum, which acquired *Woman's Cloth* in 2002, now uses a photograph from the October Gallery installation, though cropped to remove identifying details of the space, to represent *Woman's Cloth* on its website (https://www.artfund.org/supporting-museums/art-weve-helped-buy/artwork/8741/mans-cloth). Perhaps, as the importance of variability in Anatsui's work has been more widely discussed, the museum has recognized the need to represent the object's sculptural potential.

Figure 2.5 El Anatsui, *Drifting Continents*, 2009. Aluminum and copper wire. Approximately 118 × 394 in. (3 × 10 m), variable.

Installation view, Gravity and Grace: Monumental Works by El Anatsui, Museum of Contemporary Art San Diego, California, March 5–June 28, 2015. Photo by Philipp Scholz Rittermann © El Anatsui. Courtesy of the artist and Jack Shainman Gallery, New York

express creativity will not always be taken up. "Sometimes museums prefer to replicate the same thing over and over," he observes, particularly for touring exhibitions where many works must be installed in a short period of time and objects must pass through many hands (Vogel 2012, 107). Installers sometimes rely on photographic precedents in installing Anatsui's work, attempting to achieve the same effects that have been presented before, as is common practice for many other installation artworks. The initial hang of *Dusasa II* at the Metropolitan Museum of Art noticeably replicated many of the central compositional elements achieved by draping at the 2007 Venice Biennial, though the image the museum later adopted to represent the work on its website shows a quite different hang.[10]

[10] For the Venice Biennial installation, see: https://www.tate.org.uk/art/artists/el-anatsui-17306/who-is-el-anatsui. For the initial Met installation, see: http://art-unwashed.blogspot.com/2010/11/hirst-out-anatsui-in.html. For the current Met collection image, see: https://www.metmuseum.org/art/collection/search/495553.

Figure 2.6 El Anatsui, *Drifting Continents*, 2009. Aluminum and copper wire. Approximately 118 × 394 in. (3 × 10 m), variable.

Installation view, Gravity and Grace: Monumental Works by El Anatsui, Akron Art Museum, Akron, Ohio, June 17–October 7, 2012. Photo by Andrew McAllister

© El Anatsui. Courtesy of the artist and Jack Shainman Gallery, New York

Vogel feels that museums are inherently ill suited to honor Anatsui's prescription to exercise creativity in hanging the work: "I regretfully accept that the nonfixed form will only be moveable and flexible while it is still free, outside the preserve of the museum" (Vogel 2012, 107). I regard this statement as too broad: museums vary significantly in their accommodation of contemporary artistic practices, and some are both eager and able to respect the rules sanctioned by the artist even if doing so significantly modifies their standard operating procedures. The traveling exhibition Gravity and Grace, which premiered at the Akron Art Museum in 2012 and traveled to four other US venues from 2013 to 2015, was expressly designed to realize Anatsui's concept of nonfixed form, as indicated on the website for the exhibition at the Bass Museum of Art:

> As the exhibition travels, each installation of Anatsui's artwork will be quite different. The artist encourages museum staff to "sculpt" each metal piece as they install it, and so the works are condensed, expanded or reshaped to fit the space and sensibility of each institution.[11]

---

[11] See the Bass Museum of Art website: https://www.bassmuseum.org/art/gravity-and-grace-monumental-works-by-el-anatsui/.

While Gravity and Grace provides a counterexample to Vogel's pessimistic statement, her perspective undoubtedly reflects a variety of experiences Anatsui has had with museums that were so attached to the conventional idea of visual artworks as having a fixed display that they simply didn't have procedures in place to accommodate alternative practices. As Gwynne Ryan (2011) discusses, museum practices related to artworks with variable display are actively in flux, since these artworks require new conservation approaches geared toward preserving both the physical object and the work's immaterial elements, including rules for display. Well-resourced museums with a contemporary art focus tend to be at the forefront of developing new procedures and institutional roles for conservators, registrars, and others involved in the acquisition and maintenance of their collections.[12] Other museums that acquire Anatsui's work may need to realign their institutional procedures to accommodate it, and some will, of course, do so more quickly and more successfully than others.

Interwoven with these institutional factors is a shift in the understanding and treatment of Anatsui's work. Anatsui's international reception was initially as an "African artist," a label which may have transmitted expectations about his works as predominantly artifactual and as disengaged from the evolution of artistic practices seen in the international contemporary art world. Kwame Anthony Appiah notes that "talk of African art encompasses at least three quite different kinds of artifact": (1) "'traditional' African art," or "the body of materials created in Africa in traditions that began outside the influence of European conceptions of the aesthetic"; (2) contemporary "African 'outsider' art, . . . not informed by the sorts of art theory that is the global common currency of those artists trained in academies"; and (3) "African art that circulates today in the global art world," which is created by academically trained artists and informed by global art theory (Appiah 2010, 69). Nkiru Nzegwu (2019) elaborates further on the racialized and primitivizing assumptions that often lead western theorists and institutions to misperceive and dismiss key elements of works by African artists. While Anatsui's work belongs unambiguously to Appiah's third category, a perceived resemblance to traditional tapestry—perhaps combined with a default western tendency to assign works by African artists to the first two categories or even, as Nzegwu notes, deny their art status—may sometimes have led institutions to give his work the more static reception that western museums often give to traditional African art. As Anatsui notes, his own framing of the works may have contributed to this phenomenon:

---

[12] Examples include the European collaboration Inside Installations (https://www.incca.org/articles/project-inside-installations-2004-2007) and the Canadian project DOCAM (http://www.docam.ca/).

I made a mistake when I started naming [the metal hangings] after cloths. Because people seized upon that—and I'm sure that a lot of very lazy critics and curators did the same—so that all they do is build a point up to kente cloth, and then that ends everything.   (Enwezor 2011, 105)

When a work is assigned to one of the first two categories Appiah describes, for instance because it is assimilated to kente cloth, it will not trigger the acquisition, conservation, and display procedures that have developed to accommodate the immaterial elements of contemporary art. Anatsui has come in recent years to be treated as, in his words, "just an artist" rather than "an African artist"; it is thus not surprising to see a shift in the way that museums apply their procedures (Vogel 2012, 89).

As we have seen, the rules for display sanctioned by Anatsui result in variability, sometimes dramatic, in displays of his works. The rules also affect the works' prospects for meaning. As Anatsui says, his works realize a *nomadic aesthetic*, which "is about fluidity of ideas and impermanence of form, indeterminacy, as well as giving others the freedom, or better still, the authority to try their hands at forming what the artist has provided as a starting point, a datum" (McCrickard 2006, n.p.).

The rules and the resulting variability of displays, then, are essential to some aspects of what the work expresses. In addition to admiring each display for its own sake, it is important for audiences to be aware of the variability if they are to appreciate the work most fully and to recognize the nomadic aesthetic that it expresses. This is why the Bass Museum's public statement on its website is important: it not only expresses institutional willingness to comply with the rules for display Anatsui designed for his works, but also gives the audience crucial information about these rules that will enrich their experience.

As curator Yukiya Kawaguchi notes, the rules for display show through in the aesthetic impact of Anatsui's work.

A distinctive element of his recent work, I feel, is freedom from any kind of power. His recent works feel very soft and gentle, neither aggressive nor authoritative, as is often the case with contemporary artworks of European and American artists. I think this quality is deeply connected with his theory of the nonfixed form.   (Vogel 2012, 82)

The kind of feeling Kawaguchi describes is grounded in a combination of visual experience of the work and knowledge about how its displays are produced. Direct observation of the variability of displays of the same work is ideal, but as long as viewers are informed about the fact that Anatsui allows installers to hang his works in a wide variety of ways, they can add to their experience of a given display the knowledge that allows them to appreciate the work in its fullness.

As we have seen, rules for display can be deployed to very different effect. Cardoso uses them to exercise control over her work, whereas Anatsui consciously relinquishes control. Recognizing the artist's role in designing rules for display of their works, then, does not commit us to a situation in which they exert a death grip—it is up to each artist to decide whether and how they wish to engage with the prospect of designing their own rules.

Should an artist choose not to express rules for display, there are conventions and defaults that will tend to kick in, including the convention of regarding visual art objects as having a fixed form and thus a stable display. It is not surprising that institutions have sometimes replicated a style of hanging they have seen elsewhere, or have hung one of Anatsui's works like a simple tapestry, without folds: both of these express the assumption that only the artist, and not the exhibiting institution, should make significant aesthetic decisions that affect displays of the work. Anatsui's rules run against the grain of longstanding artistic practices, though Anatsui is not the first to challenge them. The fact that there has been some resistance or, at least, delay in uptake is understandable—though, to the extent that such resistance is a function of retrograde and racialized assumptions about Anatsui qua "African artist," we may not wish to explain it away uncritically.

Even when museums do comply with artists' rules permitting or mandating variability of display, they sometimes experience backlash from viewers steeped in expectations about fixed form. The Solomon R. Guggenheim Museum's object file on Eva Hesse's 1969 *Expanded Expansion* includes a handwritten letter, dated September 19, 1977, from an audience member who complains that the work was exhibited in "obvious incorrect condition," since the display he saw did not match a photo of a previous display and thus, he concluded, misrepresented Hesse's concept for the work. Linda Shearer, then assistant curator at the Guggenheim, replied on September 28, 1977:

> The artist intended many of her pieces to be placed and arranged randomly, at the discretion of the curator or collector, as the case may be. This is indeed so with *Expanded Expansion*, as the title indicates; it can be stretched to its full capacity or compressed, like an accordion, depending on the space it occupies and the person installing it . . . We have made every attempt, as we did at the time of the exhibition, to adhere to the spirit and meaning of Hesse's work.[13]

As we see from this example, artists' rules permitting variability of display are not a new phenomenon, and museums with a contemporary art focus have been accommodating them for decades. However, the uptake from both institutions and audience members remains uneven. Many viewers still arrive at the museum

---

[13] Quoted with the permission of Linda Shearer.

with assumptions that the form of an artwork is and should be fixed, and these assumptions are an obstacle to appreciation of works like Anatsui's. Institutions must, then, make an extra effort to reveal Anatsui's nomadic aesthetic through their exhibition practices. This extra effort includes creative modes of hanging the work, so that audience members who encounter it more than once will see that the display has changed. Hanging an object in very different gallery spaces with different conditions and constraints is helpful.

Equally important is the sharing of specific information about Anatsui's rules, as the Bass Museum has done on its website and many museums do through wall texts. Though information provided through wall texts is sometimes thought to interfere with the audience's immersive experience, in this instance the audience needs the information that displays of Anatsui's works are variable by design in order to appreciate the works fully. Leaving the audience to infer the rules from the display is not sufficient, as the letter received by the Guggenheim shows: a viewer who notices differences between displays is left to wonder whether a mistake has been made, a situation which certainly happens in art museums often enough (as we will see in Chapter 9).

Constrained variability: Liz Magor's *Production*

Anatsui sanctions variability of display for a whole body of works and allows installers to make a wide range of display decisions. Other artists, like Liz Magor, use variability within particular works and place more constraints on the possible displays. Magor's 1980 *Production* is an installation artwork involving 2800 bricks, along with the press Magor used to make them out of wet newspaper (Figure 2.7). Simply bringing these material components into a gallery wouldn't be enough to generate a display of the work; it is also necessary that they be arranged in an acceptable way. Magor and curators at the National Gallery of Canada had extensive correspondence by fax in which they exchanged diagrams, proposals, and principles for the work's installation. At one point, Magor stated:

> Yes, there are a thousand different ways to do it. But there's a notion or rule of thumb that eliminates some of them and modifies the others. I like it best when the bricks are trying to act architecturally—they're trying to make a wall or a column or something. The ultimate would be that they totally cover a wall, with no space at the top, bottom or sides...[14]

---

[14] Fax from Liz Magor to Germaine Koh, National Gallery of Canada, November 25, 1998. See Irvin 2006 for further discussion of this work.

Figure 2.7 Liz Magor, *Production*, 1980. Newspaper, wood, steel, machine: 53 ×
32 × 24 in. (134.6 × 81.3 × 61 cm); paper bricks: 2 × 4 × 8 in. (5.1 × 10.2 × 20.3 cm)
each.
Purchased 1984
National Gallery of Canada, Ottawa
Photo: NGC

The bricks dumped in a heap alongside the press, then, would not be an acceptable
display of the work. However, there is no one required configuration; the bricks
can be rearranged for different exhibitions. In fact, it is important, if viewers are to
understand the work fully, for the work to be displayed in different ways on
different occasions.

Why is arrangement so important? The arrangement of materials helps to
imbue the work with meaning. By titling the work *Production* and spending
many weeks of messy manual labor to make the bricks, four at a time, using the
press, Magor highlights the importance of the productive labor that generates,
literally, the building blocks of society. Through the possibility of installing the
bricks in different configurations, the work makes reference to real-world strategies of production in which modular, interchangeable components are assembled
to form a variety of different structures. The reference to real-world practices of
construction is relevant to interpretation of the work: it opens up possibilities for
seeing the work as social commentary that would be unavailable if the bricks were
always used to generate the same static structure. If the work were always installed
the same way, viewers would not be pressed to reflect on the relationship of
individual components to the final, overarching structure, or on the way that

workers' labor is a crucial complement to activities like design and architecture that are often treated as superior.

Variability has a different function in Magor's work than in Anatsui's. First, Magor does not simply relinquish the decision-making to the installation team. She is heavily involved in reviewing possibilities, and there is a clear expectation that the preferences she expresses will be translated into principles that guide future installations of *Production*. Installers thus have less latitude for choice, and where choices are to be made it seems that they should be generated from Magor's aesthetic vision rather than the installer's own. An installer who put the bricks together in a very chaotic fashion would not be respecting Magor's instructions; indeed, it is not clear the display would be a display of Magor's work at all. Someone who installs one of Anatsui's sculptures in a completely unexpected fashion, on the other hand, may be realizing Anatsui's vision par excellence.

Second, variable display is a major part of Anatsui's artistic practice: it characterizes all of his metal wall-hangings and many of his prior works. Most of Magor's other sculptural works have fixed displays. It thus makes sense to see the rule for variable display governing *Production* as connected to the specific theme of the work, rather than as an aspect of the artist's broader style or aesthetic. Variability, for Magor, is thus less connected with engaging others in the creative process or representing the dynamism of human relationships. It seems to have the more restricted aim of showing something about the different levels or stages of production.

Viewers, to appreciate *Production* fully, need to know that the display is variable, just as they would need to know for Anatsui's works. But they also need to know that the situation is not anything-goes: the variability operates within constraints defined by the artist.

Open-ended variability: Lawrence Weiner's text-based works

For both Anatsui and Magor, the rules for display govern the installation of fabricated physical objects the artists have supplied. For some contemporary artworks, arrangement of elements replaces, rather than supplementing, material components. Lawrence Weiner's (2008) *A WALL BUILT TO FACE THE LAND & FACE THE WATER, AT THE LEVEL OF THE SEA*, like many of the artist's text-based works, has no enduring physical components at all; the only thing that was transferred upon acquisition of the work by the Pérez Art Museum Miami was an authentication certificate.[15] To display the work, the museum need only inscribe

---

[15] Interview of senior curator Peter Boswell by the author, July 2010.

the words contained in the title so that they are visible to the viewer. Although text-based conceptual artworks like Weiner's are often displayed by affixing vinyl lettering to a gallery wall, for *A WALL BUILT* the possibilities for display are quite open-ended: the artist's representative told a curator "that it's ultimately totally up to us—we can carve it into the building, we can write it in lipstick on a sidewalk, whatever."[16] Any visible inscription of the words making up the work's title can count as a display of the work.

Of course, every display of *A WALL BUILT* has material components, since the words must somehow be made visible. However, the work itself is not identical to these displays or to the material components that make them up. The rule for display of elements is crucial; indeed, the rule for display and the title are the only elements of the work that persist between exhibitions. Weiner's work, like Anatsui's, is subject to highly variable display: indeed, since Weiner's work has no fixed material, there is not even a physical object to anchor its appearance. Moreover, variable display is a common feature running through Weiner's works, as with Anatsui's. However, the function of variability for Weiner is much different than for Anatsui. Weiner identifies the medium of his text-based works as "language + the materials referred to." Since "the materials referred to"—in this case, a wall built to face the land and face the water at the level of the sea—are not part of the display, all that is left to show is language: and language consists of signs that can be concretized in different ways. Variability, then, is simply consistent with the conceptual underpinnings of the work: it is not a vehicle for engaging the creativity, autonomy, and aesthetic sensibilities of others involved in constructing the display. Indeed, since the work does not purport to be about visual aesthetic effects at all, creativity in the construction of a visual display seems somewhat anathema to its aims.

It is perhaps for this reason that displays of Weiner's works tend to be stylistically similar even though variability is in principle permitted. A dramatically different aesthetic choice by the installers might serve as a distraction from the work's linguistic nature. At the Pérez Art Museum Miami, the work was ultimately installed much as it had been shown at the Marian Goodman Gallery prior to acquisition: the main difference was a change to a typeface more similar to that on the certificate Weiner supplied to the museum.[17] We see, once again, the power of the convention that the work is to be displayed in accordance with existing precedents and the artist's choices. Even where variability is permitted, its exercise

---

[16] July 1, 2009, email from associate curator René Morales to senior curator Peter Boswell regarding a telephone discussion between Morales and Andrew Richards of Marian Goodman Gallery, which represents Weiner.

[17] For the installation at PAMM, see https://frieze.com/article/pushing-boundaries-what-art-fair-can-be-new-curators-frieze-new-york-2019. For the earlier installation, see https://www.mariangoodman.com/art ists/70-lawrence-weiner/works/26159/.

may not be judged desirable, depending on the function it serves in a specific artistic context.

Variability due to rule violation: Nicholas Galanin's *Imaginary Indian*

Nicholas Galanin's *Imaginary Indian* (2016) is an installation work featuring a carved totem covered in wallpaper with nineteenth-century Victorian motifs (Figure 2.8). It is hung on a wall covered with the same wallpaper.

Galanin (Tlingit/Unangax̂), who both carves traditional totems for communities and works in the contemporary idiom of the international gallery scene, acquired the totem from a gift shop in Alaska. These gift shop totems are manufactured cheaply in Indonesia, yet sold to tourists in Alaska as though they were local Indigenous carvings. Galanin has reappropriated this commodified object and transformed it back into an Indigenous creation through inclusion in *Imaginary Indian*. The wallpaper alludes to histories of colonization and cultural genocide which continue today when Indigenous art forms are commodified and sold in a process that excludes actual Indigenous artists. In Galanin's view, this is part of a pattern in which non-Native people aestheticize Indigenous objects and

Figure 2.8 Nicholas Galanin, *The Imaginary Indian (Totem Pole)*, 2016. Wood, acrylic, and floral wallpaper, 80½ × 51½ × 11 in. (204.5 × 130.8 × 27.9 cm).
© Nicholas Galanin. Courtesy of the artist

forms but have no interest in or concern for the cultures and individual people who produced them.[18]

An important aspect of the work is that it is governed by a rule for display requiring that the object be lit from above left so as to project a shadow onto the wall adjacent to it. Though the figures on the totem are animals, the shadow forms the silhouette of a person with features often included in reductive stereotypic depictions of the American Indian. We have, then, an object (and, indeed, a whole pattern of consumption) that celebrates an Indigenous visual aesthetic while ignoring the ongoing violent histories experienced by actual Indigenous people, and projecting a generic Indian in the background as the presumed creator. Galanin notes that there is a long history of Indigenous artists being "treated as tribal representatives with no individual identities," and also of distinct tribal cultures being reduced to a single "pan-American identity."[19] Curator heather ahtone (Choctaw/Chickasaw) similarly identifies the tendency to "extrapolate some kind of useless and generalized definition for an Indigenous aesthetic system" (ahtone 2019, 5) rather than attend to the particularities of particular Indigenous cultures, whose "aesthetic systems...are not mutually informing" (ahtone 2019, 4).

When Galanin's work was shown at the Heard Museum in Phoenix in 2018, it was initially incorrectly installed: the object was illuminated from the front like an ordinary sculpture, and the raking shadow revealing the silhouette was absent. Galanin notes the irony in this, since it is an instance of precisely the phenomenon the work is designed to illuminate: "the aestheticization of object and culture without paying attention to concept," which, as he says, "is Indigenous erasure happening again, essentially, and erasure of this work." Work by Indigenous artists is often treated through what Galanin describes as a "bad practice of anthropology" that "doesn't allow space for a work to be viewed in a western idea of fine art,"[20] and thus doesn't require specific attention to the artist's creative activity beyond fabrication of the object. The phenomenon is similar to one we examined earlier for contemporary African artists: their work is often reduced, in Appiah's words, to either "'traditional' African art" or "African 'outsider' art... not informed by the sorts of art theory that is the global common currency of those artists trained in academies" (Appiah 2010, 69). Legal scholar Rebecca Tsosie (Yaqui) notes that something similar is true of works by Indigenous artists: they tend to be construed within western philosophy and law as "artifacts" rather than "art," and are thus not subject to the same theoretical attention or legal protection as cultural products recognized as artworks (Tsosie 2015, 85ff.; cf. Tsosie 2010). If one assumes in advance that the work is "traditional," primarily

[18] Interview of Nicholas Galanin by the author, July 11, 2018.
[19] Interview of Nicholas Galanin by the author, July 11, 2018.
[20] Interview of Nicholas Galanin by the author, July 11, 2018.

"artifactual," or made from an "outsider" perspective, it is easy to ignore the artist's engagement with contemporary practices of articulating rules for display, and thus to severely misrepresent—indeed, to erase—the artist's actual work.[21]

We see, then, that the rule for display Galanin has articulated, which requires lighting the object so as to produce a shadow with depictive content, is a key aspect of the work; failure to comply with this rule results in a display that severely misrepresents the work and renders Galanin's central point inaccessible. Arguably, the initial mistaken display at the Heard was not truly a display of Galanin's work at all.[22]

Rules and Meanings

As these examples show, rules for display may supplement a carefully fabricated object, or they may replace the object altogether. Some artists embrace variability of display, while others make rules designed to reduce or eliminate it. Variability may pervade all of an artist's works, or it may be used to make a specific point on a one-off basis. It may involve an invitation for installers to exercise their own creative judgment, or it may be mainly a matter of working within constraints set up by the artist.

Rules for display contribute to the work's potential for meaning, but in different ways for different works: all of the elements of the work, including the rules, operate together to provide resources for interpretation. Violation of a rule for display can undermine key elements of the work's meaning, as we saw in relation to Nicholas Galanin's *Imaginary Indian*. Where artists sanction rules for display permitting variability, this can have quite different expressive significance depending on the context: variability is used differently and for different reasons by El Anatsui than by Liz Magor or Lawrence Weiner. In the current context where both fixed and variable displays are possible, both choices are expressive: when Cardoso creates rules to make displays of her complex multi-object work as consistent as possible, this is a meaningful choice, just as Anatsui's choice to invite creative participation by the installers is meaningful. For this reason, I'll argue in Chapter 5 that rules are part of the *medium* of contemporary art. But first, we need to look at two other kinds of rules: rules for conservation and rules for participation.

---

[21] See D. Davies 2009a for a pointed critique of the concept of "outsider art."
[22] Issues of mistaken display will be taken up in greater detail in Chapter 9.

3

Rules for Conservation

In 2012, Cecilia Giménez decided that a badly damaged nineteenth-century fresco in her local church in Spain needed to be restored. She painted over most of the surface of the fresco and dramatically changed its aesthetic features, replacing a rather realistic portrait of Christ with a cartoonish face surrounded by a mane of fur that might be found on a stuffed animal (specifically a Monchhichi, for those who recall the 1970s toy monkey). Whatever one may think of the result, it is clear that if her actions cannot be reversed, she has destroyed the original work, *Ecce Homo* by Elías García Martínez.[1]

The persistence conditions for traditional works of painting, including this fresco, are such that a dramatic, permanent change to the appearance of the painted surface is sufficient for the work's destruction. This is a matter of cultural convention: on the standard understanding of painting, even something that would count as the same physical object may fail to count as the same artwork if the appearance of its painted surface is dramatically altered.

But as we saw in the introduction, practices in contemporary art have challenged this convention. Beginning in 1979, the Canadian artist Gerald Ferguson created over one hundred *Maintenance Paintings*, described as "a series of paintings in a variety of sizes and colors, on standard supports, using latex paint, installed in a reasonable manner and whose reinstallation and maintenance (repainting) is at the discretion of the end user."[2] Thus, the owners of the works are permitted to repaint them. In a later statement, the artist said, "If someone bought a green painting, for example and felt it would look better white, they could repaint it. That would be aesthetic maintenance."[3] Ferguson has, through his statements and the labels affixed to the reverse of the paintings, rejected the persistence conditions traditionally associated with painting. The persistence conditions for his works in this series are such that the works can survive total repainting of their surfaces and dramatic changes to their appearance.

---

[1] A study commissioned by the city of Borja indicates that the original work cannot be restored. To be fair to Giménez, we must note that her restoration effort was stopped before she completed it. And the story has something of a happy ending, since her work has become a moderately lucrative tourist attraction for the municipality. See Doreen Carvajal, "A Town, if Not a Painting, Is Restored," *New York Times*, December 15, 2014, http://www.nytimes.com/2014/12/15/world/a-town-if-not-a-painting-is-restored.html.

[2] This wording is from the label affixed to the back of each *Maintenance Painting*.

[3] Gerald Ferguson (n.d.), *Notes on Work: 1970–1989*, unpublished document supplied by Curator of Collections Shannon Parker at the Art Gallery of Nova Scotia. Punctuation as in original.

In this series, Ferguson has sanctioned a *custom rule* for the conservation of his work. This custom rule operates against the background of a default practice of preserving objects supplied by the artist in a state as close as possible to their original physical condition, unless the artist explicitly states otherwise. This default practice is historically well entrenched: the discipline of conservation was long concerned mainly to defend the physical material of the work from damage or decay. Renée van de Vall, for instance, speaks of "the established paradigm of 'scientific conservation,' for which the preservation of the material integrity of the work as a physical object is the central aim of conservation" (van de Vall 2015, 8). The approach to conservation on this paradigm was straightforward, at least conceptually if not technically: "Whereas a traditional painting or sculpture requires extensive research and testing prior to treatment, the parameters are relatively clear within a particular aesthetic" (Stringari 2003, 55). Indeed, as we will see in Chapter 7, even though Ferguson put in place a non-standard persistence condition by sanctioning a custom rule permitting repainting, he did not thereby eliminate the social authority of this longstanding convention of painting conservation: owners of his works have been very conservative about repainting them, owing no doubt to the recognition that judgments about provenance and the associated economic value of the work are likely to remain tied to the expectation that the surface was painted by the artist's own hand. Some of the distinctive expressive potential of custom rules lies in their ability to create confrontations with other normative elements of a situation and invite us to engage our agency in response, revealing our priorities and commitments.

Conservation of contemporary art is far from straightforward, either technically or conceptually, for several reasons. First, many artists use uncommon materials that decay more quickly or unpredictably than traditional artmaking materials. If this were the only change in artistic practice, it might pose mainly a technical rather than a conceptual challenge: we could leave in place the aim of preserving the physical object, and then we'd just have to figure out the chemistry and mechanics. But other changes in artistic practice complicate the picture. Some artists embrace deterioration for some or all of the physical aspects of their works, rejecting preservation. Other artists, like Ferguson, embrace specific kinds of change due to audience intervention. Still others allow that some or all of the physical parts of their works may be replaced, rendering preservation unnecessary.

This is not to say that the "established paradigm" of preservation, to use van de Vall's term, never applies: some artists still work in traditional media governed by conventional practices of conservation. However, Ferguson's *Maintenance Paintings* remind us that even when an artist is using a traditional technique or material, there is no guarantee that the established paradigm applies. Although preservation still tends to be the default for most art forms, it has been destabilized: institutions are more likely to ask direct questions about whether preservation is appropriate, and several protocols have been developed for conducting effective artist interviews and recording relevant information.[4] The expectation that artists may express custom rules for the conservation of their works is now built into institutional practice.

Let's look at a few examples of custom rules for conservation, with an eye to the process by which these rules are expressed and to their relationship to the works' nature and prospects for meaning.

Resisting Conservation: Zoe Leonard, *Strange Fruit*

The use of non-standard materials in contemporary art is often accompanied by custom rules for conservation. Consider Zoe Leonard's 1992–1997 *Strange Fruit*. Leonard, grieving the death from AIDS of her friend and fellow artist David Wojnarowicz, began gathering the peels of fruits that she and other friends had eaten. She used needle and thread to sew the pieces of peel back together, leaving the stitching quite visible. On some of the peels she added embellishments like zippers and buttons (Figure 3.1). To display the work, the reconstituted and decorated fruit peels are spread out in a seemingly random array on the gallery floor[5] (Temkin 1999).

Fruit peels degrade rapidly, even in a climate-controlled environment like a museum, conflicting with the typical museum mandate of preservation. As Nina Quabeck (2019) describes, Leonard's dealer, Paula Cooper, suggested that she work with a conservator to preserve the objects prior to sale. Leonard initially explored aggressive conservation measures with the well-known conservator Christian Scheidemann. But as curator Ann Tempkin, who oversaw the work's eventual acquisition by the Philadelphia Museum of art, writes,

> Leonard surprised herself and found that she recoiled at Scheidemann's hard-won results. She realized that the appearance of decay was not enough for her, the metaphor of disappearance was insufficient. I would argue that this was a reaction determined by art history—after Joseph Beuys's sausages or Dieter Rot's chocolate, the mere pretense of deterioration was no longer persuasive. Leonard set herself a criterion of honesty and rejected the twenty-five preserved pieces. (Temkin 1999, 47)

---

[4] On artist interviews, see Beerkens et al. 2012. Documentation and interviewing tools include the Variable Media Questionnaire developed by the Variable Media Network (http://vari ablemediaquestionnaire.net), the DOCAM Documentation Model (http://www.docam.ca/en/ documentation-model.html), and the Documentation Model for Time-Based Media Art developed by Joanna Phillips of the Solomon R. Guggenheim Museum (Phillips 2015).

[5] As Quabeck 2019 describes, the work was exhibited in other formats previously; however, when the work was acquired by the Philadelphia Museum of Art, the artist sanctioned a rule that the objects would be placed on the floor.

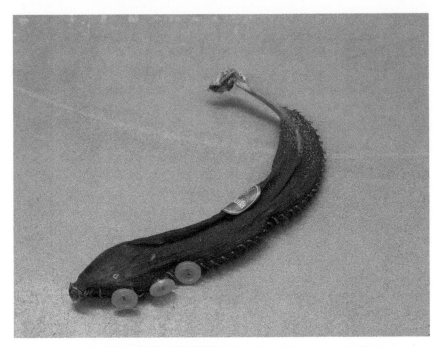

Figure 3.1 Zoe Leonard, *Strange Fruit* (detail), 1992–1997. Orange, banana, grapefruit, and lemon skins, thread, buttons, zippers, needles, wax, sinew, string, snaps, and hooks. 295 parts: Dimensions variable.

Philadelphia Museum of Art
Purchased with funds contributed by the Dietrich Foundation and with the partial gift of the artist and the Paula Cooper Gallery, 1998-2-1
© Zoe Leonard
Courtesy the artist, Galerie Gisela Capitain, Cologne and Hauser & Wirth

In a 1997 artist statement, Leonard said, "The very essence of the piece is to decompose. The absurdity, irony, pain, and humor of it is that we attempt to hang on to memory, but we forget" (quoted in Quabeck 2019, n.p.).

Leonard decided that it was essential to this work's expressive power that it directly manifest deterioration. This required the adoption of a rule for conservation that goes against the paradigm of preservation. Adopting this rule is what makes it possible for the work to *embody* deterioration rather than only alluding to it; and as Leonard's choice indicates, these acts have different communicative resonance. As Leonard described in 2018, holding the preserved objects Scheidemann produced "made it clear to me that the very meaning of the piece would be undermined by preserving it" (quoted in Quabeck 2019, n.p.).

Of course, Leonard's choice to reject preservative measures also changes what the audience potentially sees: had the work been displayed for an extended period, or displayed multiple times over a period of years, the deterioration of the fruits would have been apparent to visitors who made multiple visits. The rule Leonard has expressed for conservation, then, is not merely a background issue: it has direct effects on the display.

However, the fact that the rule for conservation has the potential to affect displays of the work doesn't guarantee that audience members have what they need to understand it fully. Merely seeing that an object exhibits damage or deterioration doesn't inform us about the significance of that damage or deterioration. Artworks are damaged in museums quite frequently: sculptures break, paintings are dented by elbows, flakes of paint fall off, and small pieces of multi-object artworks are stolen. The fact that damage is visible, or that a display has changed over time, does not yet tell us whether or how this damage or change figures in the artist's communicative activity.

We recognize that the *Nike of Samothrace* was made to be appreciated as an intact object; the breaking off of the head and arms is an unfortunate accident, not something that we figure into the meaning or message of the work itself. The statue may now be headless and armless, but it does not depict a headless and armless deity. Nor is it *about* damage or decay, though we might appropriate it to illustrate such themes. Something similar is true of a traditional painting part of whose paint has flaked off: we know that, in assigning meaning to the work, we are to bracket off this damage rather than understanding the work as an entity that was designed to embody a void or breach. The default rule for conservation, specifying that paintings are to be protected from such damage and restored where possible, supports this.

When it comes to Leonard's work, on the other hand, change in the object over time is a *feature of the work*, shaping its meaning possibilities. This is why a correct understanding of the work's nature is critical: when we are unclear on whether change in the object is a feature of the work or, instead, a violation of its integrity, we are not in a good position to begin reflecting on the work's significance. Grasping the work's features is a precursor to interpreting and appreciating it.

Thus, even for audience members who detect change in the fruit peels over time, the significance of this change is not immediately evident: we need more information about the status of the change, whether it is part of the artist's communicative act or external to that act. Moreover, the availability of information about the change depends on whether the work is displayed for long enough, or at suitable intervals, for audience members to be able to see it at different moments. And, of course, any individual viewer may be unable to visit the work more than once even if it is displayed. Seeing the change over time, then, may be impossible, either because the work is not on display or because the viewer does not see available displays on multiple occasions.

Conservation scholars argue, on similar grounds, that the public needs access to information that goes beyond what is visible in the display. As Glenn Wharton says, "Museum visitors experience a snapshot of how a variable work may be realized when it is on exhibition, but they cannot easily learn what museum staff knows about past iterations and artist sanctions for exhibition" (Wharton 2015, 181). Some works with variable or ephemeral presentations, Wharton says, "cannot be fully understood without background knowledge," and such information should thus be made more widely available (Wharton 2015, 183). Vivian van Saaze argues, similarly, that conservation and installation activities that have traditionally been kept on the "backstage" need to be brought to the "frontstage" of the presentation of art, because "providing insight into the backstage practices of museum work... is a prerequisite for understanding installation art" (van Saaze 2011, 245).

In the case of Leonard's work, the need for such backstage information is especially acute. As Quabeck (2019) compellingly discusses with extensive documentation, Leonard's expectation that the work would frequently be on display so that audience members could directly observe change in the objects was not fulfilled. The artist's initial hope had been to find a place where the work could be permanently displayed until no longer in exhibitable condition. However, though the Philadelphia Museum of Art made it clear that they would not install the work permanently, Leonard ultimately acquiesced because "it provided a very tempting context" given the presence of works by Cézanne and Duchamp (quoted in Quabeck 2019, n.p.). A "letter of intent" was developed to secure a mutual understanding of the artist's and institution's expectations for the work's exhibition and treatment. An early draft of the letter states, "We would like to display the piece at regular intervals over time, until it becomes too fragile to show. In keeping with the spirit of marking time, we will try to show it, as possible, during a period that is consistent from year to year" (quoted in Quabeck 2019). However, Ann Temkin, the curator who championed the work's acquisition by the PMA, departed in 2002, and the work was not displayed at all from 2001 until loaned to the Whitney Museum of American Art in 2018. In addition, it appears that the PMA has been subjecting the work to forms of conservation treatment for "insects, mold, and agents of decay," thereby undermining "the very mechanisms by which Leonard foresaw the work decaying" (Frasco 2009, 73; quoted in Quabeck 2019).

How should we understand the situation in which negotiation between artist and institution, and the institution's subsequent treatment of the work, result in a state of affairs substantially deviating from what the artist initially intended? First, as we saw with the rules for display sanctioned by El Anatsui in Chapter 2, artists make creative decisions about their works for a wide variety of reasons, both practical and aesthetic. Had different opportunities been available, Leonard might well have sanctioned a rule for continuous display of her work. Because of the "tempting context" of the PMA, she accepted a tradeoff whereby the institution expressed that it would "like to" or "try to" display the work regularly, without making any firm commitment. For the purposes of understanding Leonard's project, it is helpful to know that she wanted the work to be continually displayed so that the process of decay would be transparent. However, she did not in fact sanction this; and while the institution may have failed in an ethical duty to the artist by reneging on its expression of intention to display the work regularly, and it certainly prevented audiences from encountering the work during a key period of its lifespan, it did not thereby violate any rule *constituting* the work.

The institution does appear to have violated Leonard's clear sanction regarding conservation. As we will see in Chapter 9, institutions can have legitimate reasons for violating the artist's sanction, such as when complying with it endangers audiences or other artworks. I will not attempt to assess whether that was the case here, though it is plausible that the presence of organisms that promote the decay of fruit may threaten other organic materials like canvas whose deterioration the museum is bound to prevent. If the institution makes a choice, justified or not, to violate the artist's sanction, this doesn't show either that there is no sanction or that the sanction is irrelevant. Where an artist specifies a rule for conservation and the institution agrees to it, sanctioning that rule is part of the artist's artmaking activity, and the rule is part of the structure to which it is appropriate to attribute meaning. Where conservators find it necessary to alter the procedures in ways that contravene the artist's sanction, they introduce an element of artificiality into the structure of rules constituting the work, just as replacing a physical part of the work introduces artificiality. This artificiality may be worthwhile in maintaining our continued access to the work or protecting other works, but we should not now interpret the work as though the artificial components were part of the structure the artist created. To the extent that institutions can help us understand the work's original structure by providing background information as Wharton and van Saaze suggest, they promote our ability to understand the experience the artist designed for us and grasp the work's expressive import.

With the example of Leonard's *Strange Fruit*, we see that by sanctioning a rule for conservation, the artist changes what the work communicates. Rather than alluding to decay through the presentation of objects whose own process of decay has been artificially slowed, the work directly embodies decay and thus has a circumscribed life span, forcing us to confront the ephemerality of the very objects we encounter in the display in relation to the themes of AIDS, mortality, and grief. The work's deterioration and eventual loss is especially meaningful in the museum setting: the presence of objects that are actively decomposing is striking in a context where it is generally presumed that the material integrity of things will be maintained indefinitely. The fact that this rule for conservation is expressed against a background where the default practice is preservation is part of what makes the work expressive.

Artwork Destruction: James Turrell, *Tending, (Blue)*

As we have seen, the established paradigm of conservation holds that the material integrity of the objects presented by the artist should be preserved. A corollary is that preserving the material integrity of the objects is sufficient to safeguard the work: if a painting or sculpture is preserved in a physically pristine form, little or nothing else should be required to maintain its identity and existence as an artwork.

We saw with *Strange Fruit* that in contemporary art, preserving the material objects might, in fact, threaten the work rather than preserve it. James Turrell's 2003 *Tending, (Blue)* provides us with a different sort of example: one in which maintaining the physical integrity of the structure presented by the artist is not enough to ensure the artwork's survival.

Tending, (Blue) was constructed for the Nasher Sculpture Center, which opened in Dallas, Texas, in 2003. *Tending, (Blue)* is one of Turrell's Skyspaces, buildings with apertures that allow the viewer to see the sky. Optical illusions and other perceptual effects involving light are widespread in Turrell's works, and viewers often remark that the Skyspaces make it seem as though the sky is right there at the level of the ceiling, an effect intended by Turrell: "With the right size of opening and the right vantage and some careful finish work, he found that it was possible to eliminate the sense of depth, so the sky appeared to be painted directly on the ceiling."[6]

A few years ago, a high-rise condo development was constructed on a nearby lot, and the building was visible through the aperture of *Tending, (Blue)*, destroying the visual effect. A central and essential element of the visual experience the work was designed to produce is no longer available, and this is, in Turrell's view, sufficient for the work's destruction. The museum concurs, and visitors no longer have access to the site.[7]

James Turrell has thus expressed a custom rule for conservation of his work, one that extends beyond the appearance or integrity of the physical entity he designed. This rule for conservation is such that permanent encroachment of an object on the visible space framed by the aperture destroys the work.

This is not, of course, a standard rule of conservation for sculpture, whether contemporary or traditional. Richard Serra's *My Curves Are Not Mad* (1987), another work in the collection of the Nasher Sculpture Center, involves two arcs of

---

[6] Wil S. Hylton, "How James Turrell Knocked the Art World off Its Feet," *New York Times*, June 13, 2013, http://www.nytimes.com/2013/06/16/magazine/how-james-turrell-knocked-the-art-world-off-its-feet.html. Another critic notes, of Turrell's *Meeting* (1980–6), that the night sky "appears as an Ellsworth Kelly-esque black square on the ceiling." Joshua Barone, "An Artist's Eye to the Sky, Transformed at MoMA PS1," *New York Times*, October 5, 2016, https://www.nytimes.com/2016/10/06/arts/design/james-turrell-skyspace-an-artists-eye-to-the-sky-transformed-at-moma-ps1.html.
[7] Interview with curators Jed Morse and Catherine Craft, Nasher Sculpture Center, July 2013.

Cor-Ten steel between which audience members can walk. Permanent encroachment of a building on the visual space framed by the two arcs of steel has no effect on the work; it neither destroys the work nor requires relocation or reorientation of the steel arcs.

In specifying a custom rule for conservation, Turrell has established a persistence condition for his work: a condition specifying what is required for the work to persist through change. A change in which an object comes to encroach permanently on the visible space does not allow the work to persist: it is destructive of the work. This is related to the fact that acceptable displays of the work are no longer possible: we can no longer have the kind of experience Turrell designed for us in the making of *Tending, (Blue)*.[8]

It might seem surprising to suggest that an artist can sanction a persistence condition encompassing elements of the environment that are not themselves physical components of the work. But when it comes to immersive artworks, multi-object installations, and new media works, it is not uncommon for artists to specify display conditions involving wall color, lighting conditions, ambient sound, and other elements of an appropriate display site, because these can have a profound effect on the viewer's experience: and making available a particular kind of experience, with cognitive, perceptual, and affective components, is critical to how artworks function. As conservator Joanna Phillips describes, identifying and documenting the "intended experience" is a key aspect of defining an artwork's identity (Phillips 2015, 177). I prefer to speak of the experience the artist *designed*, to clarify that the experience is a function of the artist's creative activity, including both fabrication of physical objects and sanctioning of rules. The experience the artist has designed for the audience may involve what conservators refer to as specific artwork *behaviors*, such as persisting as a self-contained, relatively static object; tolerating or requiring variability of display; or being permitted to decay over time (Stigter 2017; cf. Ippolito 2003). The intended experience and behavior of a work may create "aesthetic or conceptual dependency" on specific material conditions, and these dependencies figure in the work's identity (Phillips 2015, 173).

For Turrell's Skyspaces, the intended experience is specific: the audience member is meant to have a distinctive experience of seeing the sky through a portal that frames it and juxtaposes it with conditions inside the specially constructed room. Many of the works involve periods at sunrise and sunset when the interior of the Skyspace is illuminated in gradually shifting colors, so that changes inside are juxtaposed with changes in the color of the sky as it darkens or brightens. There

---

[8] Turrell closed another of his Skyspaces for six months in 2019 when construction scaffolding temporarily encroached on the aperture. Jasmine Weber, "James Turrell Skyspace Reopens at MoMA PS1 after 6-Month Closure," *Hyperallergic*, August 2, 2019, https://hyperallergic.com/512156/james-turrell-skyspace-reopens-at-moma-ps1-after-6-month-closure/.

would be no way to have the experience of perceptual absorption that Turrell designed if an object were continually visible to anchor one's perception of space and distance. To use Phillips's term, the experience designed by Turrell involves an aesthetic dependency on unencumbered visual space. It is thus neither arbitrary nor frivolous to regard the artist as having the authority to sanction a persistence condition for the work that involves material conditions outside of its physical boundaries.

Complex Rules to Manage Change over Time:
Sarah Sze, *Migrateurs*

We will now explore a different kind of case: rather than a single rule governing conservation, the artist has sanctioned a complex array of custom rules to manage change in objects over time. Sarah Sze makes intricate, multi-object sculptures out of mass-produced materials: pencils, water bottles, tools, saltine crackers, toilet paper, ladders. Sze sometimes likes to make use of non-art spaces within the museum like storerooms, "spaces where you didn't expect to see art."[9] *Migrateurs*, which was created on top of the distinctive exit signs at the Musée d'Art moderne de la Ville de Paris, is much smaller than many of Sze's sculptural installations, but like most it is a whimsical and precarious assemblage of everyday objects (Figure 3.2). Twined lengths of colorful insulated wire of various gauges, sometimes connected by zip ties, weave over and around towers made of wooden matchsticks, of round white tablets stacked on a yellow wire nut, or of Del Monte raisin boxes. The structures, presided over by a tiny human figure, combine ingenuity, comedy, and danger: an AA battery is repurposed into, perhaps, some sort of furniture for the little person; a cotton swab stands improbably on end; and a yellow box reading "SAFETY" highlights the perils of upturned nails and thumbtacks, an open safety pin, and stripped ends of electrical wire. A clamp-on lamp with an articulated neck, far out of scale with the elaborate constructions, illuminates the scene and casts shadows on the wall behind the object.

About ten years after the work was made, Sze was interviewed by conservator Carol Mancusi-Ungaro for the Artists Documentation Program, designed to solicit information from living artists about the conservation of their work.[10] In

---

[9] Sze in a November 16, 2010, lecture in the Clarice Smith Distinguished Lectures in American Art series at the Smithsonian American Art Museum, https://americanart.si.edu/videos/clarice-smith-distinguished-lecture-artist-sarah-sze-154334.

[10] Interview of Sarah Sze by Carol Mancusi-Ungaro, Artists Documentation Program, June 30, 2008, http://adp.menil.org/?page_id=297. All quotations and details from the discussion of Sze's work in this section are derived from the interview unless otherwise noted. The work, then in the hands of a private collector who participated in the interview, has since entered the collection of the Museum of Modern Art in New York, with the title *Migrateurs (Green Lamp)*, https://www.moma.org/collection/works/216778.

Figure 3.2 Sarah Sze, *Migrateurs*, 1997. Found objects, 18¾ × 17¾ × 15 in. (47.6 × 45.1 × 38.1 cm).
Collection Museum of Modern Art
Gift of John Silberman in honor of Ann Temkin
© Sarah Sze
Digital Image © The Museum of Modern Art/Licensed by SCALA/Art Resource, NY

the interview, Sze and Mancusi-Ungaro reflect at length on specific rules for conservation of the work, on more general principles that should guide future judgments, and on how these rules and principles are related to the themes and expressive potential of Sze's work. Rather than one very significant rule for conservation that shapes the boundaries and meaning prospects of the work, *Migrateurs* involves a complex set of fine-grained rules for conservation. Looking at this case in some depth will allow us to examine the process by which rules are articulated and how they connect to the work's prospects for meaning.

Early in her discussion with Mancusi-Ungaro, Sze clarifies that the goal of conservation of *Migrateurs* is not to prevent or reverse signs of aging. Instead, "the work should look aged but not neglected." Mancusi-Ungaro then asks her how they should establish a baseline state to which the work should be restored, to operationalize the "aged but not neglected" principle. Sze responds in part by expressing specific, custom rules regarding the maintenance or replacement of various components of the work. The green Tic Tac candies, which have faded, can be replaced. This is partly to achieve a formal effect—to restore the "popping green"—and partly because putting in a new element is a way to keep the work from seeming neglected. "If you put food into the work," Sze says, "it's something you assume is going to be replaced." Sze here offers a principle that can be applied generally to her works: where a work enters a collection, there is a presumption that it is designated for extended life, and thus that rapidly decaying elements are replaceable. Sze later suggests that the Tic Tacs could be replaced with longer-lasting simulacra, because the interplay of real and fake is a theme often explored in her works. We can see, then, that Sze is expressing a precise custom rule: deteriorating organic materials can be replaced with newer materials, and in some instances artificial substitutes may be introduced. For most artists' works, the use of simulacra would be impermissible: Zoe Leonard, for instance, certainly could not accept the creation of compelling fakes to replace her decaying fruit peels. But Sze allows such substitutions because they are expressive of one of the themes she consistently explores in her work. The knowledge that such substitution is permitted, then, provides information about the artistic project Sze is engaged in.

Sze suggests that it is acceptable to replace sticks of chewing gum inside their packets with a stiff material. This is because the gum itself isn't seen, and the sagging that has developed is visually distracting. Sze says, "It wasn't the intention that this part of the aging be so dramatic." Thus, we see both an explicit rule—it is okay to replace the chewing gum with some other material—and a more general principle, namely that Sze is not concerned with the material authenticity of unseen materials. In addition, the example provides an anchor for the "aged but not neglected" guideline Sze previously expressed: the degree of sagging in the chewing gum has surpassed the threshold. Because many judgments about the aging of the work are necessarily comparative, Mancusi-Ungaro suggests that it will be important to photographically document the work periodically. This highlights the fact that the rules constituting the work cannot always be stated fully in language: other forms of documentation, including images and video, may be needed.

Sze notes that the cotton included in the work can be replaced if its appearance deteriorates, but that it has not yet reached that point. In addition, components that have separated can be reattached. However, the visible glue previously applied by Sze must be preserved, since both the specific quality of her marks and their "frenetic" aspect are important. Sze applied the original glue with a glue gun, which "has a very fast mark" and allows the artist to "make decisions really quickly." Sze suggests that the glue is, in this case, "almost like a painterly mark," with a result that Mancusi-Ungaro describes as "these wonderful really little webs." Sze suggests that she "was letting the glue really be part of the piece." If the glue were replaced with archival quality glue, "it just wouldn't be this same piece [...] not just because of the look, but because of the process."

As the discussion continues, Mancusi-Ungaro eventually states some principles she infers from what Sze has expressed. For instance, "We're not just 'accepting aging,' but we're saying, 'No, there's a spirit about this piece ... that we are trying to keep ... [W]e're recognizing that parts of it age, and those that jump out are aging in a way that [is] really distracting that we have to do something about.'" Mancusi-Ungaro then gives Sze the opportunity to endorse, modify, or reject the principle as formulated: "Does that sum up more or less what you're thinking?" Sze confirms Mancusi-Ungaro's understanding.

The yellowing of the glue, Sze suggests, is not a problem but rather a record, ten years on, of the work's material history. Mancusi-Ungaro notes that materials in the work are likely to age quite differently: the glue will get yellower, while the aspirin and cotton may whiten. She mentions that Sze is "comfortable with that dichotomy." Mancusi-Ungaro further observes that Sze's view about the conservation of *Migrateurs* fits with her general artistic practice of using a combination of materials that age rapidly and materials that don't. Sze agrees, noting that "the idea in the work was ... to make things that seemed like they were alive [...] to make it feel like ... it will have an end. [W]hen you come to it, you think about how was it made and how will it die ... how it will decay ... [I]n the piece you see different stages of a life process." But the piece is about a life cycle, not principally about degradation and death. "[N]ot everything in the piece has to be decaying. There should be locations that you know this piece is tended to. I think this idea of breathing life into objects is very important."

Some of the discussion ranges over relationships to other works by Sze. The relationship between "real" and "artificial," for instance, does not need to be achieved the same way every time a work is installed; indeed, she suggests, even works that are designed to have "real" elements, such as live plants, can sometimes be installed without them. She notes that given the complexity of elements in her works, "you can turn the volume up on what's fake and what's real in different ways." If the institution doesn't have the resources to water a plant or periodically replace real oranges, artificial elements can be substituted without undermining the work.

Sze also expresses some rules for displaying *Migrateurs*. Like many of her works, it is responsive to the history and physical structure of the sites for which it was created. This doesn't preclude reinstallation in new spaces, but it does mandate judgment about how the display can best engage with a new location. After the initial display in Paris, Sze acquired identical exit signs from the same manufacturer so that the work could continue to exist outside the museum. This fit with Sze's aim, manifest in many of her works, to "create a piece that, no matter where it goes, feels site-specific." The exit sign, showing a stylized person running toward a white rectangle representing an exit, is "a universal symbol," but also "very specifically French." When it comes to reinstallation, she suggests, "you might install it in a place that actually it would function as an exit sign, but at the same time clearly it's from another place." Installing it as a working exit sign is not necessary, however: "it functions as an object even without being lit … [I]t's a sign that's not being used as an exit sign or a light." The work's title, *Migrateurs*, provides context for understanding such rules as meaningful. Human migration often involves both experiences of shared humanity across difference and the sudden salience of aspects of oneself that, in a new location, are seen by others as distinctly connected to one's point of origin. Both people and the objects they carry may or may not continue to play the same roles after migration. Immigration often involves repurposing, improvisation, and finding ways to make things work for the time being. The fact that *Migrateurs* can be installed differently in different contexts, sometimes functioning as a recognizably "foreign" exit sign and sometimes with its function as a sign deactivated, comports with an exploration of migratory experience.[11]

The dialogue between Sze and Mancusi-Ungaro generates principles that can be applied later in practical contexts. It is unnecessary to preserve the mass-produced materials for their own sake; elements that are not visible can be replaced with different material to improve structural integrity; there is no need for everything to look like it is the same age, and indeed it is preferable for this not to be the case; where the assembly shows specific signs of the artist's touch, as with the webs of glue, these signs must be preserved; "real" things may be replaced by more durable simulacra in some instances.

There is a reason for the granularity of Sze's rules, as opposed to a blanket rule about when things should be replaced. She is designing a specific kind of experience for the spectator. She aims "to make everyone a conservator … wondering what's going to happen to certain parts of the piece." This interest can be stimulated by the juxtaposition of real and fake elements within a work, by the

---

[11] Such a reading must be tentative, since the French word *migrateurs* is used most commonly as an adjective to indicate migratory species of animals, not humans in situations of migration.

substitution of fake for real elements in different displays of the same work, and by the replacement of elements obviously subject to decay.

Viewers' conservation sensibilities can also be stimulated by a visible difference in how similar elements evolve over time. Sze and Mancusi-Ungaro observe that aspirin tablets in *Migrateurs* are in very different conditions: some have held up perfectly, while one has decayed to the point where what remains is "just the skin," in Mancusi-Ungaro's words. While Sze has mentioned that badly decayed items should be replaced to keep the work from looking neglected, she notes that "that aspirin's kind of great." Because the visual effect is appealing, and the difference in condition is likely to stimulate the viewer's curiosity, Sze resists replacing the degraded aspirin. She notes, "that's part of seeing the piece ... [Y]ou know that you are seeing it at a time in its life cycle because you've realized there are elements that are in that process of decay."

Likewise, she suggests, some aspects of the piece should "feel like they happen very quickly," whereas elsewhere "you see a kind of gesture with objects that looks more like something that accrued over time." These "different senses of time" are important in the work, and this, too, connects to the granularity of conservation instructions.

Sze's custom rules of conservation connect in various ways to broader artistic themes expressed through the work, as identified both by Sze herself and by critics and curators. First is the importance of time and process. Sze says, "Despite the fact that you're only witnessing inanimate objects, there's the strong sense of seeing an act in process, of witnessing behavior" (Enwezor 2016, 14). Critics, too, identify this theme within her body of work:

> Jean Louis Schefer: "Her devices are silent timepieces. They take up an obstinate childhood notion which resists age: the idea that everything measures time ..."
> (Schefer 2000, 21).

> Linda Norden: "This is a place, her pieces ... seem to say, in which things have happened and will continue to happen"   (Norden 2007, 12).

> Benjamin Buchloh: "Sze engages in an astonishing, at times almost comedic, staging of material and procedural conflicts ..." (Buchloh 2016, 91). Buchloh also identifies "procedures and processes of material transformation" as "fundamental features of Sze's sculptural conceptions"   (Buchloh 2016, 67).

Different rates of decay and the replacement of some elements, as entailed by the rules of conservation, signal that the work is subject to material process as well as to acts of care. Okwui Enwezor observes in an interview with Sze:

> I'm often confronted with the notion of the demand that you place on the viewer or the audience, perhaps even the institution: the demand for care, the demand

for slowness and for a certain kind of behavioural modification that one has to make when approaching the work ... [T]hat immediately locates the work in a particular type of psychological context.   (Enwezor 2016, 26)

Sze responds, "The idea that there's care, that there's tenderness, that there's intimacy, and that there's a longing for that care is an important idea in and of itself" (Enwezor 2016, 26). Sze further observes that audience members, like institutions, exhibit care in encounters with her works. While damage to and theft of components of contemporary artworks is very common, Sze's works have seen very little of either, even when viewed by hundreds of thousands of people (Enwezor 2016, 26–31).

The replaceability of elements of Sze's work connects to a theme she has discussed repeatedly over the years: the exploration of how an object that has little inherent aesthetic value, and no sentimental value, can gain value through juxtaposition with other objects mediated by the artist's touch. She eschews "objects that have the potentially romantic history of being used, like trash."[12] Norden notes,

> Sze's interest in [an] effort to create presence, and ultimately value, from insig-
> nificant things, and her insistence that those things—the objects she
> incorporated—be read as unused, 'raw' materials, not as souvenirs or symbols
> in and of themselves ... These associative images and objects function not as
> stories, not even, necessarily, as clues, but as free-floating signifiers that take their
> meaning from their placement and use within the piece.   (Norden 2007, 12)

The fact that an object included within the work can be replaced conveys that even Sze's use of it in an artwork does not transform it into a precious object or souvenir: it maintains its central identity as a fungible, mass-produced object, and another object just like it can contribute to the work in exactly the same way.

The granularity of the rules for conservation Sze has sanctioned fits with Sze's general attention to detail and with the fact that very small, subtle changes can have disproportionate aesthetic and expressive import. As Norden observes, "Sze's formal precision is crucial to the effect of her art" (2007, 8). She notes that Sze has developed "a structural, semiotic practice in which the arrangement of those parts—stacking two red, two orange, and one yellow Starburst, and twisting each to just this angle; letting the lamp cord dangle *down*, not across, the desk— and not any isolated element, determine the larger meanings of the piece" (2007, 12). Sze's works are "designed to incite recognitions hinged on the knowledge that

---

[12] Unpublished interview of Sarah Sze by Betsy Carpenter, July 2, 2002, in the file for *Grow or Die* in the collection of the Walker Art Center.

the tiniest shift in focus, balance, temperature, or movement can incite profound shifts in mood, comprehension, and behavior" (2007, 12). The details of what can be replaced and under what circumstances, just like the precise angle of a small component, are relevant to the effects the work can have on us, to how it leads us to infer behavior, ascertain an emotional tone of humor or patheticism, or recognize stages in a life cycle. The fine-grained detail of the rules for conservation fits with the fine-grained detail of Sze's works more generally.

The preceding discussion illustrates that articulating rules for conservation is part of Sze's artistic practice: the rules are specifically motivated by the kinds of experience she wishes to design for the audience and connected with the kinds of meaning she aims to make available. Moreover, the meanings she associates with these rules are meanings that curators and critics also find there. Sanctioning rules for conservation, like fabricating sculptural objects, is integral to Sze's process of work creation.

Objects, Rules, and Artworks

The custom rules for conservation sanctioned by the artist help to determine the relationship of the objects to the artwork. When Zoe Leonard sanctions the rule that the objects of *Strange Fruit* must be allowed to deteriorate, she embraces evolution of the objects as an interpretable feature of the artwork, rather than as a mere material reality that must be bracketed off for purposes of interpretation. In a context where the preservation of objects in a preferred condition has long been the central aspiration of conservation, the choice to allow deterioration has particularly strong expressive import.

The custom rule sanctioned by James Turrell for *Tending, (Blue)* has a very different effect, determining that even perfect preservation of the fabricated object in a pristine state is insufficient to secure the work's existence. This is because the work's identity requires that a particular kind of experience be available to the audience, and this experience involves a relationship between the fabricated object and its surroundings.

For works like Sarah Sze's *Migrateurs*, a single rule is not sufficient. The sanctioning of a complex array of custom rules becomes part of the fine-grained articulation of the work, and is used by the artist to shape the evolution of the material features of the work over time and the prospects for the artwork's meaning. Sze's sanctioning of particular rules tells us about the experience she is designing for the audience, as well as about which things are essential to the work and which variable or expendable. Her rules permitting replacement tell us that Sze is less concerned than, say, Leonard about having the work embody some sort of material authenticity grounded in its original materials; and she is not interested in presenting an object whose trajectory is simply to decay over time, though she does want attentive viewers to be conscious of the objects' material evolution and to speculate on the care that must be offered.

These are aspects of the expressive character of Sze's communicative act, and thus legitimate to take into account in interpretation. Learning about the rules for conservation can tell us more about the artist's purposes and bring some aspects of the artist's interests and concerns *into the work* in a material way. Knowledge of the rules, then, legitimately affects our experience of the work and the meanings we assign to it, whether or not the rules directly affect our encounters with the display.

4

Rules for Participation

Invitations to participate in some way, whether by interacting with a presented object or by engaging in some other form of activity, are widespread in contemporary art. Audience members might be invited to wander in an immersive environment, to play with a set of objects or use them in some form of activity, to interact with other people, or to make a promise or commitment. Rules for participation can take many forms. Some permit participation, while others require it: Adrian Piper's 2012 *The Humming Room* specifies, "In order to enter the room, you must hum a tune. Any tune will do" (Piper 2013, 309). Some allow for wide-ranging forms of activity, while in others the permitted activity is carefully circumscribed. Some allow anyone to enter the exhibition space and participate, while others invite participation only by the museum staff or only by people who have signed up in advance on a particular day.

Sometimes, the viewer's activity, invited by the rules for participation, is the main thing constituting the display; at other times, a specific fabricated object or environment is crucial, and viewers are interacting with or in that environment. Occasionally, audience members are invited to add something or take something away.

Of course, all art invites active engagement. The mind, the perceptual organs, and the body are active in generating the experience of the artwork and navigating around the physical space in which the artwork is situated. Theories of sculpture often note the importance of the viewer's bodily movement in gaining perceptual access to a variety of vantage points on the work, as well as the tendency of the work to alter our sense of the space around us and of our own bodily potentiality (Irvin 2013b). However, the accepted forms of engagement are standardly ones that leave the art object unaltered, and in which the spectator's activity, while occurring in proximity to the display, does not become part of it. Contemporary artworks that involve rules for participation are ones that invite the breaching of traditional boundaries that separate the participant from the display. While I have no commitment to a particular definition of "participation," I'll focus on activity that changes the display in some way, in some cases because the activity itself becomes part of the display.

Many artworks involving rules for participation are presented outside of dedicated art spaces (see, e.g., Thompson, ed., 2012). And technology-based interactive works might also be thought of as involving participation. In keeping with the focus of this book, however, I'll mainly discuss object-based and performative works presented in traditional gallery spaces.

As we will see through several extended examples, rules for participation can be an integral part of the artistic project pursued within an artwork, affecting the kinds of experience it affords and the kinds of meaning one can reasonably find in it. The prospect for participation, even if not taken up by a particular audience member, deeply shapes the expressive possibilities and themes of the work.

We will also consider cases in which, though the work is governed by a rule for non-participation, viewers regularly engage in unauthorized participation. As we will see, this phenomenon doesn't demonstrate that rules don't matter; works can be specifically designed to explore situations in which people tend to violate rules that have social, institutional, or legal force. Rules for participation allow artists to examine individual agency, temptation, and desire in relation to institutional power and control.

Adrian Piper, *The Probable Trust Registry: The Rules of the Game #1–3*

Much of Adrian Piper's body of work has involved direct address to or confrontation of an audience, often in ways that expressly invoke or invite interpretations related to race, gender, and social stigmatization. In her *Catalysis* series of performances, she traveled through public spaces covered in smelly material, with bubble gum hanging out of her mouth, or covered in wet paint with a placard indicating as much (Lippard and Piper 1972). Her *My Calling (Card)* series involved small cards she would give out in everyday situations when confronted with sexism or racism, particularly at the hands of those assuming, based on her light skin, that she was white (Figure 4.1).

In her video installation *Cornered* (1988), she speaks directly into the camera, informing the viewer of her blackness and examining some of the reactions a viewer might have to this declaration. As she says, "I'm cornered. If I tell you who I am, you become nervous and uncomfortable or antagonized. But if I don't tell you who I am then I have to pass for white, and why should I have to do that?" (Grigsby 1991, 90).

Through her approach of direct address to the viewer, Piper clearly aims to induce audience members' personal reflection about their approach to race and social interaction. "I am primarily motivated to do the work I do," she has said, "by a desire to effect concrete, positive, internal political change in the viewer" (Piper 1996, 248). *The Probable Trust Registry: The Rules of the Game #1–3* (2013) exemplifies her shift to an interactive approach, which engages the audience member not only in reflection but in deciding whether and how to engage with an ethically charged invitation (Figure 4.2).

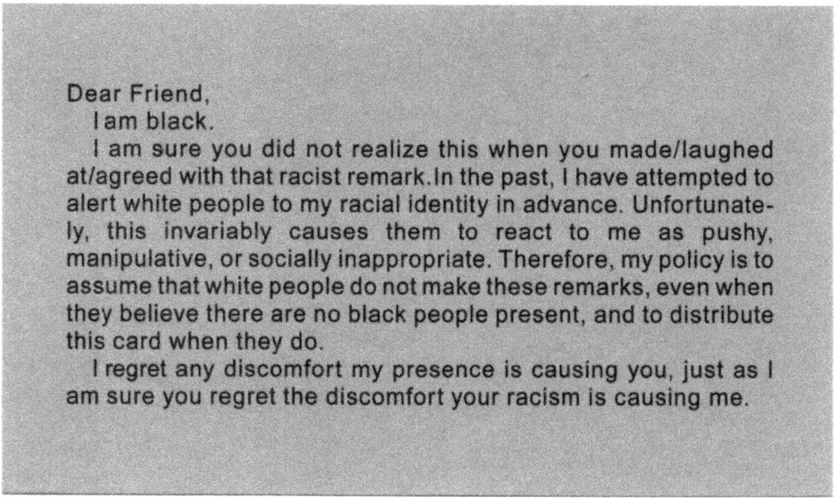

Dear Friend,
  I am black.
  I am sure you did not realize this when you made/laughed at/agreed with that racist remark.In the past, I have attempted to alert white people to my racial identity in advance. Unfortunately, this invariably causes them to react to me as pushy, manipulative, or socially inappropriate. Therefore, my policy is to assume that white people do not make these remarks, even when they believe there are no black people present, and to distribute this card when they do.
  I regret any discomfort my presence is causing you, just as I am sure you regret the discomfort your racism is causing me.

Figure 4.1 Adrian Piper, *My Calling (Card) #1 (for Dinners and Cocktail Parties)*, 1986–present. Performance prop: brown business card with printed text on cardboard. 2 × 3.5 in. (5.1 × 9 cm).
Various private and public collections
© Adrian Piper Research Archive Foundation Berlin

In *The Probable Trust Registry*, which she calls an "Installation + Participatory Group Performance," Piper invites audience members to sign agreements committing themselves to one or more of the following three statements:

1. I will always be too expensive to buy.
2. I will always mean what I say.
3. I will always do what I say I am going to do.[1]

The installation consists of three attended kiosks, one for each statement. Audience members can converse with the agent if they wish and then choose whether or not to electronically sign a contract committing them to complying with the statement. The signatures are to be archived by the Adrian Piper Research Archive Foundation Berlin (APRA Foundation Berlin) for one hundred years, and each signatory will receive the personal declarations of all others who have signed. If one signatory wishes to contact another, they can contact the gallery or exhibiting collector and request contact information (released only with the other signatory's consent).[2] Thus, the commitment has an element of public accountability.

---

[1] See http://www.adrianpiper.com/art/The_Probable_Trust_Registry.shtml.
[2] Instructions for mounting the work, which are also posted publicly at the exhibition site, are found at Piper's website: http://www.adrianpiper.com/art/docs/TPTRGeneralizedPerformanceInstructionsWebsite.pdf.

Figure 4.2 Adrian Piper, *The Probable Trust Registry: The Rules of the Game #1–3*, 2013. Installation + Participatory Group Performance: three embossed gold vinyl wall texts on 70 percent grey walls; three circular gold reception desks, each 72 × 63 in. (183 × 160 cm); contracts; signatories' contact data registry; three administrators; self-selected members of the public.

Photo credit: David von Becker
Collection Staatliche Museen zu Berlin, Nationalgalerie
© Adrian Piper Research Archive Foundation Berlin

The fact that this work is robustly participatory, rather than simply a perform-ance or installation that can be observed, gives it special potential to achieve Piper's aim of effecting change in the audience: participation engages the audience member's agency and, given the nature of the participation, invites consideration of what commitments mean, the circumstances under which we should enter into them, and the way in which our engagement with an artwork is (or is not) continuous with our experiences in everyday life: as one critic notes, the work "demands from the participant an unbreakable commitment (to keep his or her promise), while also knowing that the context of art allows an escape from it through fiction" (Zabunyan 2015, 2).

The work engages us as ethical agents on multiple levels, including the funda-mental level of contemplating the very nature of commitments and how we understand them. A critic remarks, "I noticed that some people were entirely unwilling to sign any of the statements, while others signed cavalierly. The show allows for both kinds of participation: quick and unthinking or conversational and philosophical" (Bass 2014).

A fundamental decision, then, is about how seriously one will take engagement with the work: will one consider the act of signing to constitute a genuine commitment that one should take seriously, especially given that it will be entered in a registry? Is it reasonable to make an indefinite commitment to something when we can't know what future circumstances will arise—and, indeed, when we can predict with a high degree of confidence that something will eventually undermine our full compliance? What do these statements mean, and what would it mean to comply with them? Notably, one might comply with statements 2 and 3 simply by saying less, thereby avoiding saying something one does not mean or will not be able to make good on. This may be a promising ethical approach extending far beyond the commitment invited by the work.

The prospect of interacting with the work, then, rather than simply watching a performance in which others do so, creates a distinct kind of experience, even for an audience member who ultimately chooses not to sign. Decisions, including the decision to opt out, have ethical significance, and Piper's work creates an occasion for the audience member not merely to reflect but to directly engage their agency in a way that has significance for future decisions and actions.

Marina Abramović, *Rhythm 0*

Where Piper offers the audience member a rather circumscribed opportunity to engage in a specific action, that of signing an agreement, Marina Abramović's six-hour participatory performance *Rhythm 0* (1974) provided a much more wide-ranging opportunity for ethically charged decision-making and action (Figure 4.3).

For *Rhythm 0*, Abramović supplied an assortment of objects with the following posted information:

Instructions.
There are 72 objects on the table that one can use on me as desired.

Performance
I am the object.
During this period I take full responsibility.[3]

---

[3] In 2009, Abramović created an exhibition version of the work, in an edition of three, to document the official performance. Information about the performance, including a full list of the seventy-two objects, is available from Tate, which acquired the exhibition version: http://www.tate.org.uk/art/artworks/abramovic-rhythm-0-t14875.

Figure 4.3 Marina Abramović, *Rhythm 0*. Performance, 6 hours, 1974.
Studio Morra, Naples
Photo: Donatelli Sbarra
© 2022 Marina Abramović
Courtesy of the Marina Abramović Archives/(ARS), New York

The selection included, in Abramović's words, objects "for pleasure" and "for pain," as well as "objects that can bring you to death." She later described the unfolding of the event:

In the beginning the public was really very much playing with me. Later on became more and more aggressive. It was six hours of real horror. They would cut my clothes; they would cut me with the knife close to my neck, drink my blood and then put the plaster over the wound. They would carry me around half naked, put me on the table, and [stick] the knife between my legs into the wood. And even somebody put the bullet in the pistol and put [it] in my hand and seeing if pressing it, her hand against my hand, if I would resist. But I remember after six hours when the gallerists come and say, "This piece is finished," and . . . I start walking toward the audience, naked and with blood and with tears in my eyes, everybody [runs] away, literally [runs] out of the door.[4]

In the years surrounding *Rhythm 0*, other artists were creating performance works that were extreme, visceral, and disturbing in various ways. These include Chris Burden's 1971 *Shoot*, featuring his being shot in the arm with handgun;[5] Vito Acconci's 1972 *Seedbed*, in which he masturbated under a platform on which visitors walked and had his voice amplified into the exhibition space;[6] Ana Mendieta's 1973 *Untitled (Rape Scene)*, in which Mendieta physically reenacted the scene after a sexual assault, presenting her body stripped from the waist down, tied to a table and smeared with blood;[7] and Carolee Schneemann's 1975 *Interior Scroll*, which featured her undressing, removing a scroll from her vagina, and reading from it.[8]

All of these performances provided occasion for the audience to reflect seriously on the human condition, on social norms, and on the relationship between art contexts and life contexts. But Abramović, rather than simply giving audience members a striking event to watch and ponder, gave them an opportunity to implicate themselves quite directly: they would determine, through their choices about how to use the implements and how to engage with the artist and with each other, whether the event ended up being disturbing and horrific or, instead, playful, pleasant, or frivolous.

Had *Rhythm 0* been staged as a non-participatory performance, with performers committing exactly the same actions as in the actual *Rhythm 0*, audience members would have had a profoundly different experience: they might have felt deeply uncomfortable, but the conventions of the performative arts would have spoken against an intervention to care for or protect Abramović from the performers' actions (just as no one intervened to prevent Chris Burden from being shot). In the actual case, where audience members were the ones deciding how to engage, they learned about their own tendencies to respond to a particular kind of situation in which the norms of art and the performer's instructions seemed to suspend the standard ethical rules, but the possibility of dire harm remained fully in place. The audience members' "running away" at the end suggests that they

[4] Interview with Marina Abramović, Museum of Modern Art, http://www.moma.org/multimedia/audio/190/1972.

[5] Video of the performance is available here: https://www.youtube.com/watch?v=gwh-XMFMp8U.

[6] Photo documentation of the performance is in the collection of the Metropolitan Museum of Art: https://www.metmuseum.org/art/collection/search/266876.

[7] Photo documentation of the performance is in the Tate collection: http://www.tate.org.uk/art/artworks/mendieta-untitled-rape-scene-t13355. See also Cabañas 1999 for discussion.

[8] A print related to the performance is in the Tate collection: http://www.tate.org.uk/art/artworks/schneemann-interior-scroll-p13282.

learned something unpleasant about themselves and perhaps also came to recognize the ultimate unviability of using the art status of a situation as a shield from moral evaluation.

Even those of us who were not present are an extended audience for the performance through our access to descriptions and documentation. Though we cannot directly learn about our own tendencies to respond in a situation like the one Abramović set up, we do learn something about human tendencies by knowing how other audience members behaved. Abramović's work thus extends prominent social psychology findings about interpersonal dynamics during the decade preceding *Rhythm 0*, motivated in part by an attempt to understand how many ordinary people had failed to resist, and indeed actively complied with, genocidal authoritarian directives during World War II. Stanley Milgram (1963, 1974) found that if you place people in situations with the right cues of "authority," such as an unyielding instruction delivered by someone wearing a white lab coat, you can get them to administer electric shock to a stranger with an intensity they reasonably believe to be extremely painful and harmful. Philip Zimbardo's lab found that if you assign ordinary people at random to the groups "prisoner" and "guard," the guards quickly assume a harsh and brutal demeanor despite knowing the prisoners did nothing wrong (Haney, Banks, and Zimbardo 1973). And John Darley and Bibb Latané (1968) found that ordinary people often fail to provide aid that is clearly needed, especially if they believe that many others are in a position to do so, sometimes yielding the paradoxical result that the more help is available, the less is offered.[9]

Through *Rhythm 0*, Abramović demonstrated that in a sense, the situation is even worse than that described by Milgram and Zimbardo: audience members did not need to be assigned to a specific role or instructed by an authority to perform harmful actions; they simply made these choices on their own, once they were in a situation—the art context—where they understood the usual rules of engagement to be suspended.

Abramović's work thus allows us (and the participants themselves) to observe how people understand the separation between art contexts and life contexts and the extent to which they are willing to act on this separation. But it also reveals, through the audience members' discomfort when the performance ended and they were confronted with the artist no longer in performance mode, the artificiality and potential harmfulness of this separation.

Jill Sigman, *The Hut Project*

In an ongoing project that began in 2009, Jill Sigman has built twelve huts designed out of found materials, typically items people had thrown in the garbage

---

[9] Some of these prominent social psychology findings have been subsequently questioned; for instance, a meta-analysis by Fischer et al. (2011) qualifies some elements of earlier claims about the bystander effect.

or donated. All of the huts have been presented in dedicated arts spaces, ranging from Sigman's Brooklyn studio to the Norwegian Opera in Oslo (Sigman 2017). *Hut #8* (2012) was built mostly of bundled water bottles, *Hut #9* (2014) mostly of electronic waste such as old printers and monitors, and *Hut #7* (2012) of tethered bundles of various forms of waste.

Though these huts resemble installation artworks, their genesis and point is very different. Sigman, a dancer, choreographer, and performance artist, conceived the first hut in part because she wanted a space that would contain the energy of performance, in contrast to open outdoor spaces where that energy tends to dissipate (Sigman 2017, 3). The huts were never conceived as sculptures; they were always understood as sites for events: performance, habitation, and interaction. Sigman lived in *Hut #4* (2010) for four days and invited strangers to visit by posting a phone number in a window and hanging messages around the neighborhood (Figure 4.4). Much of Sigman's choreographic and performance practice has involved inviting audience members to participate, and the huts quickly emerged as places for audience members to engage in structured and unstructured interactions with each other, with the artist, and with the material environment.

The Hut Project shares some of the concerns of Abramović and Piper: Sigman invites audience members to engage their agency, to reflect on matters of ethical significance, and to experience connections between art and life contexts (Sigman

Figure 4.4 Jill Sigman, *Hut #4*, 2010.
Photo Isabella Bruno
© 2022 Jill Sigman
Courtesy of the artist

2016). Sigman aims to use the huts as a space for interaction, prompting audience members to "[talk] to others they didn't know, [taste] things they wouldn't normally eat, and [think] thoughts they wouldn't often think" (Sigman 2017, 5) and, ultimately, to imagine new ways of living with each other and with material culture. The interactive situations she sets up offer audience members not a test— Will they sign a commitment? Will they use the knife to cut the artist?—but something gentler like an invitation or opportunity.

Sigman, like Abramović and Piper, is concerned to reunite art and life contexts, integrate life into art. While she lived in *Hut #4*, Sigman gave people many opportunities to visit her, have tea, engage in dialogue, and participate in structured activities like a treasure hunt, a trivia quiz, and a community discussion about gentrification. On some occasions, she asked people to bring specific kinds of gifts, including a handful of dirt or a floor plan of the visitor's own home (Figure 4.5) (Sigman 2017, 50). Visitors were invited to plant seeds in the dirt surrounding the hut, and Sigman asked each person a question: "What is your wish for your neighborhood?" (Sigman 2017, 52).

Sigman says, "It was with this hut that art and life blurred for me. Not just through sleeping there, but through the ongoing maintenance and dialogue" (2017, 52). The physical structure of the hut itself, the inventive use of discarded

Figure 4.5 Jill Sigman, detail from *Hut #4*, 2010. Visitors' drawings of their home floor plans.
Photo Rachel H. Eisley
© 2021 Jill Sigman
Courtesy of the artist

and repurposed materials, Sigman's practice of living there, and the occasions for relationships and community provided by the hut were all designed to stoke viewers' imaginations about possibilities for living: can we live more gently and richly in our built environments? Can we foreground experiences of surprise and beauty that are derived from values other than those inculcated by capitalist modes of production and consumption?

We can now begin to see a range of rules for participation that artists express, as well as a range of roles that material objects play in facilitating this participation. Piper's rules support a limited range of activity: the audience member may converse with the agents and sign the agreements if they desire. The built environment evokes, to my mind, a certain kind of bland corporate aesthetic associated with contracts. In Abramović's work, the rules for participation allow audience members to engage in any forms of activity they like, and the objects seem mainly to facilitate their choices. The rules for participation in Sigman's works—plant seeds, bring a gift, come for tea, take an item away—vary from hut to hut and lie in between the narrow focus of options made available by Piper and the unstructured openness of the possibilities offered by Abramović. The hut itself, with its peculiar materiality and history, is crucial in framing these interactions: Sigman notes in an interview that "when people do things in a hut they have a different relation to the space and their own bodies and each other and their ideas about what is possible" (McLendon 2015, 116). Carol Becker states that artists creating participatory works "have taken on the task of creating microutopian interventions that allow us to dream back the communities we fear we have lost" (Becker 2012, 71). Sigman's huts exemplify this project.

Paul Ramírez Jonas, *The Commons*

Through his works, Paul Ramírez Jonas often explores dynamics of power, control, and who is able to wield them. Some of his works have involved exchanging keys: at the close of his performative lecture *Mi Casa Su Casa* (2005) he gave a key to his own front door to one audience member, who was required to hand over a key that Ramírez Jonas would duplicate and give to someone else;[10] and in *Key to the City* (2010), he gave away keys to locked public parks and other public and private sites in New York City, access to which would ordinarily be controlled by an authority rather than lying in the hands of ordinary citizens (Becker 2012).

In his work *The Commons* (2011), Ramírez Jonas explores the power to shape public narratives and crystallize understandings of history (Figure 4.6). Drawing on the tradition of bronze equestrian monuments that are designed to create a

---

[10] A transcript of the lecture is available on Ramírez Jonas's website: http://www.paulramirezjonas. com/selected/refImages/Lecture_English.pdf.

Figure 4.6 Paul Ramírez Jonas, *The Commons*, 2011. Cork, pushpins, steel, wool, and hardware, 126 × 124 × 64 in. (320 × 315 × 163 cm).
© Paul Ramírez Jonas
Courtesy of the artist and Galeria Nara Roesler

long-enduring heroic tribute to a public figure, such as the famous statue of Marcus Aurelius that was erected *c.*175 CE,[11] Ramírez Jonas creates a different kind of monument: a riderless horse presented on a blank, generic pedestal, with the ensemble made of cork rather than bronze (Becker 2012, 71). When the work is displayed, pushpins are pressed into the pedestal to signal that it is meant to function as a public message board, and soon the pedestal is covered with messages, snapshots, funeral announcements (van Ryzin 2017). Audience members add to the assortment and sometimes remove items: a critic describes leaving behind a business card and removing a handwritten recipe for spinach lasagna (Wilson 2011).

In his artist statement, Ramírez Jonas notes:

> Cork is a material that can 'publish' an endless number of voices[, in] opposition to the singular voice of the state, or the singular identity of the hero portrayed riding the horse, or the immutable inscription on the public space that bronze and stone allow.[12]

---

[11] The work is held by the Musei Capitolini: http://capitolini.info/scu03247/?lang=en.
[12] http://www.paulramirezjonas.com/selected/new_index.php#22&32_2011&sub221&01_The%20Commons.

In addition to permitting audience members to add material to the display, the construction of cork means that this work will not have the long lifespan of a bronze or stone monument: the cork will break down over time as pushpins are inserted and removed. Audience intervention thus gradually pockmarks the work, changing it physically even when the temporary inscriptions are removed.

The invitation Ramírez Jonas offers here is, in one sense, banal: bulletin boards, and the attendant opportunities to publish one's opinion or post a flyer, are ubiquitous. But the act of posting one's message here has further significance added by the art context and the convention of attending seriously to every element of the visual display.

The rider, and with it the specific historical context the monument aims to vindicate, has been removed: the material supplied by the audience replaces the official public narrative which, as Ramírez Jonas has noted, "tries to be permanent, and monumental."[13] In a sense, then, the agency of the audience members who display their messages replaces the agency of the rider of the horse and the agency of whoever created the monument, just as it replaces the agency of the artist in determining the precise visual appearance of the display. At the same time, though, the sharing of power and access, here and in the artist's other works, is not unlimited: the horse, high on the pedestal, is inaccessible to audience interventions. Audience members are invited to express their voices and messages, but not to obscure the most striking visual aspects of the display. They are invited to post what they like, but these postings are removed and, one supposes, discarded between displays, not becoming part of the official material of the work. For this reason, it is easy to bracket the audience interventions as, in an important sense, external to the work: the work involves a rule that audience members may post on the cork, but not a rule that what they offer becomes part of the work in any deeper sense.

Similarly, the distribution or exchange of keys in several of Ramírez Jonas's other works takes the form of what Tom Finkelpearl (2013, 4), following a taxonomy of collaborative artwork developed by Grant Kester (2004), calls the "scripted encounter," as opposed to a more open or improvisatory situation. In *Key to the City*, for instance, audience members were invited to come to a specific site at which they could confer a key on a deserving person. "Part of preparing for the key bestowal ceremony," as noted by the informational website for the work, "involves filling out a template script, which you will read aloud during your ceremony."[14] Audience members are invited to designate a recipient for a key and to specify the reasons for which the key is bestowed, but not to design their own ceremony or transfer the key in circumstances of their own choosing.

[13] http://www.paulramirezjonas.com/selected/new_index.php#20&30_2009&sub206&06_Publicar%20I,%20II,%20III.

[14] http://creativetime.org/programs/archive/2010/keytothecity/bestow-a-key/.

As Ramírez Jonas indicated in his artist statement, a key to the city is usually given as "a symbol and an award" to someone who has performed a heroic or noteworthy service; but

> [t]his new Key to the City is for us and to be awarded among ourselves. We will give each other a key to the city for our private reasons that exist outside of history...One on one, one at a time, all the time, thousands of keys were bestowed by thousands of people on thousands of citizens for thousands of reasons that deserve to be recognized.[15]

Ramírez Jonas is concerned both to reveal how access to physical space and modes of communication is restricted and controlled, and to expand such access.

In attending to the details of Ramírez Jonas's works, then, we see that the rules for participation play a critical role in the nature of specific displays, and are essential to these works' being able to make their points about the control and dissemination of power in public and private spaces. In addition, we see that the limits on participation encoded within the rules constrain the extent to which the artist can or should be understood as sharing or distributing power. The artist is committed to revealing and to some extent challenging restrictions on access; yet, like the state, he is an official agent who uses his institutionally derived power to shape the form and content of audience members' engagement with his artworks and with each other. Interpretations of the work must attend to the specific contours of custom rules for participation; a work involving a broader permission for audience intervention would make different points about democratization and public power.

Uninvited Participation

Through the examples discussed above, we now have some sense of the range of projects that artists may attempt by sanctioning rules for participation, the range of forms of participation that may be invited, and the range of roles that that material objects or environments may play in participatory works.

But it also seems important to acknowledge that people regularly have physical interactions with sculptural objects, even where those interactions are not permitted. (I will focus here on intended interactions rather than accidental contact.) What should we say about such cases? Does the phenomenon of uninvited

---

[15] http://www.paulramirezjonas.com/selected/new_index.php#21&31_2010&sub211&01_Key%20to%20the%20City. Extensive information about *Key to the City* is available at http://creativetime.org/programs/archive/2010/keytothecity/. The artist's other projects involving keys include *Taylor Square* (2005) and *Talisman* (2008).

participation suggest that rules for participation have no significance, and that we should dedicate our attention instead to how audience members actually engage in and with the objects and situations that are made available to them regardless of the rules? I suggest that the fact that these interventions are not permitted is crucial to understanding their significance, and indeed to grasping the expressive import and social effect of the work on which they intrude. (We'll consider a variety of kinds of rule violations in greater depth in Chapter 9.)

Additions: Sarah Sze

Sarah Sze, whose small work *Migrateurs* is discussed in Chapter 3, makes sculptural works of installation art, creating whimsical arrangements of non-precious, mass-produced materials like cotton swabs, pencils, candies, and toothpicks. Many audience members act as though Sze's works are inviting their participation: they often leave small contributions. In fact, though, the works are governed by a rule for non-participation. If people frequently disobey the rule, does this show that the rule is not in fact effective? Does it show that the work is flawed insofar as it fails to convey that this rule is operative? What difference does it make to say the work is governed by a rule for non-participation, if the rule is often broken?

Sze's works are often large and complex, and presented in such a way that it would be very difficult for an institution to monitor every moment of audience contact. One might expect that people would steal objects from the work: theft of small artwork components from museums is commonplace, as is damage. But Sze notes that, in fact, displays of her work are rarely afflicted by such treatment. Of *Things Fall Apart* (2001), a large-scale work at the San Francisco Museum of Modern Art, she says,

> There was a very intimate view of part of the work, you could look at it and touch it as you came up the stairs and there were no guards. People often ask this, but no one touched it; it was not damaged. Occasionally, and this is common with my work, people would leave things. Usually no one who works in the museum even notices, but I come back and think, I didn't leave that there.   (Sze 2010)

Sze notes, "Some of the things I've found are a postage stamp, a mint Life Saver, a bus ticket, a lunch receipt, and a hair band. They're all things that people probably had in their pocket and spontaneously decided to add" (Scott 2012). There is a reason why people in the museum typically don't notice, Sze suggests: these interventions are "usually . . . in the vocabulary of the work" (Sze 2010).

When Sze's *Untitled (Thessaloniki)* was shown in New York City in 2014, part of the display, consisting of loose objects like paper clips and tablets of over-the-counter medication, was presented on the sidewalk outside the gallery (Figure 4.7). When

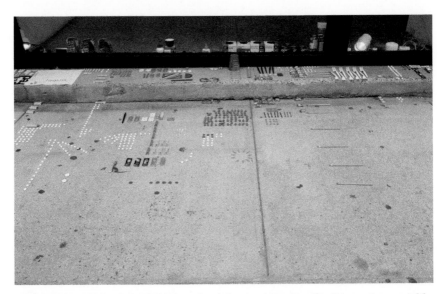

Figure 4.7 Sarah Sze, *Untitled (Thessaloniki)*, 1997. Mixed media. Dimensions variable.
© Sarah Sze
Courtesy of the artist and Tanya Bonakdar Gallery, New York/Los Angeles

I saw the work, someone had added an empty plastic cup and red drinking straw to the display. While it was not difficult to discern that the cup and straw were not part of Sze's work, they seemed to undertake a lighthearted dialogue with the artist: "So you've given us that. How about this?" Gallery staff told me that they removed the outdoor portion of the display each evening and reset it the next morning, so that each day's audience would have a fresh look at the display Sze sanctioned.

Playful intervention in the form of small, non-damaging contributions, then, is a frequent mode of engagement with Sze's works. Yet, the works are governed by a rule for non-participation: Sze says, "It's nice that people have this urge to participate when they think of my sculptures, but it's not how I usually work" (Scott 2012). But we might wonder whether this shows that something has gone wrong. If people are frequently engaging with the work this way, does this show that the rule for non-participation does not, in fact, have any force for this work? Or does it show that the work is somehow failing, because nothing internal to the display communicates that audience interventions are not invited?

There are specific things about Sze's works that might make them seem to welcome such interventions: they seem playful, unpretentious, and accessible, and might inspire an audience member to use whatever they have on hand to try out Sze's gambit of making intriguing objects from spare and ordinary materials. Moreover, contemporary art continues to be faced with audience members who resist the value of nontraditional materials and techniques, so an addition may occasionally be made in a spirit of skepticism that there is anything special about the display Sze has designed.

But audience tendency to interact with the work is also the product of precisely the broader trend we have been examining in this chapter: the proliferation of custom rules for participation. When audience members know that participation is sanctioned for some works, this destabilizes the longstanding default rule that artworks—particularly those in institutional displays—are sacred, untouchable objects. The social norm of treating artworks as unbreachable is weakened, and this leads to interventions that would not have happened in earlier contexts: once people get used to encountering artworks that can be touched, they are tempted to do the same with other works.

But this shift in tendency doesn't instantly transform all artworks into participatory ones. The act of creating a work where audience members are invited to intervene in the display is different from the act of creating a work where interventions are prohibited. Indeed, creating a work that seduces audience members to intervene even while prohibiting that intervention is a specific kind of action that has distinctive expressive potential in exploring human urges, social norms, and institutional control.

What the work expresses, then, depends not just on how audience members actually treat it, but on whether the work is governed by rules for participation that invite or prohibit that treatment. The proliferation of rules for participation has contributed to a shift in audience behavior, but this doesn't mean that rules are moot and the choices audience members actually make are the only determinant of how the work should be understood. Non-participatory works remain non-participatory. However, a consequence of this shift is that creating a work governed by a rule for non-participation has different import now, in our current art historical context, than it would have had several decades ago, when a rule for non-participation governed nearly all artworks by default. In an earlier context, the rule for non-participation would not have been specifically expressive, since so many other works were governed by the same rule. But now that rules for participation are a live option commonly taken up by artists, a choice *for* non-participation is more of a genuine choice than it was previously: and, in an important respect, it is a choice *against* participation, a choice not to avail oneself of an artistic resource that is now readily available. As an analogy, consider marriage vows. Reciting the traditional marriage vows, in a circumstance where those vows are used in every wedding ceremony, may not indicate assent to the specific content of those vows; one may simply recite them because one wants to be married, and this is the utterance one must generate to be married. But a choice to recite those same traditional marriage vows when it has become common to write custom vows has different significance: it may signal assent to the content of those vows, adherence to tradition in the face of change, or an endorsement of heteronormative gender roles.

This is not to say that the choice can have only one meaning: the significance of a choice depends on the entire context in which one's action is taken. But the landscape of options and of others' choices matters: the choice to make a non-participatory work has different significance when virtually all works are non-participatory than it does when participatory works have proliferated. Sze makes work that is whimsical and incorporates everyday materials, in a context where inviting audience participation is fairly common. Her choice to sanction a rule for non-participation, in this artistic landscape, tends to reaffirm that despite appearances, she endorses the traditional roles of artist as creator and audience as receiver, not co-creator, of the work.

What of the audience member who encounters a display of Sze's work that has been affected by an unauthorized intervention? Should this audience member care whether or not the intervention was permitted? A first thing to notice is that if Sze's works were governed by rules permitting audience members to make additions, Sze's distinctive sculptural aesthetic would no longer govern displays to the same extent. We would likely see that aesthetic spinning out into something much more diffuse and chaotic as new audience members responded to Sze's display and to other audience interventions, with ever-increasing digression from Sze's visual vocabulary. And as we saw in Chapter 3, this would make for an entirely different experience: as critic Linda Norden notes, "Sze's formal precision is crucial to the effect of her art" (Norden 2007, 8), in which specific choices about how to position elements give rise to "the larger meanings of the piece" (Norden 2007, 12). A work not governed by Sze's choices in the arrangement of elements would not have the same aesthetic effect or generate the same meanings.

Since participation is not authorized for Sze's works, there is an institutional practice of removing added elements. But it will still sometimes happen that an audience member encounters a display with an addition in violation of the rules, and even specifically enjoys this addition. Should this matter?

Where the audience member can tell that the addition was made by someone other than the artist, as with the drinking cup and straw I saw added to *Untitled (Thessaloniki)*, appreciation involves recognizing that the addition encodes a reaction to the work by someone other than the artist: perhaps an attempt to inhabit and extend the artist's aesthetic, or a protest regarding the perceived banality of the display of ordinary mass-produced objects. The fact that the addition is unauthorized but does not damage the work gives it a mildly transgressive quality; we might chuckle at its audacity and/or be a bit annoyed at the intrusion on Sze's distinctive visual aesthetic.

Should we, instead, mistake the addition for part of the display sanctioned by the artist, to that extent we will be misled about what the artist created, and about at least subtle aspects of the aesthetic and visual effects she produced through her creative activity which, as Norden describes, are critical to the function of Sze's works. Similarly, if someone other than the artist repainted part of a painting,

changing its visual appearance, and we did not notice that this was an unauthorized change, we would to that extent be misled about the nature of the work. How
deeply this misunderstanding would pervade our grasp of the work would depend
on the details of the case: a tiny visual change might nonetheless have an outsize
effect, as if someone painted out the legs of Icarus in Bruegel's famous *Landscape*.

Even though people do in fact intervene, then, the rule for non-participation
sanctioned by Sze remains important. This is true both because of its effect on how
displays unfold over time (institutions rein these interventions in rather than
allowing them to spiral endlessly), and because the act of inviting people to
intervene in the display is very different from the act of creating a display that,
while whimsical and inviting, is marked by the artist's visual aesthetic and specific
formal choices. An invitation for all to participate would suggest a democratization of artmaking and a breakdown in the artist's traditional authority; and this is
not Sze's project.

Subtractions: Janine Antoni

Two of Janine Antoni's works involve objects made from chocolate. *Gnaw* (1992)
involves two 600-pound cubes, one made from lard and the other from chocolate
(Figure 4.8). Antoni removed material from each of the cubes by chewing with her
teeth, and then made further objects from the removed materials: she added
pigment to the chewed lard to make lipsticks and cast the chewed chocolate into
chocolate candies inserted in a plastic tray. The lard cube collapses under its own
weight and is remade each time, whereas the chocolate cube is a persisting object
(Buskirk 2003, 7–8). *Lick and Lather* (1993–4) is a group of fourteen self-portrait
busts the artist created through a process that involved direct body casting
(Figure 4.9). Antoni cast seven of the busts in soap and the other seven in
chocolate and then altered them, removing detail by taking the soap busts into
the bath with her and licking the chocolate busts (Buskirk 2003, 140).

These works are governed by a rule for non-participation: touching or altering
the objects is prohibited. When asked by interviewer Klaus Ottmann whether she
had considered allowing audience members to intervene by gnawing on her
chocolate works, Antoni replied that they already do this periodically, but she
would "prefer that they didn't" (Antoni 2013). Audience members have bitten
the noses off the chocolate busts on multiple occasions (Buskirk 2003, 142), and
the Museum of Modern Art, which holds *Gnaw*, keeps spare chocolate available
for repairs (Cembalest 2013).

There are probably several reasons why audience members act on these works.
Those familiar with other works that permit participation may misunderstand
Antoni's work, believing that participation is invited. Antoni has said that when
Gnaw was acquired by the Museum of Modern Art, audience members began to

Figure 4.8 Janine Antoni, *Gnaw*, 1992. 600 lb chocolate cube and 600 lb lard cube gnawed by the artist, 45 heart-shaped packages of chocolate made from chewed chocolate removed from chocolate cube and 150 lipsticks made with pigment, beeswax, and chewed lard removed from lard cube, 24 × 24 × 24 in. (60.96 × 60.96 × 60.96 cm) (each).
Installation view The Museum of Contemporary Art, Los Angeles
© Janine Antoni; courtesy of the artist and Luhring Augustine, New York

understand it as "about an ephemeral work being in a museum," which, though not her intended reading, may have contributed to the sense that there was little harm in leaving one's mark (Barnett 2015, note 43).

Some may intervene in the "I could have done that" vein of protest against contemporary art that is perceived as unserious or unskilled. Some may simply be curious: What would it have been like for the artist to have the experience of fabricating this object with her mouth? Is this real chocolate? What will happen if I bite this object? It is not uncommon for viewers to try to smell the chocolate busts of Antoni's 1993 work *Lick and Lather* (Gupta 2015), and critics often remarked on the strong smells of the works early in their exhibition history (Weichbrodt 2013, 211–12). As Antoni remarks, "There's not a lot of time between smelling and biting" (Cembalest 2013, n.p.).

Most fundamentally, as Antoni says of *Lick and Lather*, "the piece is about desire, and if the viewer responds in that way it's actually quite an appropriate way to respond" (Antoni 2013). The first time she got a call that one of the busts had

Figure 4.9 Janine Antoni, *Lick and Lather*, 1993. One licked chocolate self-portrait bust and one washed soap self-portrait bust on pedestals. Bust: 24 × 16 × 13 in. (60.96 × 40.64 × 33.02 cm) (each, approximately). Pedestal: 45⅞ × 16 in. (116.01 × 40.64 cm) (each).

Collection of Carla Emil and Rich Silverstein and the San Francisco Museum of Modern Art (John Caldwell, Curator of Painting and Sculpture, 1989–93, Fund for Contemporary Art purchase)
Photo: Ben Blackwell
© Janine Antoni; courtesy of the artist and Luhring Augustine, New York

been bitten, she had to decide whether to leave the bite, and this prompted her to reflect on the most fundamental aspects of the experience she meant to design for the viewer (Antoni 2013).

Ultimately, Antoni determined that the works must continue to be governed by a rule for non-participation because, like many others in her oeuvre, they involve a focus on her own body and her own bodily experience. Many of her works involve casts of her body or traces of her bodily activity, and they are designed to invite audience members to "empathize with [her] process but not participate" (Antoni 2013). Antoni aims to make available a specific experience of imaginative connection. "I do these extreme acts," Antoni says,

> because I feel that viewers can relate to them through their bodies . . . Imagining the process is so much more powerful than watching me do it . . . By imagining

me, the viewer's experience turns out to be about their own wish fulfillment...
Traditionally, we stay objective and go through a process of decoding information to make meaning. I'm much more interested in the viewer empathizing with
my process.   (Horodner 1999)

The works are designed, then, for audiences to imagine and empathize with
Antoni's bodily experience, but without actually undergoing a similar experience.
Empathy is a central ethical capacity: to be appropriately morally responsive, we
may need to imaginatively identify with an experience we cannot share due to
differences in our embodiment, identity, or situation. As Antoni says, "When you
know where someone is coming from, you put yourself in their position, even if
it is a really difficult thing to do, it helps you open up and gives you access"
(Horodner 1999). Elsewhere, she notes,

> My work comes out of a deep sense of loneliness and frustration that we cannot
> truly ever know each other. I try to enter my objects, leaving traces of my
> interaction on their surface for others to discover. To understand my objects is
> to empathize with what I have gone through to bring them into the world.[16]

Inviting audience members to sculpt by using their own bodies, then, would be a
different project than the one that Antoni has pursued throughout her career.

In addition, a work with the same physical structure but governed by a rule for
participation would have very different expressive potential. The artist's act of
sculpting objects from lard, soap, and chocolate using her own mouth is very
different from an act of presenting fabricated objects that audience members are
invited to chew on. The latter artwork would challenge the taboo on eating after
strangers, raising questions (and perhaps even real medical concerns) about
communicable disease. Whereas the large scale of *Gnaw*'s chocolate cube and
the amount of chocolate that has been removed can engage vivid imagining and
empathy for the physically grueling act the artist undertook in fabrication, in a
similar work where participation was invited, the large scale might seem connected instead to the idea of the object being large enough for many people to
participate in chewing. We would know that the cube has the potential to
continually shrink with audience intervention, so the time-based nature of the
artifact would be at the forefront. A work where the artist had sanctioned a rule for
participation would, then, have very different import than Antoni's actual work.

Chocolate is an alluring material. Wharton et al. (1995) note that mouth-
inflicted damage to works of art made from chocolate is commonplace. Does

---

[16] Janine Antoni, artist statement for her 2016 artist residency at the Fabric Workshop and Museum:
https://fabricworkshopandmuseum.org/artist/janine-antoni/.

this show that the rule prohibiting such interventions is unreal or meaningless? No: articulating such a rule for a work made from this specific material is a way for the artist to explore dynamics of desire, control, prohibition, and temptation. A woman artist's act of chewing huge quantities of lard and chocolate inevitably evokes the pervasive social control and scrutiny of women's body shape and food consumption. A rule prohibiting us from consuming a highly seductive object replicates a widespread tension between availability and prohibition, thereby having special expressive force.

Touches: Kara Walker

Another work subjected to unsanctioned intervention is Kara Walker's 2014 *A Subtlety or the Marvelous Sugar Baby, an Homage to the unpaid and overworked Artisans who have refined our Sweet tastes from the cane fields to the Kitchens of the New World on the Occasion of the demolition of the Domino Sugar Refining Plant* (Figure 4.10). Walker created this monumental work, consisting of an enormous Black female sphinx figure (with a surface of refined white sugar) and a group of child worker figures (some cast in brown sugar, and others cast in resin and coated in molasses), shown holding baskets or carrying bunches of bananas, in the defunct Domino Sugar refinery in Brooklyn (Carpio 2017, 551–2).

Photographic images, the testimony of observers, and video footage shot by Walker's team all show a variety of interactions between audience members and the sculptural elements of the work, including direct touch. Children were observed licking the sculptures of the child workers, and adults were observed and photographed sticking out their tongues as though to lick the female figure's vulva. Audience member Dána-Ain Davis observed, as she waited to see the exhibit, "i am also afraid i will want to lick the sugar" and "i fear getting too close ... there are things i don't want to see—people sticking out their tongues as if they are licking her nipples or placing their fingers near her vagina ... so I take my time" (D.-A. Davis 2014).

Walker's footage, collected in her work *An Audience*, shows a variety of audience interactions.[17] A toddler is shown with his mother smiling and holding him by the upper arms, as both of his hands are dripping with sugary syrup. Someone says, "Say cheese!" as someone else says, "You got a part of the artwork!" A boy, perhaps seven years old, walks along touching the sphinx, with a man capturing him on video. He pinches at the sculpture with two fingers. The hands of many people of many skin tones, adults and children, are shown touching the surface, sometimes cautiously, sometimes with a nearly erotic caress.

---

[17] The trailer is available at https://vimeo.com/112396045.

Figure 4.10 Kara Walker, *A Subtlety, or the Marvelous Sugar Baby, an Homage to the unpaid and overworked Artisans who have refined our Sweet tastes from the cane fields to the Kitchens of the New World on the Occasion of the demolition of the Domino Sugar Refining Plant*, 2014. Polystyrene foam, sugar. Approx. 35.5 × 26 × 75.5 ft. (10.8 × 7.9 × 23 m).

Installation view: Domino Sugar Refinery, A project of Creative Time, Brooklyn, NY, 2014
Photo: Jason Wyche
Artwork © Kara Walker, courtesy of Sikkema Jenkins & Co., New York

All of these interventions occurred in the context of prominently posted signs reading, "Please…do not touch the artwork." Clearly, though, audiences found the work highly seductive, with the smell of molasses hanging in the air and wafting from the sticky puddles into which the cast sugar child worker figures gradually collapsed. Walker was unsurprised by these responses:

> I put a giant 10-foot vagina in the world and people respond to giant 10-foot vaginas in the way that they do. It's not unexpected…[H]uman behavior is so mucky and violent and messed-up and inappropriate. And I think my work draws on that. It comes from there. It comes from responding to situations like that, and it pulls it out of an audience. I've got a lot of video footage of that [behavior]. I was spying.   (Miranda 2014)

Walker's main project in the video is not to reveal audience misconduct. In many ways, the video comes across as celebratory, both of the fact that such a racially diverse audience invested their time to visit the work (not typical of contemporary art events) and that people had strong reactions of interest and delight. Of the video, Walker says,

> I want to tell about the gathering of this piece. Overall, it was a very positive environment. Large groups of people came, families came, grandmothers came, little kids—things that don't happen very often around contemporary art… People are stupid, but the greater majority are conscientious, if not always respectful, and they are aware of one another's presence in the room.
>
> (Miranda 2014)

At the same time, though, the willingness of people to touch the work, even when both posted signage and the usual conventions of art encounters prohibit touching, mirrors a broader phenomenon: the treatment of Black women's bodies as essentially public, always available for touch, in contravention of social norms that require respect for others' bodily autonomy. In real life, the fact that people frequently touch Black women's hair without permission tells us something important: namely, that under white supremacy, some of the usual rules for embodied social interactions are treated as lacking force during interactions with Black women.[18] The unauthorized participation—and the fact that it is unauthorized—serves to illustrate precisely the point the work is making.

The tendency to disregard Black women's bodily integrity and autonomy can be traced back to the sugar trade that Walker's work invokes. How is a female figure, with her vast vulva exposed by her kneeling posture, connected to the historical injustices of sugar? The stereotypical mammy figure of Aunt Jemima was long used to market some of the products of the sugar industry in the US. But a more crucial connection is to the fact that women's bodies were productive of the labor force that maintained the slave trade. Rape was a mechanism through which this labor force was reproduced; and thus the Black woman's body was treated as always available, and not subject to the conventions of respect and restraint applied to white women's bodies (A. Davis 1981; Feinstein 2018; Freedman 2013; West and Johnson 2013). The economy of sugar that extracted labor from some and produced wealth for others, then, is connected to a history of violent exploitation of Black women specifically.

The history the work examines, then, is one in which white women benefit from social conventions designed to protect them from violent assault, while those conventions—and the laws undergirding them—are suspended when it comes to

---

[18] See Davidson 2016 for discussion of Walker's work as having a corrective didactic function in relation to the treatment of Black women and their bodies. And we must note that people of all races are socialized into white supremacist norms; the fact that even Black people may enact a disregard for Black women's bodily integrity (both in relation to this work, and in general) does not undermine the point.

Black women.[19] As is typical of her works harking back to historic injustice and violence committed by whites against Blacks in the US, Walker is demonstrating the present-day legacy of this history, as Black women continue to be disproportionately subjected to treatment that undermines their bodily autonomy, failing to receive the full benefit of social conventions that apply more robustly to white women.[20] To represent and explore a similar situation within the exhibition, Walker must put in place a rule that prohibits touching the work, to see when people treat it as lacking force. A work in which audience members were invited to touch the work could not undertake the same project: there can be no exploration of the range of situations in which people violate a rule, if the rule is not in effect.

The fact that audience members frequently violate the rule for non-participation, then, does not show that this rule doesn't matter. Instead, the rule is essential to the artistic project undertaken in the work, and violations of the rule give us specific information about how audience members respond both to the work itself and to the real people it represents.

Conclusion

Rules for participation, like rules for display and rules for conservation, are implicated in distinctive artistic projects and have distinctive expressive affordances. To return to Adrian Piper's *The Humming Room* (2012), cited at the opening of this chapter: when Piper requires us to hum in order to enter the gallery space, we must engage our agency in one way or another. Will we refuse to hum, regarding the activity as too silly or the artist as too demanding? Will we hum with an attitude of resentment that we are being required to engage in a pointless activity? Will we hum self-consciously, just loudly enough to convince the guard to let us pass? Will we hum with gusto, amusing ourselves and perhaps trying to amuse others?

Even as she requires us to engage our agency, Piper engages the institution's authority. She redeploys the mechanisms that restrict access to spaces and objects to enforce a rule that is at once frivolous and vital: since the rule constitutes the work, a failure to enact the form of authority prescribed by the work would endanger it. The museum is thus faced with questions of how it does and should deploy its authority: should it truly stop people from entering the gallery if they do not hum? Merely admonish them? Or simply engage in a pretense of enforcement, knowing that most people will comply with a stated rule if it is clearly posted? And

---

[19] As Angela Y. Davis (1990, 45–6) discusses, some groups of white women receive less protection than others: working-class white women are more likely to be subjected to sexual violence than white women with more socioeconomic privilege.

[20] The line from historic to contemporary instances of sexual violence against Black women is traced by West and Johnson 2013.

then we, as audience members, must consider how we will engage with this display of authority: through compliance, avoidance, or resistance.

These questions for the institution and the audience member readily connect to a host of issues about the nature of art and the institutional spaces within which it is often presented, as well as further matters of social relationships and power. Who can make art, and how do everyday creative activities like humming connect to more "elevated" artistic activity? If we resent being asked to hand over the ephemeral currency of a hummed tune, did we also resent being required to stand in line and hand over actual currency to enter the museum? Who should have access to art, and how should this access be secured? For those of us who enter art spaces regularly, what rituals and practices do we engage in unthinkingly because we know them to be required? And who feels unwelcome and out of place in art spaces because the rules for engagement are usually unstated, or because the mechanisms of power and control in these spaces feel like an extension of other mechanisms of the carceral state? Several of the artworks we have seen, including Jill Sigman's *Huts*, Marina Abramović's *Rhythm 0*, Adrian Piper's *The Probable Trust Registry*, and the works of Paul Ramírez Jonas, address social relations and power outside of art contexts as well. This is not to say, however, that rules for participation always undermine traditional power relations: depending on the kind of participation that is invited or required, such rules might in some cases replicate or even intensify the discomfort and lack of belonging that is felt by people who have been historically excluded from art spaces.

If rules for participation were not part of our artistic landscape, works could illustrate, comment on, and engage our thinking about matters of institutional and societal power and control. But creating a situation in which we must position ourselves in relation to these dynamics, as rules for participation allow the artist to do, is a different project, which generates distinct kinds of experience and distinct expressive affordances.

The landscape created by rules for participation also affects the expressive import of works where participation is not permitted. When an artist's work is simply subject to a firm and universal prohibition on interacting with art objects, that prohibition is not an interpretable feature of the work; it does not distinguish it from any other. But against the backdrop of a plethora of cases in which various forms of participation are permitted, thereby weakening the conventional prohibition, the artist's act of reinstating that prohibition has more specific expressive import. In a context where audience members are sometimes invited to collaborate in the shaping of sculptural objects and permitted to consume edible parts of an artwork, Janine Antoni makes a specific artistic statement by avoiding these practices: her project is to engage us in empathy for the intense process the artist went through in constructing the object, not to engage us in a collective activity of exchanging bacteria as we contribute to the object's continual erosion. Moreover, when someone does bite one of her works, this is not simply an act of vandalism (though it is that), but also a display of the dynamics of temptation, control, and defiance that are set up by a landscape of increasingly complex and variable rules for engagement with art.

As we have seen, rules for participation can be finely customized: there may be either permissions or requirements; a very broad or very narrow scope of possibilities; and the possibility for engagement with objects, performative activity, or social interaction with other people. This allows artists to use rules for participation as a finely articulated artistic resource, just as physical objects gain artistic content from the details of their articulation. Rules for participation allow us to have kinds of experiences we could not otherwise have had, involving distinct sensations and vantages on art objects as well as distinct experiences of agency in specific situations. These rules are thus a powerful artistic resource for engaging our understandings of our relationships to objects, other people, and institutions, as well as our understandings of our own nature as embodied social beings.

5

What Are Artworks Made Of?

We have seen that rules play a central role in contemporary artworks. The process of artmaking frequently involves the sanctioning of custom rules for the material that must be included in a display, for the configuration and conservation of that material, and for interaction with the material or other forms of participation in the display. Awareness of these rules is sometimes essential to grasping an artwork as the work that it is; and even where the work can be substantially grasped without awareness of a particular rule, attending to the rule can provide us with resources for thinking about its meanings.

We now turn to the question: just what is the artwork? In some of the cases we've seen, the artwork has no material that survives the display; and even for those works that do have persistent physical elements, those elements alone often underdetermine the nature of the artwork more or less dramatically. We can gather up all the bricks that belong to Liz Magor's *Production* (discussed in Chapter 2), but if we lack instructions about how to arrange them, we don't yet "have" the work and aren't in a position to mount a display of it. Any claim to contact with this artwork requires knowledge of what is to be done with the objects.

Displays

We'll begin with the concept of the display, which is central to the discussion. Displays are what audience members encounter: a display is an entity made available to an audience for experience and contemplation.

Let's consider some examples. El Anatsui's *Dusasa II* is a wall-hung sculpture consisting of aluminum caps from liquor bottles and plastic disks connected with copper wire. The work has the appearance of a large tapestry. As we saw in Chapter 2, a notable feature of this and other works by Anatsui is that there are many possible ways to hang them: whoever is doing the installation has the leeway, indeed the mandate, to make choices about how to fold and drape the object. These choices can combine aesthetic and practical concerns: folds can be introduced in order to make the object small enough to fit a given space.

A display of *Dusasa II* is just a specific instance of its being presented for viewers to encounter. Different displays do and should look different from one another, since installers are to use their individual aesthetic judgment in deciding how the work will be hung.

Mickalene Thomas's 2007 painting *A Little Taste Outside of Love* is simpler in this respect. It is a self-contained object composed of acrylic, enamel, and rhinestones applied to a wood surface.[1] A particular display of it is simply an instance of that object's being hung for viewers to encounter. The appearance of the object does not inherently vary from display to display, except insofar as its materials are subject to gradual degradation over time and the possibility of contingent damage.

Displays of Anatsui's or Thomas's work are typically stable once installed, but other works have evolving displays. Katharina Grosse's untitled installation in the 2013 exhibition WUNDERBLOCK at the Nasher Sculpture Center was a room-sized work in which the artist sculpted and painted piles of dirt, also applying paint to the gallery's walls and large canvases approaching wall size (Joyce 2013). Viewers were permitted to walk around in the room, along a particular pathway worn through the paint on the dirt. (Climbing all over was not permitted.) This was the first time Grosse created a work that audience members were invited to enter and interact with in this way; most of her work is self-contained sculpture.[2] During the opening weekend, the artist observed that the work had changed much more than she anticipated as a result of viewers' walking around on it. As a result, she agreed with the Nasher that she would return halfway through the exhibition and repaint the surfaces.[3] The appearance of the display was quite different after repainting; large swaths of color were altered, and paint was applied to a region of the ceiling where none had been previously.[4]

Other displays are characterized by constant change. Each display of Jana Sterbak's 1987 *Vanitas: Flesh Dress for an Albino Anorectic* involves perpetual, though subtle, change: the dress, which is newly constituted for each display from salted flank steak, gradually desiccates.[5]

A display may be of very long or very short duration. Walter De Maria's *Lightning Field*, consisting of "400 polished stainless steel poles installed in a grid array measuring one mile by one kilometer" in western New Mexico, was installed in 1977 and has since been maintained by the Dia Foundation.[6] A work of performance art that is only performed once, on the other hand, may have a

---

[1]   https://www.brooklynmuseum.org/opencollection/objects/5044.

[2]   Interview of Jed Morse, Curator, Nasher Sculpture Center, July 2013.

[3]   Interview of Jed Morse, Curator, Nasher Sculpture Center, July 2013.

[4]   Pictures of the work both before and after repainting can be found here: https://www.katharinagrosse.com/works/2013_4003. The change is most evident in one of the two large canvases that are propped up vertically.

[5]   For a vivid description of the process of constructing a display of *Vanitas*, see https://walkerart.org/magazine/making-jana-sterbaks-vanitas.

[6]   https://www.diaart.org/exhibition/exhibitions-projects/walter-de-maria-the-lightning-field-site.

display that lasts only a few minutes. The video of Chris Burden's 1971 *Shoot*, in which he had a collaborator shoot him in the upper arm, lasts only 8 seconds, and a film also including audio from surrounding moments lasts less than two minutes.[7]

As much as they differ from one another, all of these displays can be captured under a straightforward ontological characterization: they are events. The display of De Maria's *Lightning Field* has been going on for decades, while the display of Marina Abramović's *Rhythm 0*, discussed in Chapter 4, lasted for six hours. But each of them was an event that unfolded in a spatiotemporal location.

The boundaries of displays, considered as events, may be somewhat vague or indeterminate. As we saw in Chapter 4, from 1986 to 1990, Adrian Piper did a series of performances in which, upon encountering racism, she handed out calling cards announcing her identity as a Black woman and closing with the text, "I regret any discomfort my presence is causing you, just as I am sure you regret the discomfort your racism is causing me." When does one of these performances begin? At the moment when Piper pulls a card out of her pocket to hand to another person? Or does the presentation of the card retroactively encompass the racist behavior as an essential part of the performance? Regardless of how we answer these questions, the performance, which is a display of the work, is an event.

The Artwork Is Not Simply the Display

Artists and institutions go to great lengths to put on displays, audience members spend time and effort to encounter them, and critics respond to them. Might the artwork simply be the display?

The view that artworks simply are displays would be handy if it worked out: displays are often the focus of community practices and attention, and as events they are ontologically straightforward. But as a general position about the nature of the artwork, this view must be rejected. A central reason is that community practice for most artworks treats them as susceptible of multiple displays; and the variability of these displays is often central to the work and what it expresses (Couture 2013; G. Ryan 2011). *Dusasa II* is conceived by El Anatsui, as well as by the Metropolitan Museum of Art (which owns it) and by art historians and critics, as a single work that is susceptible of variable displays. To say that the artwork just is the display would be to say, incorrectly, that every time the sculptural object associated with *Dusasa II* is installed, a new work is generated. The same is true of

---

[7] https://www.youtube.com/watch?v=gwh-XMFMp8U.

Mickalene Thomas's *A Little Taste Outside of Love* and Jana Sterbak's *Vanitas: Flesh Dress for an Albino Anorectic*: we do not say that a new work has been created each time a display is constituted, whether the displays involve a persisting object (as in *A Little Taste Outside of Love*) or not (as in *Vanitas*). When a display of Felix Gonzalez-Torres's *"Untitled" (Portrait of Ross in L.A.)* ends, the remaining candies in the pile may be thrown out or given away. The work, however, does not cease to exist at that point. Instead, it persists in the collection of the Art Institute of Chicago and may be displayed again in the future. The practices of the contemporary art community are well settled on this point: many contemporary artworks are such as to be susceptible of multiple displays that all count as displays of one and the same work, even when they employ different objects and have variable appearances.

Such works are, thus, analogous to musical works for performance: there is an underlying work, and then there are displays of that work that resemble each other in some respects and differ in others (cf. Irvin 2013a; Laurenson 2006; Phillips 2015). A fundamental aspect of the work, then, is that it is the kind of thing that is susceptible of having displays. This is part of the work's *functional role*, as discussed in Chapter 1: an aspect of how the work is encountered, used, treated, and understood within the practices of the contemporary art community.

Even where there is only one display of the work, simple identification between the artwork and the display is often not appropriate. If a vandal damaged the display of Katharina Grosse's large installation with spray paint or bent some of the poles of Walter De Maria's *Lightning Field*, the display would fail to reflect the nature of the work, even if the damage was not so bad as to lead us to say it is no longer a display of the work at all. Such displays are *non-compliant*: they do not satisfy the rules associated with the work.

The practices of the contemporary art community are such that non-compliant displays don't fully satisfy the functional role of the artwork: they don't supply us with appropriate objects for appreciation, so artists typically reject the vandalism and ask the institution to make repairs; institutions aim to prevent such damage and reverse it if it occurs; and critics exclude such elements from their interpretations and assessments of the work.

Is it ever possible for the work to be identical to the display? Yes, the artist has the authority to make this determination. Such cases are perhaps most common in performance art: insofar as Chris Burden's *Shoot* is not subject to reperformance, the work may be identical to the one display that occurred in 1971. The artist of an object-based work, too, could specify that the work just is the display, no matter what happens or how the objects are transformed by viewers or other forces. But this would itself be a normatively laden decision, involving the suspension of the conventional rules of non-participation and object conservation that apply by default to object-based works.

Constructing the Display: A Case Study

We have rejected the idea that the artwork is identical to a display, except in unusual cases. What is the relationship between artworks and displays, if not one of identity? Answering this question will help us to understand the functional artwork-role more fully.

It will help to look carefully at the process of constituting a display. The conservator and scholar Sanneke Stigter describes working with Jan Dibbets to produce a 2009 display of Dibbets's (1969) *All shadows that occurred to me in . . . . are marked with tape*[8] at the Kröller-Müller Museum in Otterlo, Netherlands, after the Kröller-Müller acquired the work in 2007 (Figure 5.1).[9] Stigter and Dibbets had two aims in their work together: first, to constitute a

Figure 5.1 Jan Dibbets, *All shadows that struck me in the Kröller-Müller Museum*, 1969. Installation view 2012. Masking tape. Dimensions variable.

Collection Kröller-Müller Museum, Otterlo, the Netherlands, purchased with support from the Mondriaan Foundation. Photo by Marjon Gemmeke
Courtesy of the artist and Peter Freeman, Inc.

---

[8] Stigter notes that in documents supplied to the Kröller-Müller on acquisition of the work, Dibbets specified the title *Alle schaduwen die mij zijn opgevallen in . . . . zijn afgeplakt met tape*. The English translation is Stigter's. The ellipsis indicates the need to fill in the details of where and when a particular installation is created in order to complete the title for the purposes of a specific display.
[9] All details of this case are taken from Stigter 2014, 2015, and 2016b.

display; second, to secure the conditions for the institution to install displays appropriately in the future, even without Dibbets's involvement. Dibbets had never worked up a set of guidelines, since he had almost always been directly involved in constituting the display. His work with Stigter was expressly designed to enable the Kröller-Müller to ascertain the rules for constituting future displays.

Dibbets's work has no enduring physical components. To install it, a team uses tape to mark the shadows they observe in a gallery space that is illuminated in part by the sun (Figure 5.2). (In effect, they are marking the boundaries of sunlight that enters through windows and doors in the gallery space.) The shadows are marked at several intervals (not a set number) as the sun moves throughout the day. The display thus has a repeating geometric pattern, though the repetition is not perfect: the intervals depend on such things as how quickly the team is able to mark off a given set of shadows and when the sun comes out on a day with passing clouds. Tape is used to mark shadows on the floor, the walls, and sometimes the ceiling. Judgment may be exercised about which shadows to mark; one may, for instance,

Figure 5.2 Jan Dibbets, Sanneke Stigter, and Evelyne Snijders installing Jan Dibbets's work *All shadows that struck me in the Kröller-Müller Museum*, 1969.

Collection Kröller-Müller Museum, Otterlo, the Netherlands, purchased with support from the Mondriaan Foundation.
Photo by Toos van Kooten, 2009
Courtesy of the artist and Peter Freeman, Inc.

omit some shadows cast by interior window framing if that makes for an excessively complex pattern.

Stigter begins her research process by looking back at all available documentation from earlier displays and making notes of what was consistent and what differed from one display to another. She then interviews the artist to discuss his views about these displays and ascertain whether he regards some as more successful than others. The kind of process Stigter describes is common: many institutions that collect contemporary artworks bring the artist in to construct a display and to be interviewed when they acquire artworks so as to ensure that they have all the information required to mount displays of the work in the future. The process of constructing the display may be documented with notes, photographs, and video.

Stigter's work with Dibbets involves a combination of open dialogue, specific questioning, and working side by side on installation. While Dibbets insists on the work's informal nature and "stated several times that he is not very precise in the execution of his work," Stigter observes that "in practice he carefully cuts the tape endings in perfect sharp tips to neatly complete the geometrical forms" (Stigter 2015, 110–11). Her observation clarifies that his expression "not very precise" does not imply certain kinds of material sloppiness.

Dibbets indicates that, contrary to what one would naturally infer from the documentation of past displays, it is not necessary to use masking tape, and that any color of tape would be fine (though mixing of colors is prohibited). "However," Stigter observes,

> the colours he mentioned...were neutral: masking tape-beige, black and white. One could deduce from this information that a neutral colour is preferable. However, this is an interpretation from the artist's literal words and, therefore, a subjective conclusion from the interview. This is something one should be aware of, especially when retrieving information from an interview to translate...into guidelines.   (Stigter 2016b, 201)

The work involves a rule for participation: typically, some of the tape is applied to the floor, and walking on the tape is permitted. Dibbets told Stigter, "If you tape on the floor, you will damage it by walking and that is actually part of it" (Stigter 2015, 111). But in the same conversation, he also said, "It is a construction that consolidates light. You would want to have it, well 'perfect' I would rather not say, but that may be just the word: as perfect as possible" (Stigter 2015, 111). Stigter posed further direct questions to ascertain the limit of damage that is acceptable, prompting the artist to confirm that "[t]he work could bear stains caused by visitors walking over it, but when the lines become disrupted the work is considered damaged" (Stigter 2015, 111).

Stigter noticed a subtle feature in the documentation of the earliest installations that had not come up in Dibbets's description of how to install the work or in her discussions with him: there were small white lines on some of the tape. When she asked Dibbets about this, he was reminded of a long-forgotten feature of the early displays: they had small labels indicating the time that various shadows had been observed. As Stigter notes, this adds an additional layer of narrative to the piece, giving us a sense of how the sun was moving and how the work of the installation team progressed throughout the day. Dibbets told her that it is up to the installation team to decide whether to include this feature in the future: it is not necessary, but he would not rule it out (Stigter 2015, 112–13). Clearly, Stigter's careful work in examining the documentation and following up with the artist was crucial in opening up a possibility for future displays by moving the artist to articulate a rule.

One earlier display of the work, the one Dibbets regarded as least successful, had included shadows cast by a figurative sculpture. When Stigter worked with Dibbets to install the 2009 display, there were two large geometric sculptures by Carl Andre in the same gallery. Dibbets said that the display should not include shadows cast by the sculptures: "The architecture determines the form and not what is in the room…So you imagine the room empty" (Stigter 2015, 110). However,

> Dibbets deviated from his standpoint, the moment he saw long narrow shadows cast by the antique display cases in the adjacent gallery. He hastily added that those kinds of shadows could be included as well. Aware of this contradiction, Dibbets finally concluded, "It is a bit to your own liking."   (Stigter 2015, 110)

What lessons can we derive from examining Stigter's work with Dibbets? First, we see that the displays do not fully reflect or determine the nature of the work. The fact that previous displays have all been constructed with light-colored masking tape does not imply that masking tape is required. Careful observation of the displays may not give us a sufficient basis for inference about the rules associated with the work.

Second, ascertaining the rules is an inferential and interpretative process. The combination of the appearance of displays and the artist's statements and activities in executing a display provides a rich basis for interpretation of the parameters associated with the work. Some of the parameters that emerge from discussion with the artist are fairly clear (such as the possibility of using different kinds and colors of tape, but the requirement that all the tape used for a given display be of a uniform color). But the degree of informality or messiness in installation is best ascertained through a combination of looking at displays, watching the artist work, and hearing how he describes his approach.

Third, the process Stigter describes is one in which the work evolves even as it is being formalized. When Stigter asks questions and Dibbets gives answers, this may result in rules being made more precise, being loosened, or being actively changed from one moment to the next, as when Dibbets allows that the shadows cast by the display cases might be marked with tape even after suggesting that only architectural elements of the building were relevant.

Fourth, both the nature of the expressed rules and the form of a particular display will depend on the individuals involved and their choices. Stigter looked carefully at past documentation and noticed something others might not have, and her close working relationship with the artist allowed her to bring it up for consideration. The specific questions she asked, too, affected which information was expressed. Likewise, individual installers will make different judgments about which shadows to capture, and their different paces of work will lead to differences in the frequency of intervals. Also, as Stigter notes, knowing how to work with the materials is a crucial aspect of installation. She advocates having on hand for every installation a conservator who has participated before as well as a conservator who is learning to install the work for the first time. She suggests that the involvement of a new conservator is an "active conservation treatment," because it keeps alive the information that is required to install the work (Stigter 2014, 141; English translation supplied by Stigter). Some of the relevant information can't be set down in words; it involves the engagement of the installer's competence with the materials. Conservator Jill Sterrett makes the related observation that keeping such a work "in dark storage" for an extended period, as one might do to preserve a traditional art object, is "a sure sign of its demise[;] you've diminished your ability to keep it because you might not be able to install it properly" (Gale, Lake, and Sterrett 2009, n.p.).

Fifth, though the installation team must engage in an inferential process, the artist has clear authority, and the artist's aesthetic and way of understanding the work serve to guide the process of inference. As Stigter says, the aim is to "parallel the artist's way of thinking during installation and to be conscious and transparent about the choices that are made, in an attempt to intervene as little as possible" (Stigter 2014, 120; English translation supplied by Stigter). Even in asking questions, she aims not to steer the discussion too directly. At one point, the installation team points out shadows cast by the windowsills in the room, and Dibbets agrees to their inclusion at that point. One of Stigter's research colleagues later suggested to her that this was too much intervention: they should simply have followed the artist's lead (Stigter 2015, 112).

Sixth, there are aspects of the institutional background that shape what can be done. This is relevant both to small details of a particular display and to the work's fundamental nature. No tape is applied to the Carl Andre sculptures that share the gallery with Dibbets's work, because there is a widespread and powerful community norm against materially altering another artist's work in such a fashion. It is thus normative for the work that when shadows are being taped, they are not applied to other artists' works, even if Dibbets never says anything to preclude this.

Even the very possibility of a work like Dibbets's, and the fact that the work can be acquired and conserved by an institution and conceived as re-exhibitable without the artist, is a function of the evolution of conventions and practices of contemporary art institutions. As Stigter notes, the work was available for the Kröller-Müller to acquire in 2007 only because, when prominent collector Giuseppe Panza acquired an entire show of Dibbets's work over the phone in 1970, the gallerist did not even think to describe *All shadows*: it was not considered the kind of work that could be transferred into a collection (Stigter 2015, 106). The very possibility of an artistic practice that consists of expressing rules for the constitution of displays is conditioned by the contemporary art community's willingness to receive such a practice, a willingness that has expanded markedly in recent decades.

What Is the Artwork?

When we examine Dibbets's interactions with Stigter, we see that they are working together to define the rules governing displays of the work. These include rules for constituting the display (shadows visible in the room should be taped off at intervals; only one color of tape should be used), rules for participation (tape applied to the floor may be walked on), and rules for conservation (if a line is disrupted it should be repaired).

The work is an entity that is susceptible of having multiple displays, just as a musical work is susceptible of having multiple performances, a game of having multiple playings,[10] and a species of having multiple members. In philosophical terms, the artwork, the musical work, the game, and the species are *universals*: entities that bear a special relationship to concrete objects or events that we can call *occurrences*. The species "giraffe" bears a special relationship to some organisms, actual giraffes. The game "basketball" bears a special relationship to some, but by no means all, events that happen on basketball courts. Likewise, the artwork *All shadows...* bears a special relation to some display events.

In each case, the universal is connected to its occurrences by a certain kind of relation. For an event to count as a playing of chess, it must have the right kind of historical relationship to the game of chess—typically, one that involves the players intending to play chess—and must comply nearly enough with the rules of

---

[10] In ordinary language, we often use the term "game" to refer both to the game itself ("the game of chess") and to a particular event ("let's play a game of chess"). To avoid confusion, I use the word "playing" to refer to the particular event.

chess. If two people were idly to move chess pieces around on a chess board in a way that happened to be a possible playing of chess, but without their knowing about the game of chess or intending to play it, this event would not be a playing of chess despite satisfying the structural constraints on a game of chess. And if two people were aware of and intended to play chess but were seriously mistaken about the rules of chess or seriously misapplied them, the event would fail to be a playing of chess due to a lack of sufficient compliance.

Similarly, to count as a performance of a given musical work or as a display of a contemporary artwork, an event must have the right kind of historical-intentional connection to that work and must comply (nearly enough) with the rules for that work. For most kinds of musical works, this means it must have a specified sound structure (or something close enough to the specified sound structure).[11] The idea is the same for contemporary art displays: a display of the artwork must have (enough of) the structural features that have been sanctioned by the artist.

Dibbets's and Stigter's work together manifests agreement about the functional role of the artwork as they aim to specify it for acquisition and conservation purposes: it is the entity that governs and unifies displays. I suggest, therefore, that Dibbets's work is a group of rules. These rules perform a dual function: they tell installers what to do to create a display of the work, and they determine which things count as displays of the work. Similarly, chess is a group of rules: namely, rules that both tell players how to play chess and determine which events count as playings of chess. And a musical work is a group of rules: namely, rules that tell musicians how to perform the work and determine which events count as performances of the work.

Now let's make a few observations about these rules.

1. The artist, as the creator of the work, has special authority over the rules.

The artist's act of creating the work is one of sanctioning rules governing displays of the work. This sanctioning occurs through a combination of constituting displays and communicating about how displays should be constituted and maintained (Irvin 2005b).

2. Other people and institutions can help to shape the rules.

---

[11] Sounds need not be the only relevant structural features. The use of specified instruments may also be required (Levinson 1980, 14–19). And some works specify a structure of processes rather than of sounds: for instance, John Cage's 1951 work *Imaginary Landscape No. 4 (March No. 2)* requires that twenty-four performers turn the dials of twelve radios under the direction of a conductor; the resulting sounds are determined by the programming of local radio stations during the performance. For detail, see https://johncage.org/pp/John-Cage-Work-Detail.cfm?work_ID=104.

Stigter's decisions to ask certain questions, and her pointing out of the time labels in the earliest displays, affect the rules that Dibbets ultimately sanctions. There may be aspects of the rules, then, that are a matter of luck: they depend on the interactions the artist had, the circumstances that arose, and the questions that were asked. The same is true for acts of physical fabrication: the final form of a painting or sculpture may be altered by a wide variety of circumstances, including feedback from others, interruptions, and the availability of materials or tools. In addition, the conventions and practices of an institution or community can shape the implicit rules for the work: if Dibbets were silent on whether tape could be applied to other artists' work to mark shadows cast there, the conventions of conservation that apply by default to object-based artworks would settle this question in the negative (cf. Irvin 2006). The situation is similar for object-based works from earlier historical periods: an artist's decision to add paint to a canvas may be shaped by feedback from others; and some of the rules for display, such as the fact that the representational content should be presented right side up, are fixed by convention without any need for the artist's explicit sanction.

3. The content of the rules need not be—and typically is not—fixed for all time.

As van de Vall et al. (2011) note, there are certain moments in the life of a contemporary artwork when it tends to undergo change. These include the moment when it is first exhibited, the moment when it is acquired by an institution, and the moment when it is re-exhibited after a long period of dormancy. If we are to say that the work is a group of rules, then, we must allow that the group of rules can be the same group even if some of its constituent rules change over time. This is not an unfamiliar situation: we allow that human bodies, cars, and other physical objects can persist through changes—even quite extensive ones—and it also seems clear that games can persist through rule changes. What allows the game of basketball to persist through changes to its rules? It is the fact that we continue to treat it as the same game, one that is subject to evolution over time. Our practices determine that a person, game, car, or artwork can survive through extensive changes produced over a gradual evolutionary process, even if it could not survive if the same changes were produced suddenly.[12] Whether the work has survived change, then, is a function not merely of the structure after the change, but also of the process through which the change was produced. This will be discussed further in Chapter 8.

---

[12] See Hölling 2017, especially chapter 6, for a rich discussion of how rates of change and other aspects of temporality figure in our understanding of artwork identity and conservation.

Dibbets's artwork, then, is made up of rules, specifically rules for display and interaction.[13] The rules are articulated through the artist's actions and statements in a particular art historical and institutional context. The context in which the artist acts helps to determine the content of the rules; they are not determined exclusively by the artist's actions. This is typical of socially constructed entities: the consensual practices that enable social construction also help to determine what is done or made through a particular set of actions taken in a context. The content of my utterance depends in part on the conventional meanings of the words I use; likewise, the content of artwork rules depends in part on conventions for displaying and conserving works of art. There is a give and take between community norms and expectations supplied by the context, and my expressive activity within that context.

What Does It Mean to Say a Work Is Made of Rules?

What *is* a group of rules, anyway? A standard metaphysical picture suggests that there are concrete entities and abstract entities. Concrete entities like physical objects can be created, experience change over time, and be destroyed. They are familiar entities in our world that have a position in time and space and can participate in causal relations. Abstract entities, like numbers and shapes, exist eternally if they exist at all: the number four existed long before anyone was around to think of it, and nothing can change the number four or cause it to go out of existence. Abstract entities can have occurrences: any group of four items is an occurrence of the number four.

Rules don't fit neatly into either the realm of the concrete or the realm of the abstract. They aren't concrete things with a particular spatiotemporal location: the records that we consult to learn about the rules for Dibbets's work may have a location, but the rules themselves do not, just as the rules of tennis or chess don't have a location. They also don't fit the model of abstract entities: they don't exist eternally, and they aren't impervious to change.

Barry Smith (2008) has coined the term *quasi-abstract* to describe entities that, although they are not spatiotemporally concrete, can come into existence, change over time, and cease to exist, and may be subject to having occurrences. Quasi-abstract entities include debts and quantities of currency that are represented in electronic records. Such entities come into existence by way of events in spacetime (such as the signing of a mortgage agreement), but once created have an existence that extends beyond their initiating events. They may be represented by physical objects, such as an IOU or a bank account statement, but the debt is not

---

[13] Evnine 2018 has recently argued that internet memes are constituted of rules; Nguyen 2019b argues that games are constituted by their rules.

identical to its representations: destruction of an IOU does not eliminate the debt (B. Smith 2008, 44). Smith suggests that we must countenance quasi-abstract entities to make sense of many familiar phenomena.

Guy Rohrbaugh (2003) introduces a similar model for artworks: some works are both subject to being created, changed over time, and destroyed, and susceptible of having occurrences. In addition, they are modally flexible, which is to say that had the circumstances of their creation been different, they might have had different properties: for instance, even if Jane Austen had given *Emma* a few different words, we would still count it as the same work (Rohrbaugh 2003, 184). Since abstract entities like types can't be created or destroyed, can't change over time, and aren't modally flexible, artworks cannot be assimilated to types. Therefore, we must recognize that not every entity susceptible of having occurrences is an abstract type. Rohrbaugh suggests that we should see both singular artworks, like paintings, and artworks susceptible of having multiple occurrences, like works of photography and music, as *historical individuals*. Works of both painting and photography, Rohrbaugh says, "are ontologically dependent items, whose creation, continued existence, and destruction are ultimately a matter of how it goes with some other historical items" (Rohrbaugh 2003, 191). The work of painting is ontologically dependent on the paint and canvas that constitute it, such that when these are completely destroyed, the painting too is destroyed; but it can survive some change and loss to this matter. Similarly, the work of photography ontologically depends on its embodiments, which may include negatives and prints. When no prints exist and it is no longer possible to produce new ones, the work of photography is destroyed. Ultimately, Rohrbaugh suggests,

> photographs are non-physical historical individuals, continuants which stand in a relation of ontological dependence to a causally-connected series of physical (sometimes mental) particulars.   (Rohrbaugh 2003, 198)

I gather that Smith's quasi-abstract entities, too, are non-physical historical individuals that ontologically depend on series of physical and mental particulars such as paper or digital bank statements, IOUs, and memories.

However, the ontological dependence here might seem mysterious. If a quasi-abstract entity is ontologically dependent on a series of particulars, what explains the progression from one member of the series to the next? Why say that the quasi-abstract entity is dependent on *these* particulars rather than *those*? In the example of a debt, this is comparatively easy to understand: it seems the debt will ontologically depend on particulars that are causally connected to the debt's initiating event and that represent the same set of facts about what is owed to whom by whom. Moreover, change in the debt's nature over time can occur through a set of conventionally specified processes, typically involving the owed sum being partly or wholly paid off or forgiven. These processes of change are inherent in the debt's nature as an obligation of one party to another: one remains obliged unless one discharges the obligation or is released by the person to whom it is owed.

A game, much like a debt, ontologically depends on particulars that represent it correctly: specifically, particulars that represent its rules. The story about change in the game over time is different: unlike in the case of the debt, the processes for change in the game are not typically generated by features internal to the game's structure. A game can change over time through (at least) two quite different processes. The first is immediate change implemented by a recognized governing body, as when two thirds of the board of governors of the National Basketball Association votes to change the rules for professional basketball in North America. The second is gradual evolution in gameplay that results in the community of the game coming to recognize a different set of rules, as happened over the centuries in the history of chess. There may be a limit to the amount of change that we regard as compatible with saying that a game has persisted as the same game over time. The ancient Indian game *chaturanga* is widely acknowledged as the precursor to chess, but chess and *chaturanga* are nonetheless regarded as distinct games, with neither being understood as a version of the other (Shenk 2006, 17).

Let's now bring this back to the case of contemporary art. Jan Dibbets's work *All shadows...* is a non-physical historical individual that ontologically depends on the persistence of particulars, whether physical or mental, that represent the rules sanctioned by Dibbets. The aim of Dibbets's and Stigter's work together is to constitute a complex particular—an institutional record—that accurately represents the rules as Dibbets intends them, and can serve to ground the work ontologically.[14] The work can change over time through changes in Dibbets's sanction, as when he indicates that the shadows cast by display cases may be marked with tape. It can also change if some information about the rules Dibbets sanctioned is lost; this is a form of damage, analogous to the change that happens when the physical object associated with a work of painting or sculpture suffers damage. The threshold at which such damage to the work is sufficient for its destruction is connected to the artist's sanction: it depends on the extent to which the damaged work can still function in a way that is close enough to providing the experience the artist designed.

El Anatsui's work *Dusasa II*, in contrast to *All shadows...*, ontologically depends both on a specific physical object (which partly constitutes it) and on particulars that represent the rule that installers are invited to make autonomous choices in constituting the display. Thus, it is a hybrid physical and non-physical historical individual. Both its physical and its non-physical components can be

---

[14] See Hölling 2017, especially chapter 3, for discussion of how the institutional archive both safeguards and complicates artwork identity. This matter will be taken up in Chapter 8.

changed over time if Anatsui sanctions such change; and both components can potentially undergo damage and loss if change happens that violates his sanction.

My position is a variety of hylomorphism, on which "some things stand in the relation of *being the matter of* to other things" (Evnine 2016, 3). In the case of a sculpture, the physical material out of which it is made is the sculpture's matter, but not identical to it (Evnine 2016, 3–7). But an artifact can have matter that is non-physical: Evnine suggests that standard musical works are abstract artifacts that have a sound structure as their matter. This does not mean that the musical work can't change over time: when a composer revises the work, it can come to have a different sound structure as its matter (Evnine 2016, 136–9).

I suggest, along the same lines, that the rules Dibbets has sanctioned serve as the matter for his work *All shadows...*, and the persistence of the work is secured through particulars that represent these rules. Anatsui's work *Dusasa II* has as its matter both a specific physical object and a rule for display; its persistence is secured through a combination of preservation of the specific object and preservation of some particular that represents the rule. To be clear, then, not everything on which the work ontologically depends is part of its actual matter: a musical work may ontologically depend on a score that accurately represents its sound structure, but only that sound structure and not the score itself serves as the work's matter.

What determines which things serve as the matter of an artwork? Evnine says that "[a]rtifacts come into being, are made, by someone's working with certain intentions on some material that becomes the artifact's matter" (Evnine 2016, 67). An artifact is "the impression of a mind onto matter" (Evnine 2016, 89). The artwork is an example par excellence of an artifact whose nature and existence depend on its maker's creative activity. The artist thus has special powers of authorization: the artist's sanction determines what serves as the artwork's matter, on which particulars the material components of the work ontologically depend, which forms of change in those material components are acceptable and which constitute damage, and which changes suffice for the work's destruction.

The act of making, Evnine suggests, is essential to an artwork in a way that specific material is not. He imagines an example in which a sculptor grabs a hunk of clay out of a rotating vat and makes a sculpture from this hunk. It could have happened that the sculptor reached into the vat a second earlier or later, grabbed a different hunk, and made a sculpture with the same form and features. Evnine suggests that there is no reason to doubt that the resulting work is the same in the two cases.

> Where the intentions and acts are the same, and operate on such indifferent matter, it seems perverse to make the matter essential to the identity of the created object, and perverse to deny the essentiality of that act of making.
>
> (Evnine 2016, 89)

The artist's action, then, is essential to the work's identity. For some artifacts, such as a marble sculpture, a specific hunk of matter may also be essential. But even in such cases, Evnine suggests, the artist's intentional act of making has priority: it is the creative action, in the form of the artist's sanction, that determines whether a particular hunk of matter is essential to the work or not (Evnine 2016, 89).[15]

Just as the artist's sanction is essential to the work's identity, it determines which things count as occurrences of the work. As Rohrbaugh notes, not all embodiments of an artwork are occurrences of it. For instance, while a negative is a critically important embodiment of the work of photography, only the prints and not the negative are occurrences.

> The 'occurrence of' relation is then a more specific form of the embodiment relation, one conditioned by the needs of the practice of a particular art form and one which picks out those embodiments which display the qualities of the work of art and are relevant to appreciation and criticism...It is the job of the 'occurrence of' relation to pick what we care about out from the historical flow which sustains the objects.   (Rohrbaugh 2003, 198)

Which embodiments also count as occurrences depends in part on the art form in question and the practices and conventions surrounding it. Literature is notational, so counting as an occurrence is largely a matter of being correctly spelled (or close enough). The occurrences of a musical work are performance events; which performance events comply closely enough with the score to count as occurrences of the work may be determined through performance conventions operative at a particular time. But in some art forms, the artist may establish specific criteria for occurrences or even select the occurrences directly. The artist, through the process of sanctioning, determines which things count as occurrences of the work and which things are failed occurrences or mere documents. Some artists working in performative idioms treat still or moving images of their work as reproductions, while others display such documents as artworks in their own right (Berger and Santone 2016). In photography, being printed from the right negative is typically a necessary but not sufficient condition for counting as an occurrence of the work: the artist may directly select and reject certain prints, may authorize a specific person to do the printing, may place limits on the number of prints that are authorized, or may establish criteria that a print must meet in order to be acceptable.

---

[15] See David Davies (2004, 60–74) for further reasons to think the artist's creative activity is essential to the work's appreciation and identity. Davies goes further than Evnine or I, suggesting that the artist's activity of producing a structure for our appreciation, rather than just the structure thereby produced, should be identified as the artwork. While I don't agree that this is the best way to account for our critical and appreciative practice, Davies makes compelling arguments about the nature of appreciation and its relevance to the ontology of art.

When it comes to works like Dibbets's, the occurrences of the work are display events. An event counts as a display of the work when it is produced with the right historical relation to the work (typically involving an intention to display it) and sufficiently complies with the rules for constituting a display. Some aspects of what counts as sufficient compliance may be directly determined by the artist: artists sometimes directly state that the violation of a particular stipulation means that the display cannot be counted as a display of their work. In other cases, a judgment must be made by others about the extent of non-compliance that is compatible with sufficiently respecting the work as the artist originally sanctioned it. We'll consider these matters further in Chapter 9.

In sum, then, contemporary artworks are historical individuals that may be made out of both rules and physical objects fabricated or selected by the artist. The work may undergo change over time in both its physical components and its rules. Where a work is made wholly or partly from rules, it is ontologically dependent on particulars that represent the rules correctly (enough). Through the creative activity of sanctioning, the artist determines what the work is made of and can generate change in the work under some circumstances. The artist's sanction also determines which items count as occurrences of the work.

Innovation in our metaphysical categories should be avoided where possible, but as Smith and Rohrbaugh discuss, we need a notion of quasi-abstract entities or non-physical historical individuals to make sense of many aspects of our social lives: those involving games, musical works, mortgages, marriages, laws, universities, corporations, and countless other entities. It is implausible to say that a mortgage, game, law, or corporation exists eternally and unchangeably, and equally implausible to suggest that it is a concrete, spatiotemporally located object. A category that can account for such entities is a salutary addition to our ontological catalogue.

Do These Works Really Exist?

Some would deny that such things exist: when we refer to mortgages, laws, and corporations as though they exist, that is simply loose talk. Andrew Kania (2008) makes such a claim about musical works: we can explain all the practices of musical composition, performance, and appreciation without postulating that musical works actually *exist*, so (for the sake of parsimony) we are better off regarding them as fictional.[16]

---

[16] An alternative to fictionalism is nominalism, whose various species treat the work as having no existence beyond the existence of its occurrences. See Irvin 2013a for discussion of reasons to reject nominalist treatments of contemporary artworks.

Like Barry Smith (2008, 37), I don't find such fictionalism about socially constructed entities attractive.[17] Some things are fictional and don't exist: Pecola Breedlove or Pemberley, for instance. But Toni Morrison's *The Bluest Eye* and Jane Austen's *Pride and Prejudice* do exist. One can believe falsely that a mortgage has been established, but once a mortgage contract has been finalized, many beliefs about the mortgage—its amount, its terms—are true. While I don't want to venture too far into metaontology, I hold, with Amie Thomasson, that many ontological questions are in fact questions about our concepts and their application. We establish terms in our language, such as "chess" or "recession," and it is up to us, collectively, to establish the conditions for the existence of such things. Once we have done this, when the conditions are satisfied a recession exists, even if no one has noticed it yet (Thomasson 1999, 155).

Even for concrete physical objects, something similar is true (Thomasson 2014). In one sense, all that exists is an agglomeration of stuff in spacetime. Then humans come along and decide that it is useful to apply concepts to certain chunks of stuff, and we call them "planets" or "hyenas" or "houses." We are interested in certain kinds of regularities of structure, behavior, or disposition, and we may establish criteria to pick out things that exhibit such regularities. Whether something is a planet, a hyena, or a house depends on whether it satisfies our criteria, which may include both structural features and historical features that explain how the thing came to exist and to have the structural features it has (cf. Rohrbaugh 2003, 184). When the relevant criteria are satisfied, a house exists.[18]

The same goes for questions about persistence over time: whether something counts as the same house or the same human body, even if it has undergone certain kinds of change, depends on our concepts and their application conditions. Our concepts are such that when a house is demolished and replaced wholesale, we typically don't count the replacement as identical to the initial house: it may be structurally similar, but we don't consider it to be *the same* house. When a gradual replacement of parts occurs, however, even a house that is wholly physically distinct from the initial house may be counted as the same house. There is nothing necessary in our choice to apply our concepts in this way. As Dominic McIver Lopes (2007) discusses, some such choices are culturally specific: in Japan, a temple may be considered to persist over centuries even if the physical building associated with it is repeatedly demolished and reconstructed on alternating sites.

---

[17] See Letts 2015 for specific criticisms of Kania's 2008 proposal.
[18] See Caldarola (2020) for the suggestion that we need not be committed to the existence of the entities seemingly invoked by our discourses and practices. I find Caldarola's agnosticism more palatable than Kania's fictionalism, though I remain drawn to Thomasson's deflationary suggestion that it is up to us to determine the existence conditions for such entities, and all it takes for such entities to exist is that our conditions be satisfied. See Evnine (2016, 113–18) for discussion of drawbacks of Thomasson's deflationary ontology.

It is thus up to us to decide which objects it is useful to pick out from among the stuff distributed in spacetime. This doesn't mean that we can never be mistaken about what exists: though phlogiston is a human concept, and humans established the conditions for applying the concept, it turns out that nothing actually satisfies those conditions, and thus phlogiston does not exist.

When it comes to socially constructed entities, we aren't simply picking out chunks of physical stuff. Chess is not an agglomeration of stuff in a spacetime region. However, the existence of chess, the nature of its rules, and any changes in the rules over time are nonetheless explained by events in the familiar physical world: actions and declarations made by people and organizations. To say that chess exists is to say that the conditions for the creation of a game were satisfied, and to say that chess consists of certain rules is to say that people and organizations took actions whereby they successfully established those rules as the rules associated with the name "chess." These actions, which may have involved direct nomination of certain rules or participation in a form of collective practice that resulted in convergence on a set of rules over time, took place against a background of social conventions for establishing the existence and nature of a game.

Something similar is true of an artwork like Dibbets's. Against a background of conventions for creating visual artworks—conventions that have evolved, over the past century, to allow that a visual artwork need not have enduring physical components—Dibbets sanctioned, through a combination of actions and declarations, a set of rules for constituting the displays of his work *All shadows...* The Kröller-Müller's process of acquiring the work was partly an economic process of acquiring rights to display, and partly a process of working with the artist to specify the rules. It is by virtue of Dibbets's actions in the late 1960s that the work initially came to exist, and by virtue of the actions of Dibbets in concert with Stigter and other agents of the Kröller-Müller that it underwent some changes in the content of its rules during the museum's acquisition process. All of these actions occurred in a specific art historical and institutional context that places some constraints on the content of the rules and also helps to fill in aspects of the rules that may have been left tacit.

Dibbets's artwork, then, is a socially constructed non-physical historical individual made out of rules. The content of those rules is determined by the actions of people—especially the artist—in a particular art historical and institutional context. The work is not a concrete, spatiotemporally located entity, but it is susceptible of having occurrences, namely displays that are concrete events. An event counts as a display of the artwork if it sufficiently complies with the rules and has the right sort of historical-intentional relationship to them. There is no hard and fast standard for when the event sufficiently complies with the rules; as we will see in Chapter 9, this judgment must be made in context, with a determination of how severely any non-compliance affects audience experience of the work.

Artworks as Hybrids of Rules and Materials

I have suggested that Dibbets's work is a non-physical historical individual made out of rules. Clearly, though, many contemporary artworks have essential physical objects, so they are not made exclusively of rules. El Anatsui's *Dusasa II*, Katharina Grosse's untitled room-filling installation, and Mickalene Thomas's *A Little Taste Outside of Love*, like most visual artworks, have key physical components. The functional artwork role for these works cannot be satisfied by thinking of them as made of rules. The objects these artists fabricated, not the rules applying to them, are the central focus of critical, appreciative, and institutional practices surrounding the works.

But even where the physical object is central, the rules also make an important contribution to the aesthetic and artistic properties of the work. Thomas's painting has a correct orientation, and it's crucial that the appearance of the painted surface be preserved; repainting or extensive deterioration would eventuate in the work's destruction. As we've seen, contemporary artists like Saburo Murakami (of the *Peeling Pictures*, Figure 0.3) and Gerald Ferguson (of the *Maintenance Paintings*, Figure 0.4) have suspended such rules for some of their works, specifying that the surfaces of their paintings may be allowed to deteriorate or may be repainted. When they replace the traditional rules with new rules customized to their works, they both give their works important aesthetic features by virtue of these rules and reveal the aesthetic contribution of the traditional rules to the appreciation and treatment of earlier works. As Arthur Danto (1964, 583) discusses, new artistic developments reveal aspects of the structure of earlier artworks that had gone unremarked, resulting in the "retroactive enrichment of the entities of the artworld" that predate those new developments.

The extent to which the rules are central varies from artist to artist and from work to work. Sigalit Landau's *Barbed Salt Lamps*, discussed in Chapter 1, are primarily in a physical, sculptural medium, namely barbed wire and salt from the Dead Sea; the artistic contribution made by her calibration of rules of conservation is small compared to the artistic contribution made through fabrication of the object. For this reason, I suggest that in most cases contemporary artworks are material-rule hybrids, or historical individuals that are both physical and non-physical: they are made of physical entities (objects or events) and groups of rules that govern the display and conservation of these entities. The respective prominence of the material- and rule-based elements may vary, and there are limiting cases on both sides. For works that have no enduring physical components, like Dibbets's, the material dimension is set to zero: the work itself, unlike its displays, has no material element.

As we have seen, the specific features of the object or the specific contents of the rules are typically not all essential to the work's identity; the work can survive through changes in these elements, though there are limits to this survival and the artist can make direct statements that contribute to the setting of these limits.

The fact that (most) artworks are material-rule hybrids is not new: as I have emphasized, any painting that has a correct configuration is governed by a rule for display. What is distinctive of the contemporary period is the potential for artists to sanction custom rules for specific artworks that contribute to the work's artistic functioning just as choices about the work's material elements do. Rules, then, have emerged from the deep background into the foreground, as resources that the artist can directly manipulate.

Artists use both the articulation of rules and the fabrication of physical objects to achieve expressive ends. When Felix Gonzalez-Torres specifies that the candies of *"Untitled" (Portrait of Ross in L.A.)* may be eaten and replenished periodically by the museum, he supplies material for interpretation; and the range of meanings suited to the work with its actual rules is quite different from the range that would be suited to a physically similar work with different rules, as we saw in Chapter 1. And when Dibbets alters the primary rules of his work, allowing that shadows from objects within the museum may be taped in some circumstances, this change alters the aesthetic potentialities of the work, much as would be the case if a composer had replaced a metronomic tempo with an indication that the work may be performed in free time. Many artists now use the explicit articulation of rules as part of the process of imbuing their works with artistic and aesthetic value or with the capacity to make certain kinds of artistic statement. In Chapter 6, I will argue on this basis that rules themselves are often part of the *medium* of the contemporary artwork.

6

Rules as Medium

Contemporary artists, as we have seen, have taken to sanctioning custom rules for display, conservation, and participation. Here, I'll argue that rules have become part of the *medium* of contemporary art. Rules are integral to the structure of many contemporary artworks, there are practices and conventions for deploying them, and they serve as expressive resources in contemporary art. While I won't claim that rules as medium are *uniquely* suited to particular artistic tasks, in Chapter 7 I discuss two kinds of subject matter that rules, as expressive resources, are particularly well suited to addressing.

What Is a Medium?

On a museum label, the medium is often identified with the kinds of physical stuff on display. But philosophers and art theorists distinguish between physical medium and artistic medium.[1] Whereas physical medium is material stuff, artistic medium emerges when a kind of stuff is used in the context of an artistic tradition. On my account, a medium is a system involving (a) materials and (b) conventions and practices, arising out of artistic tradition, for working with those materials. A medium creates a framework within which artistic choices are meaningful: the relationship between an artist's present choice and the established practices and conventions of the medium helps to determine the expressive import of the choice.

The materials involved in a medium may be physical, symbolic, and/or technical.[2] Physical materials are things like paint, bronze, or ordinary objects. Symbolic materials are things like words in a work of literature or notes in a musical score (cf. Gaut 2010, 288–9). Technical materials are systems with complex functioning, such as software and/or hardware used to support digital artworks. A medium may involve working with more than one kind of material, or

---

[1] Murray Smith (2006) and Noël Carroll (2003, 2008) tend to focus, in their discussions, on physical medium: "the physical materials from which, and the instruments by which, a work of art is made (paint, canvas, paintbrush)" (M. Smith 2006, 141). However, Carroll (2008, 36) acknowledges that physical media are distinct from artistic media, "the conventions...which are employed in the production of certain genres of artworks."

[2] Pace Carroll 2003, who denies that literature has a medium on the ground that words are not physical.

working with one kind of material by way of another: so, for instance, a composer works with sounds (which are physical), notes (which are symbolic), and instruments (which are physical cum technical); and it may be that the composer works with sounds by way of working with notes.

My understanding of artistic medium is closely aligned with those of David Davies (2005) and Rosalind Krauss (1999, 2000, 2006). Davies defines artistic medium as a framework of communicative possibilities provided by historical uses of a physical medium in art, allowing the artist to articulate an artistic statement (Davies 2005, 183). "[A]n artistic medium," Davies says, "can be thought of as a set of conventions whereby an individual's acting in certain ways—for example performing certain operations upon a physical medium— ... specifies a piece that is accessible to receivers who grasp those conventions" (2005, 189). So, for instance, when a Renaissance artist presented a carved stone sculpture, the context supplied by the medium informed us that the shape of the sculpture, but not its color or hardness of texture, was to be attributed to the represented subject. The medium, then, while it does not fully determine interpretation, constrains the artistic statement the work should be understood to make.

Krauss describes a medium as "as a set of conventions derived from (but not identical with) the material conditions of a given technical support, conventions out of which to develop a form of expressiveness" (1999, 296). The expression "technical support," Krauss says elsewhere, "welcomes the layered mechanisms of new technologies that make a simple, unitary identification of the work's physical support impossible (is the 'support' of film the celluloid strip, the screen, the splices of the edited footage, the projector's beam of light, the circular reels?)" (2006, 56). I will use "support" to encompass physical materials, symbolic materials, and complex functional systems.

My account diverges from those of Davies and Krauss in two respects. First, I include not just conventions but also, following Gaut (2010, 288) and Lopes (2004, 110), practices for working with the support. Practices, as I understand them, are established ways of working that may not rise to the level of convention, but nonetheless have enough traction that they systematically structure the artistic projects of a community or, occasionally, an individual artist. Second, Krauss's formulation suggests that the medium is constituted of conventions, raising the possibility that the supports on which those conventions operate are included in medium only indirectly. I expressly include the support itself as a component of the medium. The medium, then, is not just a set of conventions but a system comprising both a support and a set of conventions and practices for deploying that support. (There may be no substantive disagreement between Krauss and me on this point.)

Krauss develops her account of artistic medium in a series of lamentations about the "post-medium condition" into which she feels much contemporary art has fallen (1999, 2000, 2006). Due to the diversity of materials and approaches employed in contemporary art, the prevalence of hybrid works, and the destabilizing of conventions that once governed artistic media, the story goes, it no longer makes sense to speak of medium as a significant force in the creation of contemporary art. Krauss suggests that this has created a messy, anything-goes situation of directionless artworks and aborted attempts at meaning-making: artists have lost touch with the traditions and conventions that allow artistic communication to be meaningful.

Krauss celebrates artists who, in her view, construct idiosyncratic mediums to structure their artistic projects. Jeff Wall, through his use of photography presented on large light boxes, and James Coleman, through his use of timed slide shows, have constrained their material possibilities and bound themselves to prior cultural meanings associated with their chosen technical supports, thereby "reclaim[ing] the specific from the deadening embrace of the general" (Krauss 1999, 305).

The structure of medium allows us to grasp the logic of these artists' choices. Because the narrative content of Coleman's timed slide shows must be established through a limited number of still images, Coleman employs a repertoire of strategies, such as the double face-out, where two characters are shown in the same frame both facing toward the viewer (much as in a comic strip) so that we can see both of their expressions simultaneously. "The frequency of the double face-out's occurrence within Coleman's work signals its importance as a grammatical component of the medium he is using it to invent" (Krauss 1999, 301). The characters are shown this way because the support constrains how characters' relationships and reactions to events can be made visible to viewers. Krauss's mention of grammar highlights the fact that she sees the double face-out as a structural component of the work that undergirds the assignment of meaning.

How Medium Works

Like Krauss, I see medium as providing structure and purpose for artistic projects, suggesting criteria for evaluating artworks, and allowing artists to construct and audiences to ascertain meanings. How does medium perform these tasks?

First, medium-specific conventions may set the boundaries of the artwork, or identify which aspects of a presented object are eligible for appreciation. Timothy Binkley notes that "in the medium of painting there is a convention which says that the paint, but not the canvas, stretcher, or frame, must remain invariant in order to preserve the identity of the artwork" (1977, 269). He notes the contrast with architecture, in which a complete replacement of the paint may have no bearing on the work's identity. Binkley continues, "The reason we know to look at the aesthetic qualities on the front of a painting is not because the back lacks aesthetic qualities, but rather because the conventions of painting tell us to look there" (1977, 270). The conventions and practices of painting also tell the painter that if she wishes to locate the expressive qualities of her work in the place where audience members are likely to look for them, she should focus on the front surface of the canvas. In music, similarly, the sounds produced by the performers, and not other ambient sounds present in the environment, are typically the locus of appreciation.

Second, medium helps to structure artists' choices. The conventions and practices associated with the sonnet recommend particular choices of rhyme scheme and meter. The conventions and practices associated with ceramics offer a menu of techniques for constructing a vessel: throwing on the wheel, coiling, hand-building from slabs, pinching, and so forth. The conventions and practices of painting have, at various times, recommended particular geometries or pro-portional structures of images (Baxandall 1985, chapter 4). These practices and conventions supply context for the artist's choices and often function as con-straints on the artist's project, furnishing a set of expectations they know viewers will bring to their work and problems they need to solve.

Third, and relatedly, medium plays a role in our explanations of the work's features and their relationships to each other (cf. Gaut 2010, 287). Has the artist made a creative, idiosyncratic choice to position elements in just this way to express a specific meaning? Is the artist, instead, complying with a conventional expectation that certain elements should be present or should be thus oriented toward each other? Or does the inherent structure of the support leave no alternative? In a painting, the juxtaposition of elements may be due either to idiosyncratic choice or to conventional expectations, such as the tradition of showing Mary in a red garment and blue cloak. The juxtaposition of elements in an analog photograph, on the other hand, is explained by the relative positions of the real objects whose light is captured in the image. This, in turn, plays a role in our understanding of the achievement manifest in the work: the achievement of van der Weyden's *Descent from the Cross* (before 1443) is in the meticulous construction of an image in which every element is under the artist's control; the achievement of Cartier-Bresson's *Behind the Gare St. Lazare* (1932), on the other hand, is in the discovery of a remarkable scene whose elements were juxtaposed independently of the artistic act, and then the perfectly timed and executed recording of a human action within that scene.

Fourth, medium structures how we attribute meaning to the artwork's elem-ents. The conventions of painting inform us that certain gambits of color and shading should be understood as indications of three-dimensionality; for this reason, even an abstract painting whose content exhibits no similarity to any real-world form or scene can—or even must—be seen as depicting abstract objects in three dimensions. Thus Kandinsky's 1912 *Black Spot*, though largely thwarting association with real-world objects and sites, is naturally read as containing sharply defined three-dimensional objects in the foreground against a distant background composed of hazy fields of pastel colors. To take another example, the conventions and practices of sculpture inform us that not every aspect of a sculpture is to be understood as isomorphic with the depicted object: the rough texture of Giacometti's *Monumental Head* does not signal that we are meant to attribute roughness of surface to the human being depicted. The texture is certainly expressive, and may even be expressive of something about the depicted subject; but it is not directly expressive of how we are meant to understand the subject's appearance or shape. The conventions and practices of sculpture allow this sort of distinction between features attributable to the depicted object and features that are outgrowths of the artist's style or are used to expressive ends through a mechanism other than presumed visual resemblance or isomorphism (Dilworth 2005a, 2005b; Irvin 2020).

Fifth, medium-specific conventions and practices establish what is normal and expected within the medium. This helps to determine which of the work's features are salient as expressive resources, and also the character of what they express. This is related to philosopher Kendall Walton's (1970) insight that the aesthetic significance of artwork features is relative to the category to which the work belongs. *Standard* features, those shared by virtually every work in a category, don't generally convey specific expressive content. Instead, the primary locus of expression is in those features that are *variable* relative to the category. Until recent decades, (approximate) flatness was a standard feature of paintings. For this reason, we did not ask, "What is the artist trying to express in making this painting flat?" This question becomes meaningful only in a context where the options have expanded to include three-dimensional elements, and flatness is now a variable rather than standard feature in relation to painting as a category. Subject matter and color palette have long been variable features of painting: some paintings are landscapes, others portraits; some paintings have somber and restrained color palettes, while others are vivid. When we seek to understand the expressive import of an artist's choices, we locate it in the variable features that distinguish one work from another, not the standard features.

This is not to say that standard features are completely lacking in aesthetic and expressive potential. As Walton (1970) notes, the fact that a work possesses the standard features for its category helps to establish a sense of its stability and fittingness. However, when a work combines many standard features with a *contra-standard* feature, one that tends to disqualify works from membership in the category, this can be quite striking and even disturbing: for the presence of the contra-standard feature signals a rejection or violation of a central convention for that category, even while the presence of the several standard features asserts the work's membership in the category. Normally, a work with significant three-dimensional elements is a sculpture, not a painting: but when artists began to affix three-dimensional objects to stretched canvases with paint on them, they violated the conventional flatness associated with the medium. Whereas the three-dimensionality of sculpture is scarcely expressive, the three-dimensionality of a painting was striking—though, as Walton notes, it does not have the same shocking effect for contemporary viewers for whom Rauschenberg's combines are familiar as a decades'-old artistic development: the category in relation to which we naturally see paintings with three dimensional elements has expanded to encompass such three-dimensionality as a variable rather than contra-standard feature.

The history of uses to which a material or system has been put, then, serves to determine the framework of possibilities against which current choices in using that material or system must be understood. Thus, conventions determined through histories of use help to determine the current communicative potential of choices within an artistic medium. Artistic choices communicate against the background of what others have been doing in similar contexts, and artistic medium supplies a very important context for comparison.

All of these functions of medium play a role in attributions of meaning to the artwork. Presenting an artwork with particular features is a communicative action, and medium helps to determine how this action should be understood. Where a feature of the work violates a convention, the fact that the communicative action involves such a violation is part of its significance. Violation of norms or conventions heightens the salience of particular features, highlighting them as things we must take seriously in our assessments and interpretations of the work.

A feature can also become salient through novelty relative to a particular set of artistic practices, even if it does not violate conventions outright. Portraiture usually involves showing the subject at a distance and scale that allow the subject's whole face or profile to be shown, so that the subject's facial features are visible and their expression legible. A choice to zoom in on a small region of the face, fragmenting it from the rest, would stand out as atypical relative to established practices of portraiture, thus inviting special attention as we attempt to understand the artist's choices and attribute meaning to the work. On the other hand, features that lie within the bounds established by medium-specific practices connect the work to a specific tradition and invite comparisons to and associations with other works sharing those features.

Artistic media are not exclusively conventional, of course: where an artistic medium is tied to a specific kind of support, both the potential and the characteristic difficulties associated with that support shape what can be expressed within it. So, for instance, one of the ways of harnessing expressive power is by doing something that counts as extreme relative to the potential of the support. Jerrold Levinson illustrates this point:

> Beethoven's *Hammerklavier* Sonata is a sublime, craggy, and heaven-storming piece of music... The aesthetic qualities of the *Hammerklavier* Sonata depend in part on the strain that its sound structure imposes on the sonic capabilities of the

piano; if we are not hearing its sound structure *as* produced by a piano, then we are not sensing this strain, and thus our assessment of aesthetic content is altered. The closing passages of the *Hammerklavier* are awesome in part because we seem to hear the piano bursting at the seams and its keyboard on the verge of exhaustion.   (1980, 17–18)

The fact that the *Hammerklavier* Sonata is a work for piano, and is thus composed within a medium involving distinct physical limitations, is fundamental to its expressive power.

What is expressed by a work is related to what is achieved within it; and this, in turn, is related to the characteristic difficulties its medium presents, which may be due to either or both of the support and the associated conventions. Some of the characteristic challenges of traditional ballet are related to inherent limitations of the human body, while others stem from the precise and technically demanding vocabulary of specific elements that are available within the medium. Richard Wollheim notes that sometimes, the very difficulties associated with a support may form part of its appeal as the underpinning of an artistic medium: the fact that one has to wrest a desired appearance from an unpredictable material in the course of fabrication may be precisely what gives that material its expressive potential (1980, 42).

Medium Now

I have gone on at some length about the notion of medium and how it functions. But is this notion relevant now? Krauss holds that we are post-medium: after all, many artists have abandoned the standard supports associated with traditional artistic media, and those artists still using traditional supports have often rejected the conventions that constituted the associated media.

One way to argue against Krauss's claim would be to suggest that it is over-stated, for two reasons. First, there are prominent contemporary artists who work in traditional artistic media and make artistic choices that are clearly meaningful within those media. Kehinde Wiley's work, such as *Jacob de Graeff* (2018) shown in Figure 6.1, draws on many time-honored strategies within the medium of oil painting: he appropriates historical themes and images from such artists as Rubens and Velázquez, creates visually luscious images, uses realistic but painterly forms of representation, and pulls elements from the patterned background into the foreground, creating unstable spatial relationships akin to those in Matisse's (1908) *Red Room (Harmony in Red)*. By operating so clearly within the medium of painting, Wiley signals that he is intervening in the history of that medium. His choice to offer valorizing depictions of Black people and other people of color who have historically been excluded from or marginalized in works of painting, then, is

Figure 6.1 Kehinde Wiley, *Jacob de Graeff*, 2018. Oil on linen, 72 × 60 in. (182.9 × 152.4 cm).

Collection Oklahoma City Museum of Art
© Kehinde Wiley
Photo Jean-Paul Torno, Courtesy Saint Louis Art Museum
Courtesy of the artist and Roberts Projects, Los Angeles, California

readily identifiable as a form of resistance to the historical trend of aestheticizing whiteness within the medium of painting. The fact that he works within the medium of oil painting structures his project and makes it easy to grasp some of his most salient objectives.

Krauss might respond by noting that many prominent contemporary artists are not working in a medium like oil painting: they are using materials like toilet paper, soap, and chocolate, and this leaves us without a set of medium-based conventions and practices to situate us relative to an artistic project and a shared set of concepts and expectations by which we can assess these works and assign meaning to them. But the critic might reply that even everyday objects and materials have inherent limitations that help us to grasp the artist's achievement. Sarah Sze's 1996 *Untitled (Soho Annual)* involves hundreds of tiny sculptures made from toilet paper (Figure 6.2). Once we know about the material Sze was using and the fact that she restricted herself to sculptures that could be made from

Figure 6.2 Sarah Sze, *Untitled (Soho Annual)*, 1996. Toilet paper and saliva.
Dimensions variable.

Whitney Museum of American Art, New York; gift of Dean Valentine and Amy Adelson
2005.144
© Sarah Sze
Courtesy of the artist and Tanya Bonakdar Gallery, New York/Los Angeles

a single sheet of toilet paper moistened with water and saliva (Sze 2008), we are in
a good position to understand her project and even to assess the outcome, since we
are fairly familiar with the behavior of toilet paper as a material. The sculptures

employ a ubiquitous material in an uncommonly creative way, there is a rather obsessive aspect in the large quantity and the tendency to repeat certain forms, and some of the forms seem to push the limits of the material support. This work thus involves a project whose contours we can readily recognize, and we do not seem to lack a grip on what the artist was up to or how well she achieved it.

But I want to take Krauss's concern more seriously than this back-and-forth would suggest. First, Kehinde Wiley is not simply working in the same medium of painting as Matisse or Rubens: the medium has evolved due to recent developments, which affects the expressive import of Wiley's choices. His works insist on technical mastery, conventional aesthetic value, and connections to tradition and history, as against such projects as Glenn Ligon's conceptual paintings, Helen Frankenthaler's abstract canvas stainings, or Alice Neel's portraits whose expressiveness consists more in awkward intensity than in beauty. Perhaps these shifting standards and broadening of scope constitute the undermining of "conventions out of which to develop a form of expressiveness," such that painting no longer functions as a medium (Krauss 1999, 296).

Second, the inherent limitations of everyday materials, unconstrained by medium-bound conventions or practices, will often be insufficient to provide us with an adequate grip on what the artist's project is or how we should assess it. The example of Sze's toilet paper work may be unfair: in a sense, she is doing what Krauss wishes more contemporary artists would do, namely creating a sui generis medium that provides a framework for assessing her work. Compare this to the project Janine Antoni undertakes in *Conduit* (2009) (Figure 6.3). *Conduit* involves two objects: a copper sculpture and a framed color photograph that are displayed together. This might sound straightforward enough, but the sculpture is in fact a gargoyle-shaped sculptural device designed to allow standing urination, and the photograph shows Antoni, her hair blowing in the wind, using the sculpture to pee off the Chrysler Building in New York City. The sculpture's urine verdigris patina, listed as part of the medium,[3] was produced by Antoni's own urine. Even though the objects on display are both in well-established artistic media, and urine is a traditional material to produce patination (Lewis and Lewis 2013, 159, suggest that Rodin asked his assistants to urinate on his bronze sculptures), the artwork as a whole resists assessment by standards associated with sculpture or photography as artistic media. The photograph connects the sculpture to a specific action and confronts us with the fact that the sculpture has been in intimate contact with the artist's body and fluids. The juxtaposition of objects from two different artistic media, along with the invitation to consider a specific action, seems, just as Krauss claims, to undermine our ability to apply medium-based standards of value or understandings of artistic meaning-making.

---

[3] http://www.luhringaugustine.com/exhibitions/janine-antoni3.

Figure 6.3 Janine Antoni, *Conduit*, 2009. Copper sculpture with urine verdigris patina, framed digital C-print. Image: 25 × 30 inches (63.5 × 76.2 cm); framed: 27¼ × 32¼ × 2⅛ inches (69.22 × 81.92 × 5.4 cm). Sculpture: 2 × 7¼ × 2¼ inches (5.08 × 18.42 × 5.72 cm). Pedestal: 10½ × 10½ × 32½ inches (26.67 × 26.67 × 82.55 cm).
© Janine Antoni; courtesy of the artist and Luhring Augustine, New York

It is thus unsurprising that Krauss and others have interpreted the situation in art of the last several decades as involving the demise of artistic medium. In addition to the hybridity exemplified by works like Antoni's *Conduit*, the upsurge in the expression of custom rules was precisely an attack on the conventions of traditional media. When Gerald Ferguson gives permission to paint over one of his *Maintenance Paintings* in any way one desires, even if that radically changes its appearance, this is a rejection of a longstanding convention that the appearance of the painted surface is essential to the identity of a work of painting. Despite the fact that Ferguson has presented a series of canvases with paint on them, it seems natural to say that he is not working in the artistic medium of painting: he is defying one of the central conventions that have historically defined that medium.

The abandonment of traditional artistic materials may have played an even more significant role in the seeming dissolution of artistic media. When an artist like Sarah Sze, with her 1997 work *Migrateurs* (discussed at length in Chapter 3), presents an object made out of packs of chewing gum, Q-tips, matches, batteries, and aspirin tablets, it is difficult to connect her work to the kind of artistic project traditionally facilitated by the medium of sculpture: a project involving the aggregation, carving down, and/or casting of some finely articulable material like clay, stone, or bronze. How are we to read one of these creations, when the artist has used materials that bring their shapes, multiple colors, diverse deterioration rates, everyday functions, and cultural associations to the work with them? Are we to focus on the mere appearance of the object? If so, how do we assess that appearance, given that the object doesn't participate in representing something sculpturally? Is the work's success or failure simply a matter of whether we find its appearance satisfyingly whimsical? Are we to think about the everyday functions of these objects and the fact that those functions have been subverted by the objects' inclusion in the work, or is this an irrelevant distraction? If we do think about the particularities of the included objects, should we see them as interchangeable with other objects of the same type, or might these specific objects have some important history we need to know about? This work seems not to have a medium: it is made of stuff, but this stuff is not associated with a set of conventions and practices that help us to see what kind of artistic statement is being made.

I suggest, however, that these trends signal not the dissolution but the evolution of artistic media. Painting continues to exist as an artistic medium, and many of the conventions that formerly defined the medium—such as the centrality of the appearance of the painted surface to the identity of the work—remain in force. When artists create rules that violate a medium-based convention, the convention does not thereby disappear. Instead, its force may be weakened, such that it evolves from an unquestioned universal of works in the medium to a default position that is defeasible under the right conditions. This does shift the significance of works in the medium: Kehinde Wiley's choice to make paintings that operate largely under the conventional rules for the identity of works of painting over time is itself expressive in a way that, say, Mary Cassatt's operating under those same rules in the late nineteenth and early twentieth centuries was not.

Returning to the earlier discussion of Walton's standard and variable features relative to an artistic category, we can note that for Cassatt's *Breakfast in Bed*

(1897), the fact that the work has a painted surface with a stable appearance that is the main object of our appreciative efforts is a standard feature of works in the medium of painting at that time. Standard features, shared by all works in a category, don't play a strong expressive role; they are mainly part of the taken-for-granted background. The expressive features are those that vary among works in the category: the specific subject matter of a tender domestic moment between mother and child, the distinctive color palette and composition, and so forth. But by the time Wiley is creating his main body of work in the early twenty-first century, the medium of painting has evolved as a result of interventions like Ferguson's. Though the (more or less) stable appearance of the painted surface is still typical of works of painting and functions as a default for the medium, it is no longer universal; it is now a variable feature. Similarly, in the wake of mono-chrome paintings in the twentieth century, being polychromatic is now a variable feature of works of painting; and in the wake of text-based conceptual works like Ligon's and geometric abstractions like Frankenthaler's, having representational subject matter is a variable feature. When Kehinde Wiley opts to give his works variable features associated with the traditional form and aesthetic standards of painting as a medium—realistic, conventionally beautiful representational portraits appropriating historical themes, with a stable painted surface—he makes a statement about the kind of project he is engaged in, namely a critical intervention in the grand history of painting as a fine art. He is precisely not aiming to show that Black subjects must be included within painting under a *new* conception of the medium, or included within art newly conceived and with expanded boundaries: his point is that Black subjects (and, indeed, Black artists) belonged in art, and specifically in painting, all along.

When it comes to works like Antoni's *Conduit* and Sze's works made of diverse everyday materials, I will suggest that recognizing rules as a symbolic support that works along with the material supports helps us to make sense of the artistic projects being undertaken and to recognize non-arbitrary expressive qualities in these works. Rules for display, conservation, and participation have emerged as a symbolic support, and conventions and practices for articulating and understanding rules are now identifiable across a wide range of art institutions and artistic projects.

Rules as Support

Some aspects of the evolution of the medium of painting are more dramatic than others. When we say that the (approximate) stability of the painted surface is now a variable rather than a standard feature of painting, this is a kind of change that goes well beyond the introduction of abstract or monochromatic appearances as possibilities. This means that now, *the kind of rule governing the identity of the work* is variable in the medium of painting (and, as we will see, in other artistic media as well). This means that the rule has come to function as part of the support for the work: which rule the artist chooses is part of the very structure of the work, and helps to determine what it expresses. Ferguson's *Maintenance Paintings* would not be the works that they are without the rule permitting repainting; the artistic statement, which in the actual works issues a challenge regarding the role of the artist and the nature of artistic creation, would be entirely different in works without this rule. This is why I claim that these works are made not just out of physical objects but out of rules. (See Chapter 5 for further discussion.)

Rules are a symbolic rather than material support for the work. They are like the words in a poem or, better, like the notes in a musical work. Just as the notes are part of the very structure of the musical work, the rules are part of the very structure of the artwork: to change the notes, or to change the rules, is to make a substantive change in the content of the work and what the content can express. The notes in a score serve as an instruction to the performers, just as the rules articulated for a visual artwork serve as an instruction to those who interact with it in various capacities. The rule is sometimes a requirement (as when Saburo Murakami requires that his *Peeling Pictures* not be subjected to conservation treatment) and sometimes a permission (as when Ferguson allows the owner to repaint a *Maintenance Painting*), and sometimes the same rule has both implications (as when Felix Gonzalez-Torres permits audience members to take candies from his candy spills, requiring the institution to allow such interaction).

The articulation of rules is sometimes how the artist works with the physical material, just as specification of notes is part of how the artist works with sound. When Murakami issues a requirement not to conserve his *Peeling Pictures*, he is thereby working with the material: designating it for a certain kind of future in which it will, if the rule is complied with, undergo dramatic and unimpeded degradation. But it is less clear that we should that say that Ferguson works with paint or that Gonzalez-Torres works with candies by permitting audience interaction.

We saw above that physical supports sometimes furnish constraints on creation that help to determine the expressive quality of the work. Levinson describes how the *Hammerklavier* Sonata is expressive partly by virtue of the physical limitations of the piano. Michelangelo's sculptures, similarly, are expressive partly by virtue of the physical limitations of stone: our knowledge that stone is materially cold and hard, as well as difficult to work and susceptible to unpredictable breakage, conditions our appreciation of both the virtuosity of Michelangelo's *Pietà* and the artist's ability to eke out textural softness and emotional tenderness. Rules, too, have inherent limitations that condition how we will grasp the work's expressive quality. Some constraints arise by virtue of what is practically feasible: rules are articulated within human contexts where it is unreasonable (and sometimes unlawful) to expose one's audience, other artworks, or major architectural structures to certain kinds of danger. When an artist articulates a rule that strains these boundaries, the expressive quality of the work is likely to read as aggressive. Sometimes the expressive quality of a rule is shaped by the way that it interacts with the ordinary workings of the museum, or the standard conception of the museum's mission. When, in *SLOTO: The Secret Life of the Onion* (2002–3), Jason Rhoades prescribes that museum staff go through a complex process of putting prescribed quantities of elements together in large bulb-shaped glass containers to create "onions," and then ride around the gallery in a carnival train with cars in the shape of pigs before placing the "onion" on a shelf, he is on the one hand asking them to do something absurd and whimsical, and on the other satirizing the complex administrative procedures that already condition staff members' interactions with the objects in their care.

When Zoe Leonard rejects conservation treatment for the fruit peels constituting her work *Strange Fruit*, in the collection of the Philadelphia Museum of Art, she strains the museum's convention of preserving the works in its care for future generations. The fact that her rule for conservation challenges the limits of institutional conventions in this way contributes to the rule's expressive import, as discussed in Chapter 3: Leonard has made a conscious and deliberate choice because traditional conservation undermines the artistic statement about loss and grief that she is articulating through the work.

Rules are part of the support of these works, then—they are part of what the works are made of—because they share many of the features of other material, symbolic, and technical supports: they constitute the structure of the work, they serve as expressive resources, and their expressive import is conditioned by constraints on what kinds of rules are feasible or conceivable in a given context.

Practices and Conventions Governing Rules

I have argued that rules function as part of the support for many contemporary artworks. But this is not yet sufficient for medium: within a medium, use of the support must be governed by practices and conventions that lend coherence to artistic projects and help to determine what is expressed. And, indeed, practices and conventions have emerged for the articulation of rules. Articulating custom rules for conservation, display, and participation is now such a common artistic practice that many institutions that collect contemporary art now use a standard artist questionnaire for every new acquisition to collect information about these rules. Working closely with the artist to establish the parameters and methods of display is common (e.g., Stigter 2015; see Chapter 5 for discussion), as is consulting with living artists when unanticipated questions about display or conservation arise. International research projects involving collaboration across institutions have worked to establish such practices in relation to installation artworks, artworks subject to variable display, works in time-based and digital media, and works with complex conservation requirements.[4]

Museums and galleries increasingly share information about these rules with audiences, on the view that audiences need to know about the rules if they are to recognize and appreciate the artworks. Conservation scholars Vivian van Saaze (2011) and Glenn Wharton (2015) have argued that more needs to be done to bring these "backstage" practices into the foreground.

Many artists routinely put together a "package" related to their works, detailing the fine points of display, conservation, and permitted audience participation. Such a package is sometimes a thick booklet of illustrated instructions. Moreover, specific practices have emerged around such rules. A default practice of replacing degradable materials has become widespread, though it remains defeasible (as the example of Leonard's *Strange Fruit* indicates). The background of such practices and expectations shapes the possibilities for artistic expression: when Robert Gober subjects the donuts of his 1989 *Bag of Donuts* to extensive conservation intervention, aspiring to imbue them with the sort of longevity characteristic of traditional art objects (Buskirk 2003, 146), his action is extreme and comical partly by virtue of how it resists a practice of replacement that has become established (and reasserts, for a very modest set of objects, a convention of stubborn preservation that used to be taken for granted, but has since weakened).

Rules as Medium in Contemporary Art

We are now in a position to see that rules as support, governed by a recognizable set of practices and conventions, perform all the functions of medium discussed earlier. First, medium helps to set the boundaries of the work and identify which aspects of a presented object are eligible for appreciation. Rules as medium are compatible with the persistence of default expectations about the artwork's boundaries and appreciable features, but also allow that the artist may articulate custom sanctions that deactivate these defaults. Thus, if an artist who creates a painting makes no specification, the appearance of the painted surface will be understood as essential to the work's identity and subjected to treatments designed to preserve it. But it is open to artists to articulate custom rules that set the work's boundaries differently.

---

[4] Projects include Inside Installations (https://www.incca.org/articles/project-inside-installations-2004-2007), DOCAM (Documentation and Conservation of Media Arts Heritage, http://www.docam.ca), Forging the Future (http://forging-the-future.net), the Variable Media Initiative (https://www.guggenheim.org/conservation/the-variable-media-initiative), and the Artists Documentation Program (http://adp.menil.org).

Second, medium helps to structure artists' choices. This is certainly true when we consider rules as medium: there are now practices of specifying three types of custom rules, those governing display, conservation, and participation, and an artist's choice to participate in the articulation of custom rules in one or more of these areas is meaningful against a background of related choices made by other artists and default practices that have emerged from those choices. When it comes to object-based installation art, for instance, a repertoire of strategies and practices has emerged. These practices lie at various points along the following spectrums:

- from presentation of ordinary found objects to presentation of objects specifically fabricated by the artist
- from use of relatively stable materials to use of highly degradable materials
- from total replacement of all objects after every display to maintaining and conserving all objects indefinitely
- from configuring the objects the same way for every display to permitting or requiring a different configuration for every display
- from the artist determining the permissible configurations of the objects to the installers deciding on the configuration for each display
- from forbidding any audience interaction with the objects to permitting all forms of audience participation

Because practices have emerged of specifying rules within these ranges, choices about where to position one's work relative to these possibilities are part of the structure of the creative activity of artists who work with rules as artistic medium.

Third, medium-specific conventions and practices play a role in our explanations of the work's features. This is clearly true for rules as medium: the fact that the artist is using rules as medium will help to explain aspects of the boundaries of the work and the features that are salient in appreciation. We will explain these features in terms of specific choices made by the artist in relation to an established range of possibilities rather than in terms of generally applicable conventions that determine them.

Fourth, medium structures how we attribute meaning to the artwork's elements. Rules as medium are expressive because they make particular elements of the work available for appreciation or highlight their salience; they can also, by virtue of resisting entrenched conventions or aspects of the institution's mission or recruiting people to unaccustomed forms of activity, be expressive by butting up against constraints on what is normally understood as feasible or reasonable to demand or permit. El Anatsui's choice to make works with no set configuration, and to invite installers to exercise their creativity in constituting the display, is expressive of a questioning of the characteristic roles and social relations of artists and museum professionals, and of the ideas that everyone should have opportunities to exercise creative autonomy and that no one, including the artist, needs to have absolute control over all aspects of the display. This expression is possible against a background of a historical conventions for fixed artwork display, as well as the background of more recent choices by artists to sanction custom rules for variable display, which still typically locate the creative autonomy and authority in the artist's own hands.

Fifth, medium-specific conventions and practices establish what is normal and expected within the medium. This is true of practices and conventions that have emerged surrounding rules. Through practices of articulating custom rules, some prior conventions have weakened, thereby bringing within the range of normality possibilities that were not within that range before. It is now within the range of normality to display a work in quite different configurations on different occasions, to allow audience members to interact with art objects in various ways, and to replace some or all of the objects between displays. As Sarah Sze (2008) notes, it is now a common practice to replace parts that degrade rapidly, but it is possible for artists to articulate custom rules to resist this practice from either direction, as we see when Leonard sanctions degradation for the fruit peels of *Strange* and Gober sanctions rigorous preservation for the donuts in his *Bag of Donuts*. Rules as medium, then, provide a framework to locate particular choices within a range of practices and possibilities, thereby helping to determine their expressive qualities. Where an artist violates a convention or common practice, such violations are understood as expressively salient, such that they must be accounted for in appreciation and interpretation. The fact that something is expressively salient, we should note, does not determine what it expresses: particular artistic choices are expressive in the context of the whole work, not independently. But when a choice goes against the grain of conventions and practices, understanding it as going against the grain is part of grasping the work's expressive import.

We can see, then, that rules and their associated conventions and practices have all the functions of other artistic media: they structure and constrain artistic projects in similar ways and provide a framework for understanding particular artistic choices as meaningful. We can even think here of a repertoire of strategies that serve as grammatical elements in artistic creation, to use Krauss's metaphor. Felix Gonzalez-Torres, for instance, has developed a repertoire of strategies such as letting people take things away from his work—typically either candies, which can be consumed on site, or sheets of printed or embossed paper—and charging the displaying institution with replenishing the materials. This enlists the institution in certain forms of material generosity, breaks down the characteristic barriers between the audience and the artwork, involves the gustatory and/or tactile senses in art experiences that are usually just visual, and requires that the audience member decide whether and how to engage actively with the work rather than simply remaining passive. Gonzalez-Torres uses the act of consuming candies as a symbolic resource: *"Untitled" (Placebo)* (1991) invites the audience member to regard the candy as a placebo, a metaphor which opens into a range of thoughts about whether art itself may often serve as a placebo, what kind of ill the placebo might be aiming to treat, and (given the theme of AIDS that runs through much of Gonzalez-Torres's work) the extent to which much of contemporary medical practice might be relying on placebo effects. *"Untitled" (Portrait of Ross in L.A.)* (1991), on the other hand, invites the audience member to symbolically ingest a portion of Gonzalez-Torres's lover Ross, who by virtue of being gay and HIV positive was socially treated as untouchable. (See Chapter 1 for discussion.)

Nearly all of Gonzalez-Torres's works are indefinitely replenishable, with the prospect for enduring as long as the right kind of materials can be created or procured. But a few of his stacks of removable prints have only a finite supply. In the context of an artistic practice usually characterized by expansive generosity, these works confront the audience member with a very different kind of choice: should one take a sheet from the stack, hastening the work's demise? Does one value the sheet, or the experience of taking it, enough for it to be worth it? The non-replenishable works, by virtue of their grammar, deal in expressive content related to scarcity and finitude.

Krauss, recall, worries that the introduction of everyday materials and objects foists art into a state of post-medium chaos, because there are no conventions that tell us the boundaries of such works or where to seek the works' salient features for expressive purposes. I suggest that rules as medium help to retrieve the ability of everyday materials and objects to serve as a meaningful artistic support. Artists use rules to signal the salience of some aspects of everyday materials while suppressing the potential salience of others.

When Sarah Sze expresses custom rules about whether and when the objects in her works may be replaced, as discussed in Chapter 3, she is telling us what matters for purposes of appreciation and what is less important. Color and structure matter: when a bright green Tic Tac has faded, it should be replaced, and when a pack of chewing gum sags, the sagging should be reversed. The object should look cared for: if the Q-tips start to look shaggy and unkempt, they should be replaced. Preserving signs of the artist's touch is important: the glue from the glue gun can't be removed or replaced, because the spidery networks Sze created are aesthetically important. At the same time, preserving an unchanged original appearance is not the point. It is fine to keep the aspirin tablet that has degraded to a mere skin, at least until it completely disintegrates, because it shows a remarkable aspect of the object's change over time. It is fine that the glue has yellowed, thereby showing its age. Sze is happy if the different objects visible in the work clearly have different timelines that have been braided together: one object has been aging continually since the work's creation, while others are periodically replaced. What seems to be a three-dimensional work of sculpture, then, takes on a very intentional and perceptible four-dimensional (time-based) aspect.

We also learn from the rules Sze expresses that some things are not expressively important in this work. Since everyday objects in the work can be replaced, we can conclude that the specific items initially included have no nostalgic significance. Also, the material authenticity of unseen objects is not a focus: it is fine to replace the chewing gum inside the pack with a rigid object that won't sag. Indeed, in other works Sze is explicit about blending the real with the artificial—a work might include both real and fake plants, for instance. In combining the real with the fake, including items that require care, and specifying that different objects are replaced at different moments, she aims to induce a conservator's interest in every audience member (Sze 2008).

Rules, as governed by conventions and practices, perform all the functions associated with medium. Rules themselves are symbolic resources that serve as part of the support for many works of contemporary art. Sometimes, as in Sze's case, the artist works with the materials partly by working with rules: Sze shapes the future evolution of the material supports for her work by specifying rules to govern how her objects are treated. There are now practices of specifying how rules should apply to display, conservation, and participation, and these practices and related conventions supply a context within which particular choices made by the artist are meaningful. The fact that specifying such rules is now commonplace helps to ground the claim that rules function as medium. Some art forms, including object-based installation art and time-based media art, typically include the deployment of these symbolic resources in tandem with physical or technical resources. This provides a context for seeing specific choices about the rules as expressive.

Though there may have been a period of post-medium chaos in which artists' choices were difficult to position in a meaning-giving framework, we are no longer in such a period. Medium emerges and functions historically, and the practice of sanctioning custom rules now has enough of a history to structure both artists' choices and our ability to make sense of them. In Chapter 7, we will explore the distinctive expressive potential of rules as medium.

7

Rules and Expression

Medium Specificity?

I have argued that rules function as medium in many contemporary artworks. Typically, rules are one component of a hybrid medium involving rules as a symbolic support along with a material or technical support. Rules have expressive import in themselves, and they also help to constrain the expressive import of the accompanying material or technical support.

Sometimes, discussions of artistic media are associated with claims about medium specificity: descriptive claims that an artistic medium is uniquely or especially well suited to perform certain kinds of artistic tasks, sometimes giving rise to a further normative claim that works in that medium ought to capitalize on this special potential, such that a work failing to do so is assessed as less valuable. Such claims have a long history: Lessing (1766/1984), for instance, thought visual arts ought to show beautiful bodies while poetry ought to show actions, since poetry (like action) is extended in time while visual arts show parts in relation to one another at a single moment (see Gaut 2010, 285, for discussion).

Noël Carroll (2008) rejects the idea of artistic medium in large part because he regards such medium-specificity claims as overblown and uninformative, in both their descriptive and their normative guises. I am sympathetic to Carroll's position: both of Lessing's claims, for instance, are dubious. Poetry can offer powerful representations of objects—indeed, because we imaginatively reconstruct the object in reading, poetry can lead us to engage multiple senses in grasping the object described, whereas an object rendered in painting may engage us primarily visually. Moreover, despite being restricted to a still image, a well-constructed painting can both refer to and present a perspective on an unfolding event, as A. W. Eaton (2003) argues. The problem is not simply that Lessing's particular claims are ill-judged: it seems perfectly legitimate for an artist to use a medium to pursue an artistic project that does not maximally exploit the unique elements of that medium (see, for instance, Murray Smith's discussion of Louis Malle's "uncinematic" 1981 film *My Dinner with André* in M. Smith 2006, 140–1), and a very creative artist may be able to achieve projects that exceed what a given medium seems best suited to support.

While I, along with Carroll, reject the strongest medium-specificity claims, I nonetheless find the distinctive resources and expressive potential of artistic media an interesting topic of inquiry. The philosophical literature on the function of art in moral development (e.g., Nussbaum 1992) tends to focus on works like novels and films, our encounters with which are necessarily extended in time. Such works, which have greater prospects for the inclusion of extended narratives, seem best suited to effecting shifts in morally relevant knowledge or perspectives. This is not, however, to say that all works of film or literature are or should be morally didactic. It is also not to say that a work of painting, sculpture, or still photography could never serve such a function: Davidson 2016 argues that still photographic images have historically served an (im)moral didactic function in training people to deny appropriate respect to Black women, and that contemporary installation artworks like Kara Walker's can ameliorate this immoral perspective.

Even if claims about uniqueness or exclusivity are too strong, then, it may be true that some artistic media are more readily suited to exploring certain kinds of subject matter or having particular expressive effects. In that spirit, I want to explore two aspects of the distinctive expressive potential of works that use rules as medium. First, rules allow artists to emphasize the time-based element of object-based works, which facilitates the exploration of content related to mortality and loss. Second, the use of rules as medium draws attention to and in some cases resists forces of social control. Works with rules for participation often go further and invite audience members to actively position themselves relative to such forces. For this reason, works using rules as medium are well suited to examine social relationships and power structures, especially (though not only) as they occur within institutions of art.

Expression and Exemplification

How do rules facilitate expression? Nelson Goodman and Catherine Elgin discuss *exemplification*, which is a key expressive resource: as Goodman says, "Not all exemplification is expression, but all expression is exemplification" (Goodman 1976, 52). Exemplification is a matter of a work's both *possessing* a feature and *referring back to* that very feature. Goodman gives the example of a tailor's swatch: the swatch shows us the nature of the fabric it exemplifies by referring back to its own color and texture. While the swatch also possesses other features, such as size and shape, it does not refer back to those features. The size of the swatch is not exemplified; it is merely incidental, giving us no insight into what the fabric is like (Goodman 1976, 53; see Irvin 2020 for further discussion).

Elgin explains what is involved in an object's referring back to its own properties. "An exemplar refers to certain of its properties: it exhibits them, highlights them, shows them forth, makes them manifest ... In highlighting some properties, an exemplar overshadows, marginalizes, or downplays others" (Elgin 2011, 400).

And, elsewhere: "To highlight, underscore, display, or convey involves reference as well as instantiation. An item that at once refers to and instantiates a feature may be said to *exemplify* that feature" (Elgin 1993, 15).

Exemplification is relative to use. Though a tailor's swatch normally exemplifies color and texture but not size or shape, it can be deployed to exemplify something it does not exemplify in typical uses, including the very property of being a tailor's swatch (Goodman 1976, 53). And in contexts where it exemplifies that property, it will also exemplify its own size and shape, since these properties are relevant to our understanding of what a tailor's swatch is like. An exemplar does not exemplify all the properties it possesses, and may not even exemplify those that appear most conspicuous (Elgin 2011, 401). Exemplification, Elgin suggests, is a matter of "present[ing] features in a context contrived to render them salient" (Elgin 1993, 17).

Our awareness of the tailor's swatch's conventional function informs us that in standard contexts, its colors and texture but not its size and shape are exemplified. Artworks do not have this sort of established function; and a central point of this book has been that artists have done a great deal to overturn and destabilize the conventions that would once have made certain features of artworks, such as the appearance of the painted surface, naturally salient while suppressing the salience of others, such as the reverse of the canvas. As we saw in Chapter 6, Rosalind Krauss worries that the undermining of conventions leaves us with limited resources for making sense of artists' choices. But I suggest that rules function to render certain features of the work salient, thereby securing exemplification of those features.

The literal exemplification of some features of the work facilitates a central expressive process that Goodman (1976) and Elgin (1993) term *metaphorical exemplification*. Goodman notes that a work may metaphorically exemplify properties it does not literally possess: "A picture literally possesses a gray color, really belongs to the class of gray things; but only metaphorically does it possess sadness or belong to the class of things that feel sad" (Goodman 1976, 50–1). Elgin offers further examples: "[A]n experiment can metaphorically exemplify properties like power, elegance, panache, and promise; a painting, properties like electricity, balance, movement, and depth" (Elgin 1993, 16). Narrative or representational works can metaphorically exemplify by way of representation or depiction: "*A Doll's House* metaphorically exemplifies discontent; the figure in *Guernica*, grief" (Elgin 1993, 24). *Guernica* represents people in the throes of violent emotion; the marked salience of the states we are led to attribute to the characters leads Goodman to conclude that these states are metaphorically exemplified by the work.

As Elgin's examples of painting imply, metaphorical exemplification may be secured through means other than representation. It appears, from the examples, that if a painting tends to give us a strong impression of or call to our minds properties like movement and depth, these properties should be understood as metaphorically exemplified. I suggest that for contemporary object-based works, metaphorical exemplification is often fed by literal exemplification: the properties a work literally exemplifies—such as being made from certain materials—call to our minds, by virtue of those materials' sensuous qualities, everyday uses, and historical associations, properties that are metaphorically exemplified by the work. Rules can shape both which properties are literally exemplified (rather than merely possessed) and which further properties they call to mind, thereby constituting the metaphorical exemplification through which the work is expressive.

Rules, Decay, and Loss

Rules for display, conservation, and participation affect the unfolding of the work over time, so they have frequently been used to explore themes related to mortality and loss. Their expressive content is typically secured through a combination of literal and metaphorical exemplification. Rules for display, conservation, and participation provide resources for the literal exemplification of decay, damage, finitude, and absence, both by creating the conditions in which these states arise and by making them salient as products of the artist's choices.

As we saw in Chapter 3, Zoe Leonard's 1992–1997 *Strange Fruit* is made from the peels of fruits the artist and her friends ate which Leonard then sewed back together with thread, adding occasional embellishments. The work's title refers to Leonard's friend and fellow artist David Wojnarowicz, who died from AIDS. Because they show very obvious signs of having been sewn back together, the fruit peels literally exemplify hollowness. In addition, because Leonard pointedly rejected conservation measures that would have prevented the objects from decaying, they literally exemplify degradation. Leonard made this choice precisely because she recognized that literal exemplification, as opposed to mere appearance, has expressive power. Literal decay activates a powerful metaphorical exemplification of mortality; the literal exemplification of hollow shells that have been futilely stitched back together, only to continue their process of disintegration, metaphorically exemplifies emotional emptiness, loss, and the persistence of grief.

Works sometimes implicate audience members in choices that exemplify our responses to loss and mortality. Jamelie Hassan's 1981 *Los Desaparecidos*, in the collection of the National Gallery of Canada, involves a collection of porcelain handkerchiefs that are displayed in an array on the gallery floor. Hassan's instruction is that viewers are to be permitted to walk among the handkerchiefs, which represent people who were disappeared during the reign of the Argentinian junta from 1976 to 1983. The objects are fragile, and by allowing viewers to walk among them, Hassan makes this property salient, such that the work literally exemplifies fragility. The situation in which the objects are exposed to damage metaphorically exemplifies human vulnerability and the choices we each must make about whether to exercise care or to produce harm through malice or indifference. (See Chapter 9 for further discussion of this work.)

Exemplification of finitude or loss can engage our reflections on mortality and grief. Micah Lexier's 1995 *A work of art in the form of a quantity of coins equal to the number of months of the statistical life expectancy of a child born January 6, 1995*, in the collection of the Art Gallery of Ontario, involves two boxes and 906 copper coins. The coins started out arranged neatly in rows in a box on the left. However, the work involves a rule that a coin must be transferred from the left box to the right on the sixth day of every month, until all coins have been transferred. This transfer is to be done regardless of whether the work is on display. The arrangement of elements thus evolves as months and years pass: the supply of coins in the neat rows on the left dwindles as coins are dropped into the box on the right. Eventually, all coins will have been transferred, and the display will serve as a relic of an extended ritual the institution facilitated (McElroy 2006, 36–8). The work's literal exemplification of the dwindling supply of coins on the left and the transition from order to disorder provides resources to understand it as metaphorically exemplifying the finitude of life and, perhaps, the gradual shift across the lifespan from idealized hopes and expectations to more complicated realities.

Danh Vo's 2010 *Tombstone for Phùng Vo*, in the collection of the Walker Art Center and installed on the center's grounds, is a tombstone for the artist's father, Phùng Vo, who is still living (Figure 7.1). The text, inscribed in gold leaf on the black granite tombstone, reads, "Here lies one whose name was writ in water." Once Phùng Vo dies, the tombstone will be shipped to Denmark, where he lives, to mark his grave; and four items that are meaningful to him—a lighter, a watch, a ring, and a crucifix—will be shipped to the Walker to be displayed in a vitrine designed by Danh Vo. These arrangements are specified in Phùng Vo's will and have been contractually agreed to by the Walker (B. Ryan 2012). After Phùng Vo's death, *Tombstone for Phùng Vo* will remain in the Walker's collection but the tombstone will no longer be physically present or available for display there. This is an extremely unusual arrangement: collecting institutions normally go to great lengths to safeguard the objects in their collection, requiring complex contractual arrangements even to loan the objects temporarily to other institutions. By virtue of the rule requiring that the tombstone be relinquished on the death of the artist's father, the work exemplifies the finality of loss associated with mortality. The tombstone will still "belong" to the Walker, but the death of Phùng Vo will irrevocably change the nature of that relationship, making the precious unique object created by the artist unavailable. The situation created by the work thus literally exemplifies loss and metaphorically exemplifies mortality and grief. Of course, the exemplification is imperfect, since the Walker entered into this

Figure 7.1 Danh Vo, *Tombstone for Phùng Vo*, 2010. Black absolute granite and gold, engraving from writing by Phùng Vo, 25¼ × 35⅖ × 3⅕ in. (64 × 90 × 8 cm). Inventory #DVW93.

Installation view: *"To the Arts, Citizens!"*, Serralves Museum of Contemporary Art, November 21, 2010–March 13, 2011
Collection of Walker Art Center, Minneapolis. T. B. Walker Acquisition Fund, 2011
© Danh Vo
Courtesy of the artist

arrangement voluntarily and contractually, whereas the loss of our parents is not an eventuality we can refuse.

Felix Gonzalez-Torres's (1987–1990) *"Untitled" (Perfect Lovers)* and Tobias Wong's 2002 *Perfect Lovers (Forever)* help to demonstrate the specific effect of custom rules on meanings related to loss and grief by virtue of the fact that they are formally quite similar but differ in their rules.[1]

Displays of Felix Gonzalez-Torres's 1991 *"Untitled" (Portrait of Ross in L.A.)*, discussed in Chapter 1, involve a pile of colorful, wrapped hard candies that audience members are permitted to consume, with periodic replenishment by the museum. The rules that viewers can take the candies and that the institution can continue to replenish them indefinitely are critical to the expressive content of the work: a similar work without such rules could not serve in the same way as a warm, joyous, and generous tribute to Ross Laycock, the artist's lover who died of AIDS in 1991.

---

[1] Irvin 2005b discusses the effect on interpretations related to mortality and loss when the rules for a specific work are changed by the artist, in relation to Liz Magor's 1976 *Time and Mrs. Tiber*.

Gonzalez-Torres's *"Untitled" (Perfect Lovers)* makes a different sort of comment on relationship and loss. The work involves two round analog clocks of the same model, often seen on the walls of professional spaces. The instructions for installation specify that

> [t]he clocks must be installed together on one wall, adjacent to each other and touching... Both clocks should be synchronized to the same time disregarding the second hand. When synchronized the clocks should be set to the correct time.

If they fall slightly out of sync during the course of the exhibition, "it is not necessary to resynchronize the clocks since this natural occurrence is part of the piece."[2]

The temporality of love was a major theme of Gonzalez-Torres's work, and *"Untitled" (Perfect Lovers)* expresses both the ideal and the unreality of love as a state of perfect synchronization. During the same period, Gonzalez-Torres authored a letter to Ross with a drawing of two clocks at the top, reading:

> Dont be afraid of the clocks, they are our time, time has been so generous to us. We imprinted time with the sweet taste of victory. We conquered fate by meeting at a certain TIME in a certain space. We are a product of the time, therefore we give back credit where it is due: time.
>
> We are synchronized, now and forever.
>
> I love you. (Gonzalez-Torres 1988, 155; punctuation and orthography are as in the original)

The letter, read alongside the installation of clocks, forestalls a pessimistic reading of *"Untitled" (Perfect Lovers)*: characteristically, Gonzalez-Torres is celebrating love as it occurs in a real human life, through moments of incredible good fortune and periods of excruciating loss and grief. The title is not ironic; the fact that the clocks will go out of sync is compatible with the perfection of love.

A work with a similar appearance but without the rules for displaying ordinary clocks and letting them fall out of sync evokes a different set of meanings about relationship and loss. This claim was tested in real life, when designer Tobias Wong appropriated Gonzalez-Torres's idea in Wong's 2002 work *Perfect Lovers (Forever)*. As critic Kevin Buist says of Wong's work,

> It also consists of two mass-produced clocks. At first, it seems to be a direct copy of [Gonzalez-Torres's] iconic piece, but the wry difference becomes clear over

---

[2] Sample loan invoice prepared by Andrea Rosen Gallery, undated, in the Dallas Museum of Art object file for the work.

time. Wong's clocks are outfitted with radio receivers that keep each clock synchronized with the U.S. Atomic Clock, ensuring they both stay accurate to within one second over a period of a million years.   (Buist 2011)

As Buist notes, this changes utterly the significance of the display of the two clocks.

> *Untitled (Perfect Lovers)* is such a beautiful and touching piece because Gonzalez-Torres creates a problem without giving the viewer the comfort of a solution. The two clocks, despite the fact that they seem to be a perfect pair, are flawed. They differ, they can never really be one. They will drift apart, they will disagree, they will measure and reflect the world in different ways. The fabric of their being ensures that eventually they'll end up in conflict.
>
> Wong's *Perfect Lovers (Forever)* does what design does, it provides a solution. But in doing this, Wong removes all the tragic beauty from the original. This conceptual twist has its own poetic power, however. By fixing Gonzalez-Torres's "problem," Wong brings to light a new problem: the utopian ambitions of design itself. What if design's ambition to fix the world has a dark side? When we fix a problem, what do we lose?   (Buist 2011)

The rule sanctioned by Gonzalez-Torres serves as an expressive resource: a rule to resynchronize the clocks would have resulted in fundamentally different meanings, aligning Gonzalez-Torres's work more closely with Wong's. The "perfection" secured by Wong is mechanistic, inhuman: both practically impossible and conceptually dystopian. The contrast highlights for us that there is beauty and richness in a human condition that involves inevitable asynchrony and loss.

Saburo Murakami's *Peeling Pictures*, discussed in the introduction, offer a related perspective. By exemplifying surfaces designed to erode, the works express that loss is not only loss: every change is a ceding of one state to another, and if we hold on too tightly to one preferred situation, we lose out on the complexity and unpredictable beauty that emerges as things evolve over time.

By deploying custom rules, artworks manifest forms of change over time that are thematically significant in exploring a variety of dimensions of and attitudes toward mortality, grief, and loss. Decay and damage such as we see in Leonard's, Hassan's, and Murakami's works can happen to art objects even in the absence of custom rules, but the custom rule is what secures exemplification: the fact that the work not only possesses but refers back to these states. Damage or decay that is merely present but not exemplified in this way can be appropriated to speak to themes of mortality and loss, as in Shelley's "Ozymandias"; but when these states are secured by the artist's sanction, they become relevant to interpretation of the work itself, making it appropriate to attribute meanings that account for the salience of these states. The same is true of Gonzalez-Torres's clocks: had the artist been silent on whether the clocks should be resynchronized, the status of a display in which the clocks are out of sync would be ambiguous. The articulation of a specific custom rule has the effect that the tendency of the clocks to go out of sync is made salient, and thus exemplified; this makes it ripe for the assignment of meaning, as Buist's discussion indicates.

Rules, Conventions, and Art Institutions

Another content domain to which rules as medium are particularly apt is that of social relations and power structures, both as they are manifest in institutions of art and more broadly. When artists sanction rules that contravene established conventions, they set up a dilemma: should we do this strange thing that the artist is telling us we may or should do? Will this damage or devalue the work, or get us into some sort of trouble? What adventures are we interested in having, and what risks are we willing to take?

Though Gerald Ferguson sanctioned a rule allowing purchasers to repaint his *Maintenance Paintings* as desired, I have found no instance in which someone has exercised the full permission implied by this rule. A 1984 exhibition catalog notes that Ferguson

> condones—even appreciates—the fact that, to his knowledge, none of the numerous paintings sold from the series has been overpainted. It would seem that the new owners are treating the works as traditional art by electing to accept disrepair rather than "maintain" the original perfect surface of the paint. But these decisions are not inappropriate to Ferguson's own motives and perceptions, nor are such ironies unanticipated.[3]

Maintenance was done later on some of the paintings, but even this showed a reluctance to interfere with the original surface. One collector, Bruce Campbell, contracted with Ferguson himself to repaint *Maintenance Painting No. 30* in 1994; the process included the affixing of a new maintenance contract to the back of the painting.[4] Another collector, the artist and curator John Murchie, did maintenance on a few of the paintings himself:

---

[3] Peggy Gale, catalog essay for the exhibition Gerald Ferguson: Works 1978–1984, October 4–November 11, 1984, Dalhousie Art Gallery, p. 3.

[4] Email correspondence with the collector, Bruce Campbell, July 17, 2012. Campbell explains that he chose to have Ferguson maintain the painting "as [a] very deliberate and specific conceptual addendum [,] evoking the original sales contract without compromising the integrity of the artist's hand," framing the patron as an investor while also alluding to "the dialectic of artist as worker / labourer."

When I repainted the walls of our living room a light grey, I used the same paint on the four edges of each painting. The "painting surfaces" themselves remained bright green. Sometime later I told [Ferguson] who seemed none too pleased although I deduced that more from body language etc. than anything he overtly said.[5]

The Art Gallery of Nova Scotia, which owns eight of the works, has never repainted their surfaces.[6]

The reluctance to repaint the works tells us something about the force of the convention that the painted surface created by the artist is precious and to be conserved: when the artist both creates a unique painted surface and declares that this surface need not be preserved, this sets up a clash of understandings about the work, and this clash is not automatically resolved in favor of acting as the artist's custom rule permits. Collectors and institutions may rightly fear that were they to exercise the full permission to repaint these works, their market value would diminish; community understanding of artworks and their value does not immediately update when artists begin to challenge longstanding conventions.

The shift over time in institutional treatment of El Anatsui's works, discussed in Chapter 2, manifests a related dynamic, though with a different outcome. The early reluctance to innovate in displays of the works eventually ceded to willingness to exercise the full permission sanctioned by the artist. This evolution may be related both to the fact that Anatsui became internationally prominent—with the effect that his work was increasingly displayed in spaces well equipped to accommodate novel contemporary art practices—and to the fact that, in contrast with fully following Ferguson's permission to repaint his surfaces, sculptural installation of Anatsui's work does not irreversibly alter the object.

Both institutions and audiences have embraced Felix Gonzalez-Torres's permission for audiences to take away components of displays of his work—either wrapped hard candies or prints—that institutions may indefinitely replenish. However, when an audience is unaware of the permission, the convention of treating the artwork as inviolable kicks in. Philosopher Amie Thomasson has recounted to me that a few years ago when she saw one of Gonzalez-Torres's candy spills on display in Miami, no one was interacting with the work. Recalling a talk in which I had discussed the works, Thomasson knew that taking a candy was permitted, so she did so; after this, other audience members began to take candies as well. It is possible that no one else present knew that taking candies was permitted until they saw Thomasson's action; however, equally likely, given how well known Gonzalez-Torres's work is in Miami, where he had a home and where

---

[5] Email correspondence with John Murchie, July 18, 2012.
[6] Email correspondence with Troy Wagner, Assistant Registrar of the Art Gallery of Nova Scotia, December 6, 2018.

several members of his family were based, is that while some audience members were aware that taking candies was permitted, they were reluctant to break the convention of non-participation until someone else had done so. This might be for fear of institutional repercussions—for institutions sometimes enforce prohibitions on actions the artist permitted, as we will see in Chapter 9—or for fear of social stigma in the event that other audience members are unaware of the artist's invitation. Nicolas Bourriaud makes a similar observation:

> At a Gonzalez-Torres show, I saw visitors grabbing as many candies as their hands and pockets could hold: in doing so they were being referred to their social behaviour, their fetishism and their cumulative concept of the world... while others did not dare, or waited for the person next to them to filch a candy, before doing likewise. The candy pieces thus raise an ethical problem in an apparently anodyne form: our relationship to authority and the way museum guards use their power; our sense of moderation and the nature of our relationship to the work of art.   (Bourriaud 2002, 56–7)

The simple possibility of taking a candy activated by the rule for participation in these works thus engages our agency in grappling with institutional power and social pressure.

While various kinds of interactions with contemporary artworks are now permitted, removing a component remains prohibited in the overwhelming majority of cases. For this reason, a prohibition on removing a component of the work typically is not strongly expressive. But taking a component of Gonzalez-Torres's works is so often permitted that on the rare occasions when it is not, the expressive quality of the prohibition on removing part of the work is reanimated. His 1991 work *"Untitled"*, in the collection of the Solomon R. Guggenheim Museum, consists of 161 signed silkscreens that are not replenishable and removal of which is not permitted.[7] The print is visually similar to a 1989 billboard Gonzalez-Torres created to commemorate the twentieth anniversary of the Stonewall uprising for LGBTQ rights. The white text, presented near the bottom of a field of black, lists a number of critical moments in the movement both before and after Stonewall: *"People With AIDS Coalition 1985 Police Harassment 1969 Oscar Wilde 1891 Supreme Court 1986 Harvey Milk 1977 March on Washington 1987 Stonewall Rebellion 1969."*

By requiring that the stack, which is displayed on the floor, remain intact, Gonzalez-Torres created a monument, a low monolith resembling a tombstone. This formal structure, combined with the rule for non-interaction, instills a sense of reverence in commemorating the members of the LGBTQ community who

---

[7] See the collection website at https://www.guggenheim.org/artwork/24264.

died of AIDS during the long period of obstinate government non-response, and others who have been subjected to anti-LGBTQ violence up to and including death. While many of Gonzalez-Torres's works are joyful and generous even in their acknowledgement of loss, through the rule of non-interaction, *"Untitled"* stops us in our tracks and encourages us to take time to honor and grieve those who have suffered and died due to anti-LGBTQ oppression and those who have resisted it. Gonzalez-Torres thus deploys the institutional power of protecting objects in the service of a commentary on mortality and loss, unifying the two expressive themes explored in this chapter.

Some works seem directly designed to reveal, poke fun at, or test the limits of institutional practices. Jason Rhoades's 2002–3 *SLOTO: The Secret Life of the Onion* is a large, complex installation work whose appearance varies. It involves a set of yellow shelves; large, green glass bulbs shaped rather like onions; vats of various materials and substances; and a carnival train shaped like a pig. On the walls are a series of posters, written faintly in pencil, offering instructions visible to everyone but intended for museum staff to follow. These instructions specify how to construct "onions" by adding materials available in the room to the green glass containers. Having constructed an onion, the staff member is instructed to "[g]et into the head of the pig train, and with a constructed onion on your lap go around looking in not forward," before placing the completed onion on one of the yellow shelves. This work is in the collection of the Vanabbemuseum in the Netherlands, whose contemporary art curator, Christiane Berndes, told me that they actually follow the instructions.[8]

SLOTO is silly. It asks museum staff members to engage in a series of frivolous rituals: following an "onion" recipe, riding in a pig train, and so forth. The rituals involve seemingly pointless rules, such as which way to look. (Sometimes, another artist's work has been installed in the midst of *SLOTO*, giving the participant something to look at.) The rules Rhoades has sanctioned for interacting with the objects of *SLOTO* invite reflection on the institutional context. Art museum procedures are, generally speaking, highly ritualized. To what extent are the usual rituals more meaningful than Rhoades's frivolous ones? Can an artist secure compliance with silly rules? Does the invitation to ride the pig train perhaps liberate the museum staff from a routine that is often more bureaucratic, offering an occasion for play? Why is full engagement with the work available only to museum staff and not to all?

Tino Sehgal's 2002 *This is propaganda*, in the Tate collection, plumbs the limits of institutional practices in a different way. At one level, it is a work of performance art involving a docent who, each time an audience member enters the exhibition space, begins to sing a particular song with lyrics and melody designated by Sehgal.

---

[8] Interview of Christiane Berndes by the author, Vanabbemuseum, December 2011.

(See Laurenson and van Saaze 2014, 35, for a detailed description.) But at another level, Sehgal controls the very process by which the work is institutionally acquired and maintained: for there are very strict rules about whether and how museum staff are permitted to create records related to the work. The work has a very minimal institutional footprint: no contract or written instructions accompanied the work on acquisition, and the museum is not permitted to maintain an official file with instructions for generating a display. (See Lubow 2010 for a description of the process of sale, which involves a verbal contract witnessed by a lawyer or notary.) In lieu of written instructions, Sehgal personally trained museum staff on how to audition and train the performers, and on the nature of the performance including the words and melody to be sung. While museum staff members are permitted to make notes for their own individual use, these notes are not to become part of any official file or shared with others; instead, all information about the work is to be personally transmitted from staff member to staff member through demonstration and verbal description (Laurenson and van Saaze 2014; van Saaze 2015). This represents an extreme departure from the usual institutional practice of meticulously documenting every aspect of the instructions in writing, and thereby invites reflection on the bureaucracies of art and their tendency to dampen personal experiences that museum professionals have with the artwork and with each other. Sehgal's prohibition on written documentation enlivens a performative and interactive practice within the institution that harks back to longstanding oral traditions that have served as a "conservation" practice for works of music, dance, poetry, and religious ritual in cultures around the world for centuries or millennia.

Rules, Social Dynamics, and Power Structures

When an artwork involves custom rules contravening the conventions and power structures of art institutions, the situation is ripe for metaphorical exemplification of social dynamics and power structures as they occur outside of art.

Tlingit and Unangax̂ artist Nicholas Galanin's series of three works titled *Indian Children's Bracelet* (2014–18) involves three pairs of found child-sized iron handcuffs that Galanin, who is a contemporary artist as well as a jeweler and carver, has carved with Tlingit formline (Figure 7.2) (Steinhauer 2018). The handcuffs were used to separate Indigenous children from their families and transport them to residential schools, where they experienced treatment designed to extinguish their language and culture as well as other forms of abuse. The three works in the series are governed by a rule that no institution is permitted to acquire more than one.[9] Through the literal separation of the works, Galanin

---

[9] Nicholas Galanin, public lecture at the University of Oklahoma, September 20, 2018.

Figure 7.2 Nicholas Galanin, *Indian Children's Bracelet*, 2014–18. Hand-engraved iron, 3 × 7½ × ½ in. (7.6 × 19.1 × 1.3 cm).
© Nicholas Galanin
Courtesy of the artist

metaphorically exemplifies carceral practices of separating Indigenous children from their families, cultures, communities, and each other. Through the carving he has added to the handcuffs, Galanin metaphorically exemplifies the persistence of Tlingit culture and identity even in the face of forces aiming to secure cultural genocide; the beauty and resilience of culture sit alongside the pain caused by anti-Indigenous violence.

As we saw in Chapter 4, many works with rules for participation set up situations in which social relations and power dynamics are salient, becoming part of the subject matter of the work. Kara Walker's 2014 *A Subtlety* set up a situation in which many audience members violated a prominently posted rule prohibiting touching the objects, a huge Black female sphinx figure with a surface of white sugar and life-size child laborer figures with surfaces of molasses or cast brown sugar. Some of the touching of the woman, both real and simulated through photographs juxtaposing the hand or tongue of the viewer with parts of the woman's body, metaphorically exemplified disrespect for the body of the Black woman. But other touches—gentle caresses of the white sugar surface or fascinated manipulation of the sticky pools that gathered as the child laborer figures melted—exhibited loving, reverent, and delighted reactions to the work. Setting up this situation and documenting how audience members engaged with the objects was an important part of Walker's project, eventuating in a 2014 video work, *An Audience*.

Paul Ramírez Jonas's several works in which people bestow keys on each other—sometimes keys to the bestower's own home, and sometimes keys to commercial or public spaces—invite reflection on the many mechanisms by which space is controlled and some people have access while others are excluded. We lock our private spaces to protect ourselves and our possessions, exemplifying a lack of trust in others and perhaps also an assumption that we have a legitimate claim to whatever we have managed to acquire, no matter how unequal the distribution. When public spaces are locked, this even more strongly exemplifies lack of trust and forces of social control: those who need the space most, perhaps as a place to sleep, are excluded because they are not trusted to safeguard it. By having people distribute keys to these various spaces, Ramírez Jonas highlights the attitudes surrounding property and ownership and literally exemplifies relations of trust and expansion of access to spaces and their contents.

In several of her performance works, Marina Abramović creates direct encounters between people to explore the limits of social relationships. In Chapter 4, we discussed *Rhythm 0*, a six-hour performance in which Abramović was passive as audience members subjected her to various forms of treatment including humiliation, injury, and danger, revealing the willingness of some people to abuse others as long as the treatment occurs under the guise of some situation in which the rules in force appear to permit it. Abramović's 2010 work *The Artist Is Present*, performed at the Museum of Modern Art, invited a very different sort of relationship: the artist sat in a chair, clothed in a long gown, and gazed into the eyes of audience members who chose to occupy the chair opposite. The performance lasted over 700 hours during a three–month period, and over 1500 audience members participated (Cotter 2010; Stigh 2010). As Abramović said, "Nobody could imagine...that anybody would take time to sit and just engage in mutual gaze with me. It was [a] complete surprise...this enormous need of humans to actually have contact."[10] Because Abramović had achieved tremendous celebrity by 2010, it is not in fact surprising that so many people participated. But the depth of meaning and connection many people seemed to find in the experience was striking. Audience members could choose how long to sit, and there was social pressure to sit for a relatively short period of time, for there were typically long lines of other viewers waiting. But some audience members stayed for long periods, including one who participated twenty-one times and, on one occasion, sat for an entire day.[11] In Abramović's view,

[10] Quoted on the MoMA web site at https://www.moma.org/learn/moma_learning/marina-abramovic-marina-abramovic-the-artist-is-present-2010/.

[11] As indicated on the official flickr site for the work, Paco Blancas was the only person who visited the work on March 13, 2010. https://www.flickr.com/photos/themuseumofmodernart/4479591262/in/album-72,157,623,741,486,824/. See also http://artobserved.com/2010/03/ao-on-site-new-york-marina-abramovic-the-artist-is-present-at-moma-march-14-through-may-31-2010/.

It was much better if the people sat longer than shorter because there was more time to work with the material, with the energy. When they sit for a short time, it's kind of a short investment and they can't get as much out of it...[P]eople came and sat with me for forty minutes and they were thinking it was ten minutes, so they lost the sense [of time]. The longest sitting is definitely a more transformative experience for me and for the audience, too.   (Stigh 2010)

The contrast between *The Artist Is Present* and *Rhythm 0* is striking: whereas in the situation set up by *Rhythm 0*, some audience members descended to abuse and violence, the audience for *The Artist Is Present* was largely respectful (leaving aside a few mild shenanigans that occurred on the final day) (Chen 2010). Many people were moved to tears by the simple experience of encounter with the artist. As shown in a film about the piece by Matthew Akers, "Many of the sitters... seem to be having a transcendent experience. Their eyes grow bright; tears well and fall; they bow their heads or touch their hearts—and Abramović occasionally touches hers" (Thurman 2012). The man who visited twenty-one times arrived the final time with the number twenty-one tattooed prominently on his arm, visible to the artist (Stigh 2010).

Custom rules allow artists to set up situations in which power dynamics are metaphorically and literally exemplified, the agency of audience members is engaged, and normal conventions governing social interactions are temporarily suspended, providing opportunities for new forms of social engagement. Some artists have taken this potential even further, creating works designed for extensive community participation that outstrips the usual circumscribed nature of art encounters.

Contemporary Art and Community Formation

While *Rhythm 0*, created in 1974, appeared to confirm some of the most pessim-istic social psychology findings of 1960s and 1970s, according to which it doesn't take much setup to get people to treat others quite badly and even to engage in behaviors that tend toward fascism, *The Artist Is Present* demonstrates that another kind of situational structure can promote depth of feeling and meaningful connection. Other artists have gone further, creating expansive occasions for social engagement and community formation, sometimes in ways that affect a community's prospects in the long term. Over time, the sanctioning of custom rules for participation has destabilized the longstanding convention according to which audience members are mere spectators. This has made way for new forms of deeply participatory art practice that often involve an open-ended invitation to the audience and a willingness to see projects evolve in response to community needs and interests. Some projects are now understood as artworks that would previously have been seen only as art-adjacent: community development projects undertaken by artists but not themselves constituting part of the artist's artistic practice.

This evolution from custom rules toward new participatory art forms is manifest in the work and thought of Joseph Beuys, who initiated the idea of "social sculpture." Beuys held that artists should create art "that relates to thought and to the development of an idea, so that it later becomes a practical idea within society" (Michaud 1988, 39). Beuys's 1982 work *7000 Oaks*, as initially exhibited at Documenta 7 in Kassel, involved an enormous triangular pile of 7000 large basalt stones adjacent to a newly planted oak tree. The pile was eventually dismantled as a tree was planted using each stone as a marker. Andreas Huyssen thus describes the work as "art for vanishing" (Huyssen 1984, 5).

In making this work, Beuys specified rules for display and participation: an initial display was constituted, but this display was to be dismantled and the stones used as markers for trees, with the plantings understood as elements of the work. In addition, he suggested that the aim of the work was to spur further action beyond the bounds of the initial 7000 plantings:

> The planting of seven thousand oak trees is thus only a symbolic beginning. And such a symbolic beginning requires a marker, in this instance a basalt column. The intention of such a tree-planting event is to point up the transformation of all of life, of society, and of the whole ecological system.
>
> (Beuys, quoted in Cooke n.d.)

The Dia Art Foundation, which helped to fund the initial work in Kassel, subsequently installed additional stones and trees in New York City, presenting these as parts of Beuys's work *7000 Oaks*.[12]

Despite Beuys's aspiration for his work to inspire a wide-ranging transformation, the actions and objects that seem clearly susceptible to be counted as belonging to his work are fairly narrow: the planting of trees marked by large stones and institutionally tied to Beuys's original creative activity. But the rules for participation and forms of practice he and other artists initiated have given rise to further projects and practices that increasingly involve audience members in diverse activities that lend themselves to rethinking and reconstructing the nature of community. These practices fall within what Nicolas Bourriaud describes as "an art form where the substrate is formed by intersubjectivity, and which takes being-together as a central theme" (Bourriaud 2002, 15).

Jill Sigman's ongoing *Hut Project*, discussed in Chapter 4, involves Sigman's traveling to a site, gathering found and cast-off materials, and using them to

---

[12] See the Dia website: https://www.diaart.org/visit/visit/joseph-beuys-7000-oaks.

construct a hut that reflects the material culture and history of the surrounding community (Sigman 2017). Sigman dwells in the huts and welcomes the public to visit for a wide variety of structured and unstructured encounters: musical and dance performances, chats over tea, workshops on sustainable practices, meals, and participation in rituals such as offering or receiving gifts. The *Hut Project* aims to get people thinking in new ways about community, about our engagement with the material world, and about possibilities for human life. As Sigman says, "In the unfamiliar but intimate context of the huts, I witnessed people talking to others they didn't know, tasting things they wouldn't normally eat, and thinking thoughts they wouldn't often think" (Sigman 2017, 5). As the hut is deconstructed, Sigman tries to find new homes for any objects that still have potential life or use; the *Hut Project* thus often reclaims objects that would otherwise have gone to the dump.

Important to Sigman's project is that the work is not simply a physical structure: it is, instead, an extended event that involves the construction and use of a physical structure. The boundaries of the event are vague—does it begin when the work is conceived, when the plan to travel to the site is formed, or when the materials begin to be collected? Does it end when the hut is deconstructed, or when the last object from the hut has been given away? Or does it persist as these objects continue to be used and enjoyed by their new possessors, and as these possessors continue to engage with the material world and with their communities in ways informed, even subtly, by their engagement with the huts?

Sigman's work exemplifies the potential of participatory artworks and practices, even if they began under the auspices of a gallery or museum, to extend into public and private spaces that normally have no particular connection to art. Fritz Haeg's 2005–13 series *Edible Estates* is another contemporary art practice that aims to change how people engage with material culture and community. Haeg has worked with families and communities in many cities and nations to design and create enduring gardens that offer both beauty and literal sustenance, in the form of edible produce, while also bringing people together. Haeg announces the aspiration for the project to "stitch communities back together, taking a space that was previously isolating and turning it into a welcoming forum that reengages people with one another" (Haeg 2008, 23). There are indications that this aspiration has been realized: "Most of the participants in Haeg's Edible Estates have remarked that they have never known their neighbors better—their gardens fostering interaction as well as providing shared vegetables" (Cross 2011, 33). While the projects often begin with a commission by a local art institution and their early stages are typically commemorated by an exhibition, the works exist on residential properties and are largely created and exclusively maintained by people for whom the project may be not chiefly an artwork, but a form of domestic and communal beautification and engagement.

Whether and to what extent such projects really do have broad effects on community formation depends on the details of execution and uptake. Critic Susan Cross suggests that Haeg's projects produce a shift in perceptions among "the passersby realizing that a gift economy is a possible alternative to capitalism [and] the city kids learning not only that they can grow their own carrots but that they can create their own idea of community" (Cross 2011, 33). This claim may be overstated: Cathy Lebowitz notes that at the time she visited in 2009, *Edible Estates regional prototype garden #6* (2008), in west Baltimore, had provoked "conversations about the standard blanket of grass and the benefits of growing one's own produce," but it had not spurred any neighbors to undertake a similar project— and even less, one supposes, to rethink the system of property rights or to reconceive their concepts of community (Lebowitz 2009, 103). But projects created with residents of public and low-income housing, like *Edible Estates regional prototype garden #4* (2007) on the grounds of the Brookwood House Council Estate in London, seem to have significant potential to attract people out of their individual residential spaces into an appealing community space and to engage them in a collective project (Figure 7.3). Perhaps most important, the

Figure 7.3 Fritz Haeg, *Edible Estates regional prototype garden #4: London, England,* established 2007.

Owned by the tenants of the Brookwood House Council Estate
Commissioned by Tate Modern
Photo Heiko Prigge
© Fritz Haeg
Courtesy of the artist

investment of creative and physical labor to install and maintain a rich and varied landscape expresses something about the valuing of the space and of the people who inhabit it. Housing for low-income residents is often boring or ugly, with little attention paid to the aesthetic qualities of built elements or landscaping. Projects that go against this current, aiming to produce rewarding aesthetic experiences, convey a respect for the full humanity of people who are often marginalized and disregarded. In addition to providing direct opportunities for interaction in the garden and fresh produce for people with limited access, then, this project may invite people into the broader community as well, by expressing that they are full and valued members of it.

Sigman's Huts and Haeg's Edible Estates both have the recognizable artistic form that characterizes a carefully constructed display: Sigman's consisting in the structures of the huts and the performances and other planned activities that occur in and around them, and Haeg's in the design of the landscape. Other forms of participatory art move away from the model of carefully planned form and display. *Project Row Houses*, founded in 1993 by Rick Lowe with artists James Bettison, Bert Long Jr., Jesse Lott, Floyd Newsum, Bert Samples, and George Smith and still thriving over twenty-five years later, is an iconic example of participatory art practices forming deep and sustained community (Figure 7.4). The project started with the purchase of twenty-two row houses that had fallen into disrepair

Figure 7.4 Project Row Houses, founded 1993. Opening of the exhibition Round 46: Black Women Artists for Black Lives Matter, March 25–June 4, 2017.
Photo by Alex Barber
Courtesy of Project Row Houses

in Houston's economically marginalized Third Ward. As the *Project Row Houses* website indicates, "Where others saw poverty, these artists saw a future site for positive, creative, and transformative experiences in the Third Ward. So, together they began to explore how they could be a resource to the community and how art might be an engine for social transformation."[13] The project has grown to encompass thirty-nine structures and communal outdoor spaces that host both artistic and other activities. Some of the structures are affordable artists' studios, residency sites, and exhibition spaces, while others are used as housing for young single mothers and their children, as incubation space for new small businesses with a focus on creative activity and community development, and as a site where children and adults can seek free tutoring. *Project Row Houses* periodically hosts public events such as markets for creative vendors, drawing the broader Houston community into the neighborhood. Larne Abse Gogarty describes visiting *Project Row Houses* in 2013, twenty years after its founding, and being "struck by how it seemed to act as a nerve centre, or world-unto-itself, abundant with possibilities for experimentation for both residents from the Third Ward and the artists who take up residencies and studios there" (Gogarty 2014, 8).

Project Row Houses succeeded as its founders envisioned, becoming an engine of creative activity as well as economic development. The resulting gentrification in the surrounding area motivated a strategy of buying up further properties to ensure that affordable housing would remain available to Third Ward residents. In addition, Gogarty suggests, the participatory art form that Lowe and his collaborators pioneered has itself been gentrified. Lowe has expressed concern about "white social practice MFA graduates launching projects in African-American communities without validating the cultural activity already present," and Gogarty suggests more broadly that participatory art is exhibiting "a troubling shift towards the banal, 'post-political' smoothness that typifies the art world at large. This, I believe, epitomises the codification of the field into a medium rather than an experimental strategy or practice" (Gogarty 2014, 9). Tom Finkelpearl has suggested that *Project Row Houses* escaped the fate of being absorbed into the post-political art world: it "truly is an alternative space, whereas a lot of alternative spaces have become just part of the art industry, like farm teams for the museums."[14]

We see, then, a situation in which artists' sanctioning of custom rules for participation has destabilized an earlier convention of non-participation, and thereby made way for the emergence of a participatory art form in which the involvement of community extends beyond clearly defined rules for participation. *Project Row Houses* is understood not only as a community development project

---

[13] https://projectrowhouses.org/about/mission-history.
[14] Michael Kimmelman, "In Houston, Art Is Where the Home Is," *New York Times*, December 17, 2006, https://www.nytimes.com/2006/12/17/arts/design/17kimm.html.

undertaken by a group of artists, but as part of their artistic practice, even though it does not employ sculptural forms or culminate in events that are identifiable as performances or displays (Thompson 2012, 256–7).

Should we be skeptical that Lowe and his collaborators, Haeg, and Sigman have created works of art, as opposed to art-adjacent community practices or sites? Sigman's works seem less likely to trigger such skepticism, since the displays are typically time-limited and presented under the auspices of an art institution, the huts' construction involves practices standardly understood as sculptural, and some of the specific events that occur in and around them have recognizable elements of dance or performance art. Haeg's edible gardens are deliberately designed, and each project typically involves collaboration with a recognized art institution; but many of the participants in constituting, maintaining, and living with the garden may not understand it as art. *Project Row Houses* was created by a group of artists working independently of art institutions, and discussions of it frequently allude to questioning of its art status. Lowe has said,

> As a piece of art, the form of Project Row Houses reveals something that you lose at a larger scale, when a project is not as thought through and collaboratively produced. We're trying to create a framework—a form in which questions of creative economies and community housing can come about from within a community—as we provide programs and space to a neighborhood in need.
>
> (Lowe 2013, n.p.)

Lowe suggests that, taken together, the aims, scale, and conceptual framework of the project are distinct from those of related non-art practices, such as housing development or nonprofit social services administration.

Project Row Houses is frequently discussed in art contexts and has received uptake as part of a movement of participatory or socially engaged art (Thompson 2012). Lowe was recognized as a 2014 MacArthur Fellow for "reinventing community revitalization as an art form," with *Project Row Houses* characterized as a "visionary public art project" that has been "the focus of [Lowe's] artistic practice."[15] In my view, whether something counts as an artwork depends on the practices of relevant communities: the fact that Lowe himself has identified *Project Row Houses* in a sustained way as part of his artistic practice, and that it has been recognized as an art project by critics, curators, and institutions, is a strong indicator of if not sufficient to establish its art status.

However, in a sense little hangs on whether we regard Haeg's and Lowe's products as clear cases of artworks, borderline cases, or instead art-adjacent projects that are not properly identified as artworks. The practice within

---

[15] https://www.macfound.org/fellows/920/.

contemporary art of sanctioning custom rules for participation clearly played a historical role in the development of projects that have successfully engaged and enriched communities that might never have visited traditional art institutions or engaged with artworks lacking an expansive participatory vision.

When asked about the art status of *Project Row Houses*, Assata Richards, who had previously lived in one of its houses designated for single mothers, replied,

> Well, I had heard Rick was an artist when I got there, but I thought, what kind of art does he do? Then I realized we were his art. We came into these houses, and they did something to us. This became a place of transformation. That's what art does. It transforms you. And Rick also treated us like artists. He would ask, "What's your vision for yourself?" You understood that you were supposed to be making something new, and that something was yourself.[16]

Whether or not we understand *Project Row Houses* as an artwork, its generative power for the community is difficult to deny.

Rules as medium remain of central importance in many contemporary artworks, and as we have seen, they have particular potential in exploring themes related to mortality and loss, the functioning of art institutions, and social structures and power dynamics both within and outside of art. The deploying of custom rules is also itself a form of direct intervention in institutional structures: it forces the rethinking of habitual practices and destabilizes longstanding conventions. In so doing, it fosters the development of art deeply permeated by structures and forms of activity that were not previously part of the repertoire of visual art. Participatory and socially engaged art, characterized by invitations to the community to join in a wide variety of forms of activity, has emerged in the space created when rules for participation drove a wedge into the conventions distancing art from audience.

---

[16] Michael Kimmelman, "In Houston, Art Is Where the Home Is," *New York Times*, December 17, 2006, https://www.nytimes.com/2006/12/17/arts/design/17kimm.html.

8

Rules, Indeterminacy, and Interpretation

I have argued that contemporary artworks are partly constituted by rules, that rules function as medium, and that rules as medium have distinctive expressive potential. A question immediately arises: which rules? I've given a number of examples in which artists sanction specific rules for display, conservation, and participation, as when Felix Gonzalez-Torres tells us it's okay to eat the candies in his candy spills. But often, the situation is not so clear cut. When an artist's statements at different times about how to display a work conflict, how should we decide which statement to follow? When an artist never expressly pronounces on an aspect of the display, must we try to follow precedents that appear to be set in displays the artist was involved in, or may we assume that we are free to innovate?

These questions are not merely practical or peripheral, because I have argued that the rules are actually *part of* the work. To the extent that questions about the content of the rules remain open, we don't completely know what the work itself is. And perhaps there is an even deeper implication: that there is *no fact* about some aspects of the work's very nature. That is, it's not just that we don't know these facts about the work's nature: it's that there is nothing there to know. This might seem to be a serious problem: if my view implies that artworks have a partly indeterminate nature, wouldn't we be better off rejecting it in favor of a different understanding of what the artwork is?

One approach would be to try to wave this problem away, claiming that there is a way to resolve the indeterminacies. When I first introduced the concept of the artist's sanction which fixes the rules, I was drawn to this approach. However, for reasons I will explore here, I no longer find it compelling. There are deep and irresolvable indeterminacies in the very nature of many contemporary artworks. However, as I will argue, this is not a reason to reject the idea that rules are part of the structure of contemporary artworks. Indeed, indeterminacy can itself be artistically fruitful, as we will see in relation to the works of Tino Sehgal and Yoko Ono.

Outward Expression and Knowability

In Irvin 2005b, I suggested that the artist sanctions a rule for the work only if they successfully communicate it to someone who is in a position to enter the communication in the official record. If the artist intends something but never communicates it, then no sanction has been established, just as an artist who intends to add a brushstroke but never does so has not changed the painted surface. Moreover, the artist's sanction can come apart from the artist's intention if the artist misspeaks in communicating the sanction; an artist who says one thing but means another has established a sanction through what they say, not through any thought or intention that may conflict with their outward expression.

I acknowledged that the artist's outward communications cannot possibly settle all questions about the treatment of the work or how possible future circumstances—unexpected evolution of the objects fabricated by the artist, changes in the available gallery space, and so forth—should be handled. However, I suggested that artworks are created against a background of practices and conventions that tend to settle such questions by default, as long as the artist issues no sanction that contravenes them. Unless the artist expressly says that an object they supplied may be replaced or should be allowed to decay, it should be treated in accordance with well-established practices of art conservation, which dictate that the matter and appearance of objects should be preserved, to the extent possible, in the state they were in shortly after their creation.

If this picture were viable, the artist's outward communications would combine with background practices and conventions to settle the most glaring potential indeterminacies about the work. However, I've come to feel that this picture oversimplifies many elements of the situation; and once we acknowledge this, we must take seriously the prospect of deep indeterminacy in many contemporary artworks.

One difficulty with the simple picture is that, as Amie Thomasson (2010, 125–7) has moved me to recognize, for works that have been exhibited but not yet acquired by an institution, the idea that the artist must have outwardly communicated a rule for it to be partly constitutive of an artwork is not viable. In Chapter 5, we considered the 1969 work *All shadows...* by Jan Dibbets, which was acquired by the Kröller-Müller Museum nearly four decades after its initial creation. A display of this work consists of lengths of tape applied to surfaces in the gallery, outlining sunlight that enters the space through windows and other openings. The patches of sunlight are outlined multiple times as the sun moves across the sky, so the display typically consists of overlapping geometric forms. When Dibbets created the first display of the work, he already had a concept of the rules that constitute it, though if he did the installation himself he may have had no call to explain those rules to anyone else. Moreover, the creation of the display is not itself sufficient to communicate the rules outwardly: for the display alone doesn't tell us how or even whether the practices through which the display was generated may be extended to other circumstances. But none of this seems a good reason to deny that the rules Dibbets had in mind already constituted the work, even if the situation had not yet warranted any outward communication of those rules.

Of course, one might take a hard line here and hold that until the rules are communicated outwardly, they are merely notional and not work-constituting. One motivation for this is epistemic: rules that cannot be derived, even indirectly, from what has been outwardly expressed cannot be known. A consequence is that some works are on display, yet substantially inaccessible. One might object to the idea that there can be facts about an artwork, which is by nature an entity for public consumption, that are completely unavailable to the audience.[1]

Another motivation is metaphysical: one might be skeptical that there is a fact of the matter about the content of a mental state that has not yet been outwardly communicated. After all, many snatches of thought and idea may flash through the mind as we are acting and preparing to act. The mind may change continually and never light on a final conception; or the conscious mind may settle on a conception even as there are reasons to think the action is guided by an independent sub-rational process (Nisbett and Wilson 1977). How, then, can we identify some mental states as rule-constituting, and thus work-constituting, when those mental states are not fixed and may not in fact explain the features of the display?

These considerations might lead us in one of two quite different directions. First, one might suggest that because mental states that have not yet been outwardly expressed are not a reliable basis for constituting the work, any aspects of the work's identity not determined by what has been outwardly expressed must be fixed by other factors: for instance, background conventions, such as the convention that objects presented by the artist should be conserved, which can be assumed to be in effect as long as the artist does not specify otherwise. Or, instead, one might suggest that because the rules that would fix its nature have not yet been outwardly expressed, the work is deeply indeterminate as regards all matters left open by the display. On the first position, the work is largely fixed, but by factors that do not originate in the artist's creative activity. This position resolves the problem of indeterminacy but is clearly incompatible with the account I've been offering here. On the second position, the work is indeterminate to a degree that might appear objectionable.

Ultimately, I reject both of these alternatives, though I see the appeal of each. As I argued in Chapter 5, contemporary artworks depend ontologically on particulars, and the particulars in question may include mental states. Just as a poem may come to exist and have a determinate word sequence before the poet writes it down, the artwork may have a determinate structure of rules before the artist

---

[1] Considerations about the publicity of the artwork are frequently raised in discussions about interpretation. As Stephen Davies (1982, 69) says, for instance, "The aesthetic concern is with a public object which belongs to the poet only in the aesthetically unimportant respect that he caused its existence." Noël Carroll (1992), on the other hand, suggests that art is continuous with ordinary conversation, such that our concern need not be exclusively with the publicly available aspects of the work but may extend to other indicators of what the artist actually meant.

communicates them outwardly. Especially when the work isn't yet in a collection, it can depend ontologically on the artist's mental states. Some matters in the artist's mind are fixed, and these are work-constituting. There are, of course, complications. The first, and simplest, is that the artist's conception of the rules may change over time even before they have been outwardly expressed. This is just as a poet might revise her poem before ever writing it down or reciting it aloud. Creating displays contributes to the artist's thinking about the work and thus contributes to how the rules are ultimately constituted in the artist's mind; constructing the display is often part of the ongoing creative process for these works in a way that it is not for works that don't centrally involve custom rules.

But we must acknowledge a deeper worry. When the work is in the early stages of its existence and the artist has not yet expressed the rules outwardly, the rules may not be fixed in the artist's mind. When Dibbets was creating the first display of *All shadows...*, he may not yet even have contemplated whether the work was repeatable.[2] And even once he created additional displays and the question of repeatability was settled, his thinking about the rules constituting the work likely evolved over time, and there may have been moments where there was no settled fact about some aspect of the rules even in his mind.

But these do not seem to be good reasons to deny that there may be facts of the matter about some aspects of the work's identity, even if the artist has not yet outwardly communicated them. The fact that some matters remain unsettled in the artist's mind is perfectly consistent with the possibility that others are settled. And the possibility of change over time does not undermine the fact that there may be an established state of affairs at a given time. Just as a writer might compose a poem with a particular determinate word sequence prior to writing it down or reciting it, the artist may sanction the rules of an artwork prior to expressing them outwardly. And the fact that the writer might later make changes to that word sequence does not prevent the poem from having a determinate word sequence at a given time. There may be some moments when it is indeterminate which words constitute the third line of the poem, but this is no reason to conclude that the entire poem is indeterminate or, worse, doesn't exist.

What about the fact that elements of the work that have not yet been outwardly expressed are not epistemically accessible to others? We may note first that there

---

[2] Shifts in artists' thinking about whether and how their works are repeatable are not uncommon. As Claire Bishop (2012) discusses, attitudes about the repeatability of performance art have shifted over time from an expectation that works can be performed only by the artist, often as unique one-off events, toward a notion of "delegated performance," in which others are engaged to enact the work, which is conceived as indefinitely repeatable. Some artists, including Marina Abramović, have shifted over time from the former conception to the latter, with Abramović stating, "In the seventies, we believe in no repetition. [B]ut now is a new century, and without reperformance all you will leave the next generation is dead documents and recordings" (Thurman 2010). Several of her performance works originally conceived as non-repeatable were reperformed in a 2010 retrospective at the Museum of Modern Art in New York.

are plenty of things that exist but are not epistemically accessible, at least given our epistemic positions and current tools. Now, the unknowability of rules that have not yet been outwardly expressed should not be overstated: some aspects of the rules can often be inferred from the display, just as a person's intention may sometimes be inferred with a high degree of confidence from their behavior in a given context. However, as a matter of logic, the rules constituting a work cannot simply be derived from displays. If there has been only one display, we can reasonably infer that a display with this structure is *permitted* by the rules constituting the work; but is this specific structure mandated? Are some aspects of it mandated? Increasing the number of displays is of only limited help. When we have two displays with different structures, we can infer that both structures are permitted; but does this mean that anything within the range defined by these two structures would also be permitted, or are these our only two options? The fact is that any given set of displays, no matter how numerous, could have been generated from indefinitely many sets of rules either mandating these very specific structures or permitting anything within (and perhaps even other structures outside) the range that seems to be defined by the structures displayed so far. The pattern of commonalities and variability reflected in the displays may lead us to infer some things about the artist's aims, and these may lead us to make inferences about the rules. But this is a matter of reasonable inference, not certainty: the displays themselves do not uniquely determine a set of rules that must have been used to generate them. And the smaller the number of displays, the smaller our basis for inferring the principles on which the artist was operating.

For these reasons, some aspects of the rules constituting the work may simply be unavailable to the audience at a given time. The fact that something is unknown to or unknowable by a particular group of people does not mean there is no fact of the matter about it. It does mean, however, that it cannot be meaningful to them. So, to the extent that the specific content of a rule is to be a source of meaning, it cannot serve in this way until it is outwardly expressed.

However, there is no general problem with the idea that artworks can have elements that are not epistemically accessible, and some artworks even use epistemic inaccessibility itself as a source of meaning. Fiona Banner's 2007 *Shy Nude*, the principal marked surface of which is displayed facing the wall, frustrates the gaze of a viewer who arrives at the gallery accustomed to experiencing a full reveal of the nude body whose display under many non-art circumstances would be considered shameful; and even a viewer who manages to glimpse a bit of the marked surface discovers not a pictorial representation of the body but a text.[3] By virtue of the work's nature, the contents of the ninety sealed metal cans constituting the edition of Piero Manzoni's 1961 *Artist's Shit* cannot be inspected

---

[3] For images of both sides, see the RISD Museum collection web page for the work: https://risdmuseum.org/art-design/collection/shy-nude-200911.

without destroying the object: and even if the contents of one or another can were verified, it would remain possible that the contents of some other can were different. The wry humor of the work derives in part from our wondering whether the artist truly had the audacity to can his own shit, and whether the collectors and museums who acquired it really do now have literal human excrement in their collections. The institutions that hold the work acknowledge the uncertainty in various ways: Tate lists the medium as "tin can, printed paper and excrement," but acknowledges "a lingering uncertainty about whether [the cans] do indeed contain Manzoni's faeces" (Howarth 2010). The Museum of Modern Art, on the other hand, lists the medium as "metal, paper, and 'artist's shit,'" acknowledging with scare quotes the possibility that the "shit" consists not of excrement but of bullshit.[4]

Babak Golkar has made a series of *Time Capsules (2016–2116)*, sculptural works each of which contains a concealed object that may not be exposed until a hundred years after the work's creation (Figure 8.1). The agreement Golkar executes with the purchasers specifies that early revelation of the object would destroy the work. While the works were produced in 2016, the title of each work also includes 2116, the year in which the inner object may be exposed, and "concealed object" is listed as part of the medium of each work.[5] Golkar says he is interested in the sort of frustration people experience when he tells them there is a concealed object that they are not permitted to expose (Sandals 2016). Clearly, there is a fact about the concealed object (or absence thereof) within each sculpture, even though this fact cannot now be known without destroying the work. The fact that the works are advertised as containing concealed objects is clearly a meaningful aspect of them; and it seems that the specific nature of the concealed object, once known, will also contribute to the meanings we should attribute to them, even though we are not now in a position to do so. Something similar may be true of rules: the fact that we are not now in a position to know some rule associated with a work does not mean there is no fact of the matter about this rule, and it does not mean the rule will fail to be a meaningful element of the work once revealed.

Just as some information about the rules constituting the work may be unavailable early in the work's lifespan, information that was previously known about the rules may be lost temporarily or permanently. If all of the particulars on which some aspect of the rules ontologically depends—memories, notes, digital files—are lost, then the rule itself may be lost. In this case, the work loses a component and we lose the ability to know about this component, just as if the work had lost some of its physical material. The fact that information about the rules may be unavailable at a given moment, or may be lost over time, does not suggest that the rules never constituted the work or that they are insignificant or meaningless; it's just a

---

[4] See the collection web page: https://www.moma.org/collection/works/80768.
[5] See the Studio Babak Golkar web page for this series: http://babakgolkar.ca/timecapsules-.

Figure 8.1 Babak Golkar, installation view of works from the series *Time Capsules (2016–2116)*. Date of production: 2016.
Photo by Sebastiano Pellion di Persano
© Babak Golkar
Courtesy of the artist and Sabrina Amrani Gallery

fact about aspects of culture with symbolic import that the loss of information over time may lead to loss of our ability to fully comprehend or even know of the existence of some elements of the work. As we will see later, Tino Sehgal plays precisely with this element of loss of information in a series of performance artworks (or, as he would have it, "constructed situations") governed by meta-rules about how information about the rules for constituting displays of the work may be transmitted (Laurenson and van Saaze 2014, 35).

Contemporary Art and the Archive

The museum acquisition process for contemporary artworks now standardly involves working with the artist to secure outward communication of and to formalize the rules. Some of the most extensive consideration of this process has occurred in relation to technology-based works, which are deeply afflicted by problems of obsolescence and thus require direct attention to rules for display and conservation. Curator Jon Ippolito (2003) discusses the importance of working with artists to identify the "medium-independent behaviors" of artworks, whether object- or media-based: some works are *installed*, a process that may involve new decisions for each display, while a work is *performed* "whenever the re-creators have to reenact original instructions in a new context" (Ippolito 2003, 48–9). Some works permit *duplication*, which includes practices like cloning a work of computer art or constructing a display of a Felix Gonzalez-Torres work by constituting a new pile of candies (Ippolito 2003, 49). As Ippolito notes, it is important to work with the artist to document both the behaviors that are central to the work and the acceptable actions to take if the original objects or equipment begin to deteriorate. Richard Rinehart (2007), likewise, describes a formal notational system for capturing the "score" of a media artwork in a way that identifies both essential elements and variable components. Gwynne Ryan (2011, 111) notes that "the preservation of the conceptual and intangible components of contemporary artworks can take precedence over the materials themselves." Conceptual and intangible components, medium-independent behaviors, and the score are standardly preserved through paper or electronic documents.

This process eventuates in an *archive* on which the work ontologically depends, as Hanna Hölling (2017) discusses at length. As we will see, the ontological dependence of the work on the archive raises acute concerns about indeterminacy, since the complexity of materials in the archive may demand a robust process of interpretation to reconstruct the rules that are understood to constitute the artwork. The archive comprises both the institution's official files for an artwork in its collection and other elements that are relevant to the institution's engagement with the work. Some items are contributed by the artist: formal written text, instruction manuals, acquisition questionnaires, diagrams, email messages, and transcripts or videos of interviews. These may have been generated at different times: as we saw in Sanneke Stigter's work with Jan Dibbets in Chapter 5, the artist is sometimes asked decades after the initial act of creation to help an institution formalize the rules for display, conservation, and participation.

The archive may also contain detailed photo or video documentation of displays of the work, installation diagrams made by museum staff members, copies of internal correspondence and handwritten notes about the work, and copies of reviews or articles in which the work is mentioned. In addition, there may be conservation reports, photos, and drawings that capture the condition of the work and record any treatments that have been applied to the objects. There may also be a registration record that contains information about the initial acquisition of the work and the history of loans of the work to other institutions.

As Hölling (2017) discusses, the archive doesn't stop at the boundaries of the official files. There may also be information held within the museum or elsewhere that has not yet made it into these files. Hölling describes the situation as involving "micro-archives" that not everyone has access to, and she notes that curators, conservators, and other museum staff may serve as gatekeepers who determine what is incorporated into the official file and what is excluded, as well as who has access to it. In addition, Hölling notes that the archive contains information that cannot in principle be incorporated into a file: crucial parts of the archive are often stored as tacit knowledge or memory rather than recorded in writing. Even where notes are included in the file, correct interpretation of those notes may rely on memories of earlier displays or of details expressed by the artist that are not formalized. In addition, as Sanneke Stigter (2014) notes, some aspects of correct installation may rely on know-how, the internalization of a skill set that may have been learned directly from the artist and cannot be readily articulated in words. Jill Sterrett concurs: "one of the things we've found is that the best documentation methods involve old-fashioned storytelling—somebody teaches you how to install the work, and you teach me" (Gale, Lake, and Sterrett 2009, n.p.). For these reasons, Stigter argues that inclusion of new installers each time a complex work is displayed is an active conservation treatment: it helps to ensure that the mental particulars on which some elements of the work ontologically depend are con-tinually revitalized and transferred to new staff members who can serve as their ongoing guarantors. Displaying the work, then, becomes part of preserving it (cf. Laurenson and van Saaze 2014, 36).

The process of gathering the initial information on a complex artwork may take months as the artist formalizes instructions for display, the museum requests clarification, and the artist is brought in to create a sample display, discuss locations and parameters, and train museum staff on how to install future displays. Micro-archives and memories are generated during this process, and a process of gradual filtration determines which of these items ultimately end up in the archive that is available for consultation by those involved in conserving and displaying the work. The archive grows and changes over the lifespan of the work as new circumstances arise and new documentation and communication are generated (van de Vall et al. 2011). These changes in the archive are especially prone to happen when the work is displayed: each display affords an opportunity both to assess and treat the condition of the objects and to consider new installation possibilities, which may involve correspondence with or direct involvement by the artist. And, of course, new communication with the artist may lead to refinement of or outright changes to the rules for display, conservation, and participation as the artist considers a new installation location or changes in the condition of the objects. In addition, documentation of the new display is often added to the archive, helping to shape future understand-ings of the work.

As may be obvious from this description, the archive is not a straightforward, linear, perfectly organized enumeration of rules for display, conservation, and participation. Even where the artist has offered such an enumeration—a practice that has become increasingly common, but not universal—the archive contains a great deal of other information, both explicit and tacit, that informs how we understand the rules as stated. In addition, over time the artist may make new statements that conflict with the earlier ones; and circumstances—such as changes to the condition of the objects or reconfiguration of the original gallery space—may arise that were not anticipated and that the rules as initially expressed do not speak to.

The archive, in summary, is a complex text containing information in many forms—including words, diagrams, photographs, videos, and memories—that is gathered over time from many sources in a variety of contexts. It may contain internal tensions and outright contradictions, and some information may be lost or transformed over time as memories erode or are reconstructed.

Interpreting the Archive

In Chapter 5, we saw that the rules constituting the artwork are non-physical entities that ontologically depend on physical or mental particulars like documents and memories. For works in collections, this amounts to ontological dependence on the archive, which evolves over time and exhibits lacunae and contributions by many different people at different times. Some rules are stated clearly and straightforwardly by the artist with no variation over time; grasping these rules may require only limited engagement with the archive and no particular interpretative effort. But for works subject to variable display and composed of materials that exhibit varying rates of change over time, the situation may be much more complex: the artist's communications may have been generated over an extended period and may contain tensions, shifts in perspective, and even contradictions. They may leave some matters unsettled—even, in some cases, leaving it indeterminate whether or not the work still exists after certain types of change. Two competent and thoughtful conservators, looking carefully at the same information about the artist's communications, may come to different conclusions about the contents of the rules the artist has sanctioned. In such cases, ascertaining the rules requires inference and reconstruction, which are interpretive processes. Something similar is true of technology-based artworks subject to obsolescence: "Because these works don't self-record, self-document, or exist in a stable medium, preservation is an interpretive act" (Rinehart 2003, 25; see also Dekker 2013). The very identity of the work, then, may be a contested matter.

These issues arise acutely in relation to the works of Nam June Paik, a great innovator in media art whose works often comprise television sets used to play back original content. Paik was known to make explicit statements about the replaceability of elements of his works. *TV Cello* (1971), in the collection of the Walker Art Center, is a working cello (though with a non-traditional sound profile) made up of Plexiglas boxes housing three television sets of different sizes and equipment enabling the performer to manipulate the playback of video content on the TVs. On the artist's questionnaire he filled out for the

180 RULES, INDETERMINACY, AND INTERPRETATION

Walker, Paik wrote, "If TV sets get old, throw away and buy a new set. It is still the authentic original."[6]

While this statement seems straightforward, it leaves a number of questions open. Must the new TVs resemble the old? The Plexiglas boxes are designed to fit rather precisely around the original TVs, which are the deep, boxy models prevalent in the 1970s. What if TVs in the same size or of similar depth are no longer available when replacements are needed? Should the museum acquire a bunch of TVs in the same model as the original ones, so that it can swap out or repair non-functional units with others that look the same? Should it replace the guts of the TV cabinets with contemporary components, thereby preserving the sculptural appearance but undermining the historical authenticity of the objects and resulting in the video content's having a look and feel that does not fit the historical moment of the playback devices? Notably, Paik is silent on the permissibility of refabrication of the Plexiglas components to fit new television sets. To preserve the original Plexiglas boxes coheres with the traditional conservation practice of preserving sculptural materials fabricated by the artist. It also limits the options for TV replacement. Should we conclude that Paik did not mean for the Plexiglas boxes to be replaceable, or might it be that he mentions only the TVs because they are the elements that will become non-functional and thus drive the need for replacement? Did he, perhaps, even take it to be obvious that new Plexiglas boxes would be required to fit televisions in a different size and format?

In her work as conservator for Paik's 1990 *Canopus*, Hölling encountered a similar conundrum. The work, which hangs on the wall, includes an engraved hubcap at its center, ringed by six small monitors that play back specific content. The hubcap was damaged when the work fell off the wall. Hölling's proposal to replace the damaged hubcap with an undamaged one, replicating the markings found on the original, was rejected by colleagues on the grounds that replacing a unique physical object supplied by Paik would constitute forgery. This is despite the fact that Paik's statements about his works often endorsed the idea that elements could be replaced or reconfigured, with a clear priority for keeping the work available for audience access. As Hölling (2017, 6) puts it, "Among Paik's greatest innovations...was his rejection of the singular authentic object." Her colleagues, however, thought it inappropriate to extend this rejection to an object with unique markings whose replaceability Paik had not specifically pronounced on.

As this discussion suggests, there can be reasonable but conflicting understandings of what the artist has sanctioned by presenting a set of objects and communicating about their display and conservation. The TVs originally incorporated in displays of Paik's works have a sculptural presence that is historically marked.

---

[6] Undated artist questionnaire filled out by Nam June Paik for *TV Cello*, Walker Art Center, unpublished.

When an entire work is composed largely of TVs playing specific content, to replace those TVs with very different ones dramatically alters the material presence of the work; yet, such replacements have been undertaken for some of Paik's works, as Hölling recounts. Due to issues of obsolescence and equipment breakdown, the long-term functionality of his works will require that his original video content be periodically migrated to different media and that the playback devices (or at least their innards) be replaced by others with a different look and feel; preserving the original material appearance indefinitely is simply impossible. May Paik's statements about replaceability be generalized to some or all material elements that are not subject to obsolescence and loss of function, but can nonetheless suffer other forms of deterioration and damage? A line of thought that adheres to traditional conservation practice and privileges preservation of the appearance and original material of the work would suggest that such generalization is not permissible. But a line of thought that privileges Paik's innovative spirit and willingness to understand his works as inevitably evolving with new technological developments, and that values the idea of applying a common approach to replaceability of all elements of the work, points in the opposite direction.

Paik's works also illustrate the limitations of relying solely on the artist's own statements. Hölling notes that Paik's initial instructions for displaying his works were often verbal, and he would routinely make changes from one display to the next. While some of his works entered collections accompanied by explicit instructions, she notes, the question arises: "How did instructions for Paik's works come into being? Ambiguity surrounds this question. Paik was known for his reluctance to create conventional scores or instructions" (2017, 32). Paik worked closely with assistants who traveled to realize his works, and his expression of minimal verbal instructions occurred in the context of his knowledge that these instructions would be interpreted and realized by close collaborators who had long histories of working with him, tacit awareness of his preferences, and deep knowledge of his aesthetic and artistic priorities. To regard Paik's minimal instructions as fully specifying the work, without acknowledging the importance of these other factors in fleshing out the rules constituting the work, would yield a conception of the work that is too thin to ensure displays that are expressive of Paik's artistic values and aims, and arguably too thin to meaningfully guide the practical decisions installers must make in constructing displays.

Hölling notes that ultimately, conservators are responsible for formalizing instructions that will allow the institution to conserve and display the work.

Collaborators' and assistants' firsthand experience, tacit knowledge, and memory provide the basis for, and shape the initial recording of, instructions, whereas the conservator's reformulation of those instructions is necessarily secondhand. The reformulated instructions are drawn from the archive, which contains all known information about the artworks, and they re-enter and enrich that archive to shape subsequent materializations of the work.   (2017, 32–3)

The archive, as Hölling's discussion indicates, gives us materials to work with in making decisions about these matters, but it may not settle them in a particular direction. The archive often includes fragments whose relation to each other and to the work is not self-evident. As we see with Paik, the artist's statements about other works in his oeuvre, and the facts about how his other works have been displayed, are part of the archive for any given work; they supply context about how we should understand the overall artistic project in which the work participates.

To identify rules that will effectively generate displays of the work that respect the artist's artistic aims and priorities, we must engage in a deeply and essentially interpretative and value-laden process that involves identifying some items in the archive as more significant and authoritative than others; rejecting some items as irrelevant, obsolete, or erroneous; deciding how to handle changes over time in the artist's own views about the work; ascertaining which elements of background context and tacit knowledge may have been assumed by the artist in making particular statements; and, ultimately, actively constructing rules that manifest a set of values that we have identified as essential to the work.

As Hölling notes, this is a reflexive process: the rules as they are understood at a given time guide conservation efforts and the creation of displays, and as conservation processes and displays are realized and documented, new items enter the archive. These items both reflect new interpretation of the archive's prior contents and influence future interpretative efforts.[7]

Artwork Identity and Genealogy

"The archive," Hölling notes, "participates in creating the identity, and maintaining the continuity, of works of art" (2017, 9). But the archive, as we have seen, is not fixed. Moreover, given the complexity of the archive, the role of tacit elements and memory, and the need to engage in a value-laden interpretative process, there may not be a unique ideal reconstruction of the rules constituting the work at any given moment: two different conservators reviewing the archive might reasonably reconstruct the rules in different ways, yielding different decisions about some matters of conservation and display.[8] Moreover, on a given construction of the

---

[7] See Stecker 2003, chapter 7, for a related argument about the iterative nature of interpretation in law and the resulting evolution of laws over time.

[8] See Stigter 2011 for a compelling case study related to Joseph Kosuth's 1965 work *Glass (one and three)*.

rules for a work subject to variable display, many different displays are permissible. Whichever actual display happens to be chosen will generate new documentation for the archive; and this in turn may influence future interpretative efforts.

Reasonable individual judgments and contingent historical processes, then, influence how the rules are constructed at a given time, what new information enters the archive as a result, and how the archive will subsequently be reinterpreted. The result is that the artwork itself has no fixed state: its identity can be pinned down in more than one way at a given time, and it is susceptible to evolution along more than one trajectory.

The continuity of the work over time, then, is not grounded in the unchanging structure of either the rules themselves or the archive. Instead, the conception of identity over time relevant to the work is genealogical (van de Vall et al. 2011). The set of rules constituting the work, and thus the work itself, is not frozen in time at or around the initial moment of creation; instead, the work persists over time insofar as the archive and the rules derived from it exhibit appropriate historical continuity with the structure generated through the artist's initial act of creation.

Something similar is true of the physical objects associated with artworks. Paintings exhibit a great deal of change over time, including change due to material instability and environmental conditions and change due to intentional conservation treatment. Whether a work of painting persists through such change—whether the painted surface before us today can still be appropriately described as the artist's work—depends on the type and extent of change the object has undergone as well as the historical processes through which the change occurred.[9]

The current state of the object alone, then, may be insufficient to determine whether the artwork has persisted. If the current state has been produced over several centuries of gradual conservation efforts in line with the conservation norms in place at the historical moments of intervention, we might identify the object as exhibiting sufficient continuity to ensure the persistence of the work. But a sudden, radical intervention that imposed similar changes on the object all at once might reasonably prompt our judgment that the work has not survived.

The story is similar for works that persist through oral traditions and other forms of person-to-person transmission. Gradual historical changes in these works are compatible with their persistence as living cultural expressions. However, if all the changes accrued over several centuries were instead imposed on the work at once, the sudden and dramatic discontinuity in the work's structure would lead us to deny that the new structure embodies the same work. At the same time, not all acceptable change must be gradual: if someone digs back into the archive and offers a well-warranted reconstruction of the rules based on

---

[9] See Haslanger 2003 for a survey of philosophical accounts of object persistence through change, and Scholl 2007 for a survey of both philosophical and psychological treatments.

the artist's communications and related materials, rapid evolution of the work along a quite different trajectory might be appropriate.

A work constituted by rules, then, may persist by way of an evolving, not stable, structure. The structure's evolution is compatible with the work's persistence as long as there are no disqualifying irregularities such as reconstruction of the rules in ways that ignore a central aspect of the artist's explicit instructions. If the work evolved along a trajectory in which the artist's instruction was consistently neglected and eventually lost, the work would be damaged and perhaps destroyed, just as loss of a major physical component of a sculptural work would constitute damage and perhaps destruction.

The fact that the process of reconstructing the rules is interpretative, then, doesn't mean that anything goes: there can be clear errors, such as failure to respect statements the artist consistently made, failure to consider the artist's decisions about comparable issues in relation to other works, or neglect of well-established tacit knowledge that provides further context for those instructions. (We'll see relevant examples in Chapter 9.) Because erroneous reconstruction of the rules often leaves both the archive and the material elements of the work intact, it is possible to recover from such situations: a careful analysis can retrieve the information that has been neglected and incorporate it into a new reconstruction of the work. For this reason, reconstruction of rules in a way that does not adequately respect the artist's original creative act typically will be a situation of damage to the work but not destruction. As may be evident, there is no sharp boundary between "damaged" and "undamaged" states of the work. People will disagree about which forms of change respect the artist's original creative act and exhibit the right sorts of historical continuity with earlier reconstructions of the work.

Even where a reconstruction of the rules is (from the perspective of a careful interpretive analysis of the archive) manifestly incorrect, as long as this reconstruction of the rules is guiding display and conservation of the work, these rules *are* currently constitutive of the work, just as a damaged canvas might be currently constitutive of a work of painting. A work may exist, at a given moment, in a state of compromised authenticity; and when this is the case, the work's displays may be misleading with regard to the artist's creative act and artistic project.

The situation is rather like that of a musical work: a performance might be inauthentic either because it violates the score, or because the score itself has been compromised and does not connect in the right way to the artist's creative act in making the work. However, the situation is more complicated in the case of contemporary art, because there is no set structure or notation to capture the work's "score"—the artist's instructions may pertain to many matters of display, conservation, or participation, and they may leave parameters rather open with latitude for the judgment of others, or be quite specific and fine-grained.

Thus, it can be the case both that the work *is* currently in a particular state, which involves being constituted by a set of rules that have been reconstructed based on the archive, and that the state is not ideal, because the reconstruction was flawed in some way. Sometimes this situation is discovered through careful study of the archive, and the rules are then reconstructed in a way that more closely accords with the artist's creative act, just as a flawed conservation treatment might sometimes be discovered and reversed. And sometimes the work may simply continue to evolve with an element baked in that is not ideal.

The specific issue of information loss is worth highlighting here. In part because the rules constituting an artwork can be highly idiosyncratic, tacit knowledge and memory are likely to play a prominent role in interpreting the information in the archive. Where a statement by the artist is included, there may be tacit knowledge in grasping what the artist meant by that statement or how broadly it is meant to apply. Where notes by someone in the institution are included, the notes may be synoptic of a fuller understanding that is not expressly stated. For this reason, as Jill Sterrett notes, regular engagement with the archive and display of the work is itself a form of conservation, making it more likely that information will remain active, will be transmitted from person to person, and will be explicitly recorded rather than gradually forgotten (Gale, Lake, and Sterrett 2009). For a work partly constituted of custom rules that must be reconstructed based on the archive, dormancy is the enemy of the work's persistence in an authentic state.

Who Really Makes the Work?

As we have seen, artworks constituted by rules evolve over time through processes to which many people other than the artist contribute. Even the artist's direct utterances reflect others' influence: Sanneke Stigter describes "the co-constructed nature of the artist interview as a negotiated text" (2016a, 227). Moreover, the archive may contain contributions made independently of the artist and even long after the artist's death; and reconstruction of the rules based on the archive is an interpretative process conducted, for works in collections, by representatives of the institution. Vivian van Saaze argues, for related reasons, that the artist's intention, which is often understood in conservation circles as central to the identity and authenticity of the work, is a product of a constructive and interpretive process:

> '[A]rtist intention' is not simply derived from the artist or the artwork, a view still commonly held in conservation practice, but is *produced* instead. Artist's intent, in other words, is the result of what is *done* in knowledge and documentation practices. This implies that rather than being a facilitator or 'passive custodian',

the curator or conservator of contemporary art can be considered an interpreter, mediator or even a co-producer of what is designated as 'the artist's intention.'

(van Saaze 2013, 115)

If the work depends so heavily on interpretation and other contributions by others, to what extent is it really the artist's work?

The answer is multifaceted. The artist's original creative activity is the touch-stone for decisions about which items to incorporate in the archive and how to reconstruct rules based on the archive's contents. The artist's explicit statements, particularly those made around the time of initial creation, are clearly authorita-tive relative to other items in the archive, and the interpretative effort is norma-tively guided by a conception of the artist's values and a sense of the artistic project that was undertaken in the creation of the work.

But not all of the artist's statements have the same import, and in some circumstances an explicit statement by the artist may be overruled. First, an artist will sometimes make a statement that expresses a preference but not an actual rule. In a fax exchange with curator Germaine Koh of the National Gallery of Canada, Liz Magor said of her work *Production*, "I like it best when the bricks are trying to act architecturally—they're trying to make a wall or a column or something. The ultimate would be that they totally cover a wall, with no space at the top, bottom or sides..."[10] Magor is not stating that this form of display is required, and the bricks have been displayed, with her approval, in a variety of different configurations. Her statement is indicative of her artistic priorities and is thus relevant to decisions about display, but it does not have the force of a rule constraining future displays.

Second, sometimes the artist expresses a rule, but the expression is weakened through subsequent negotiation with the institution. When the Dallas Museum of Art acquired his installation work *Drum Solos*, which consists of custom-designed sound equipment accompanied by two records recorded by the artist, Brad Tucker initially indicated that audience members should be permitted to play the records on the included turntable (see Chapter 9, Figure 9.1). However, he later revised this to allow that perhaps only museum staff should play the records once per day in order to conserve them; and he ultimately permitted the Dallas Museum of Art to display the work without any use of the sound component at all. Tucker's instructions for the piece, found in the DMA object file for the work, specify,

It is my intent that the piece allows interaction with the viewing audience. While no advertisement or wall text inviting the viewer to play the records should be

---

[10] Fax from Liz Magor to Germaine Koh, National Gallery of Canada, November 25, 1998. For further discussion, see Chapter 2.

presented, viewers who present the desire to play the records should not be discouraged. For obvious reasons, I do intend for public intervention with the artwork to be supervised.

Tucker goes on to say that pursuant to a discussion with a DMA staff member in relation to the Come Forward exhibition in which the work was shown prior to acquisition, he "will allow a mediated participation with the records. Museum staff play the records at appropriately scheduled intervals of time throughout the duration of an exhibit" (Brad Tucker, email to Elayne Rush, March 13, 2003).

An undated memo of installation instructions in the DMA's object file for the work acknowledges the rule that viewers should be permitted to play the records: "Artist intent: No wall text or advertisement should invite the viewer to play the records, but they are allowed to do so under supervision of a gallery attendant." However, this text is crossed out by hand, and "Incomplete" is written in the upper right-hand corner of the document. An internal email message (Elayne Rush, message to Suzanne Weaver, March 10, 2003) indicates that the records were not played at all during the Come Forward exhibition, and an unsigned handwritten note (dated March 3, 2003) in the file indicates that "artist makes suggestion to have viewers play but at our discretion—we have to go by our policies." The fact that Tucker initially conceived the work as having a robust participatory element is relevant to our understanding of his artistic project, but given his subsequent acceptance of marked limits on audience participation, we must now understand this as a permitted but not required element of the work, contrary to his initial statement.

Another example of change in rules over time due to institutional consider-ations is Marina Abramović and Ulay's *Imponderabilia*, initially conceived in 1977 as a non-repeatable work but then reperformed in Abramović's 2010 retrospective at the Museum of Modern Art in New York. In the 1977 performance, the artists stood naked and facing each other in the narrow entrance to the Galleria Communale d'Arte Moderna in Bologna, Italy (Figure 8.2). To enter the gallery, audience members had to squeeze between them, which inevitably involved contact with the bodies of the artists due to the small space.[11]

In the 2010 MoMA reperformance, involving professional performers rather than the artists themselves, the space between the performers was wider, such that it was possible for many audience members to avoid physical contact. And as Thurman 2010 (n.p.) describes,

MoMA will provide an alternative access to the space, an accommodation that Abramović thinks is a pity. Her role as an artist, she believes, with a hubris that

[11] This is evident in video documentation of the performance: http://www.li-ma.nl/lima/catalogue/art/abramovic-ulay/imponderabilia-1977/7094.

Figure 8.2 Ulay/Marina Abramović, *Imponderabilia*, 1977. Performance, 90 minutes.
Galleria Communale d'Arte Moderna, Bologna
© 2022 Ulay/Marina Abramović
Courtesy of the Marina Abramović Archives/(ARS), New York

can sound naïve and a humility that disarms any impulse to resent it, is to lead her spectators through an anxious passage to a place of release from whatever has confined them.

It is not difficult to see why MoMA insisted on this adjustment. Attitudes about sexual harassment evolved significantly between 1977 and 2010, and the risks of forcing audience members into unwanted contact with nude bodies as a condition of full access, as well as the risks to the performers of experiencing assault, are highly salient in the current context. In addition, the narrow passageway between the performers' bodies, even in the wider 2010 version, raises serious accessibility concerns, at best creating an awkward situation for fat audience members and those using some kinds of mobility aids and at worst excluding them from the exhibition space.

Abramović did not veto the alternate access to the exhibition space, so apparently this form of display is not precluded by the rules constituting the work as she presently conceives them. But it is relevant to note both that her acceptance is reluctant—she sees such a display as non-ideal, not fully realizing her artistic aims—and to note that this represents a marked evolution in the work. Indeed, as a non-repeatable work, *Imponderabilia* as conceived in 1977 was not constituted by rules at all: it was simply an event. A reconstrual of the work as repeatable involves a change in the work's ontological status, such that it is now constituted by rules for display. Moreover, the rules as formalized allow for displays that diverge significantly from what Abramović and Ulay initially conceived. *Imponderabilia* as conceived in 2010 departs from the original to such an extent that it might be best identified as a distinct version of the work.

This raises an important issue: when an artist offers input about a work created decades earlier, this input may be guided less by the original creative act and more by current artistic projects and priorities. Given her artistic priorities at that time, Abramović in 1977 might well have rejected the suggestion that *Imponderabilia* could be repeated at all, much less by different performers, with a wider aperture, and in an exhibition space also affording an alternate entry. Conservator Christian Scheidemann (2010) suggests both that "the artist is always right," in the sense that the intuitive, subjective creative process is not subject to rational criticism, and that after the work is complete, the artist transitions from creator to consultant, one whose input is valued but not always definitive. Abramović, as an artist who is still actively creating, has the right to generate a new version of an earlier work (assuming that her collaborator is in agreement), but when her much later statements diverge significantly from the initial conception of the work, there may be reason to deny that the reconceived work is continuous with the original. With respect to a work created in 1977, Abramović is now a consultant, not in the same position of authority as during the period of initial creation.

Is the artist, then, an authority on all matters when the work is initially created? Whereas Scheidemann says, "The artist is always right, even if [they are] technically wrong," Jill Sterrett suggests, in relation to decisions about conservation, that

> [a] work made yesterday that enters into a museum or gallery today is, for all intents and purposes, in its infancy. To capture the artist's thoughts at that moment in the work's life is important to do. That said, it's not the only opinion we are after. There are curators, scholars—and the public. All of these opinions come together with that of the artist to tell a story. (Gale, Lake, and Sterrett 2009)

While artists sometimes articulate rules for conservation informed by a highly accurate understanding of how the objects they have presented will evolve over time, at other times the objects evolve in ways the artist did not anticipate. In such cases the artist's initial statements, even when they express clear rules for conservation, may not offer sufficient guidance about how the objects should be treated. Liz Magor initially rejected aggressive conservation measures for her 1976 work *Time and Mrs. Tiber*, involving found jars of preserves supplemented by jars of preserves created by the artist (Figure 8.3). She changed her mind when it turned out that the objects were evolving far more rapidly than she had anticipated and, in some cases, developing deadly botulinum toxin that could endanger museum staff members and audiences. She agreed to remake some elements of the work

Figure 8.3 Liz Magor, *Time and Mrs. Tiber*, 1976. Wooden shelf with jars of preserves, recipe box, forks, glass tops, rubber sealers, metal lids, cardboard boxes, enamel cup, tin can, 85 × 36 × 13 in. (215 × 91 × 32 cm).
Collection of the National Gallery of Canada
Courtesy of the artist and Catriona Jeffries, Vancouver

and to permit intensive conservation treatments for others. (See Irvin 2005b for details.)

Magor's initial conception of *Time and Mrs. Tiber* contained an internal tension that became apparent over time: she both wished to allow the objects to evolve naturally and expected that the objects would have at least a life span on the order of her own, more like fifty years than five. As it turns out, she was available for consultation about how to address this tension and agreed to change the conservation protocol. Even if she had not been available or agreed, however, it would not have been unreasonable for conservators, reviewing the archive as a whole, to conclude that the best way to realize Magor's artistic aims—including the aim, which is typically prominent when a work enters a museum collection, of having the work continue to be accessible to audiences for some time—would be to conserve the objects to slow the deterioration and remove the dangerous elements to facilitate ongoing display.

The archive, in this case or others, may in fact support divergent interpretations: both an interpretation supporting conservation measures that the artist expressly rejected and an interpretation opposing them might reasonably emerge from careful readings of the same archive. The trajectory of the work's evolution, then, may depend on who is doing the reconstruction and which interpretation corresponds to their own weighting of various interests and priorities that cannot all be jointly satisfied.

If this situation seems to compromise the artist's authorship of the work, it is important to note that while artists do not control the surrounding artistic context in which conventions have weakened and the sanctioning of custom rules has become more common, they do control how they engage with this context. It is possible for an artist to express a rule in a way that makes it clear that it cannot be rethought in light of competing considerations: for instance, in relation to her 1999 work *Soliloquy* in the collection of the Dallas Museum of Art, Shirin Neshat specifies, of some of her rules for display and conservation, that if the purchaser fails to comply, "the work shall no longer be a work by Shirin Neshat and Shirin Neshat's name may not be used in connection therewith."[12]

As we saw in Chapter 2, artists can choose to be extremely specific and detailed in their specification of rules for displaying and conserving their works, or can choose to take a more schematic approach that leaves latitude for others' judgment. As we have seen in relation to the works of El Anatsui and others, the latter choice can be centrally integrated into the artist's project and have expressive import.

The choice to offer an extremely detailed package of instructions for their works or to express a relatively loose score that is quite open to interpretation is, like the choice of whether and how to fabricate an enduring physical object, a creative choice through which the artist constitutes the work. These choices occur in a historical context in which they are read as expressive in relation to past artistic

---

[12] Certificate for *Soliloquy*, signed by Shirin Neshat on September 29, 2000, found in the object file for the work at the Dallas Museum of Art.

projects undertaken by the same artist and others. An artist who wishes to control the evolution of the work in great detail can take measures to do so; an artist who chooses not to is exercising a different sort of creative authorship through that choice. If artworks created through choices of the latter sort are more subject to evolution along a variety of trajectories, this is characteristic of the artist's project, not in opposition to it.

Ambiguity, Indeterminacy, and Evolution as Expressive

Artists sometimes play both with deep ambiguities in their works' nature and with the trajectories of evolution that are inevitable as information is recorded and re-recorded over time. Yoko Ono's 1961 *Smoke Painting* is, on one level, a text:

> Light canvas or any finished painting with a cigarette at any time for any length of time. See the smoke movement. The painting ends when the whole canvas is gone.   (Ono 2000, n.p.)

The text was published in her book *Grapefruit*, initially in 1964. However, the text was first displayed in 1961 alongside an actual canvas, in a display that a reviewer described as follows:

> Yoko Ono...has made a "smoke" painting. It consists of a grimy unstrung canvas with a hole in it. Into the hole she stuck a burning candle, withdrawing it when the canvas began to smolder and smoke on its own. The painting's limited life was shortened by half a minute for this report, its living presence snuffed out by a damp cloth as soon as the idea became clear.   (Swenson 1961)

Arthur Danto says of Ono's text, "Now these are instructions for the execution of a work, not the work itself. They exist for the purpose of being followed, like orders" (Danto 2000). But this oversimplifies the situation. Ono was a participant in the Fluxus movement, which was known for conceptual and "intermedia" works that challenged conventional boundaries (Higgins 2002). While performativity was central to many Fluxus works, some textually specified Fluxus works were manifestly unperformable, either entirely or in some of their particulars. La Monte Young's 1960 *Piano Piece for David Tudor #1* specifies,

> Bring a bale of hay and a bucket of water onto the stage for the piano to eat and drink. The performer may then feed the piano or leave it to eat by itself. If the former, the piece is over after the piano has been fed. If the latter, it is over after the piano eats or decides not to.   (Nyman 1999, 84)

Nam June Paik's *Danger Music No. 5* famously instructs the performer to enter the vagina of a living whale (Nyman 1999, 86). Or consider Ono's own 1962 *Painting for the Skies*, which opens,

> Drill a hole in the sky.
> Cut out a paper the same size as the hole.   (Ono 2000, n.p.)

Many of the other texts published in *Grapefruit* contain instructions for impossible performances or actions—such as *Tape Piece I* (1963), which specifies, "Take the sound of the stone aging"—or for careful perception or contemplation:

> Collect sounds in your mind that
> you have overheard through the week.
> Repeat them in your mind in different
> orders one afternoon.   (*Collecting Piece* (1963) in Ono 2000, n.p.)

As Ono said to curator Hans Ulrich Obrist in 2001, "I discovered that by instructionalizing art you did not have to stick to the two-dimensional or three-dimensional world. In your mind, you can be in touch with a six-dimensional world, if you wished. You can also mix an apple and a desk" (Ono and Obrist 2009, 17).

I suggest that with *Smoke Painting*, Ono is playing with ambiguity over whether and to what extent her text should be seen as a freestanding work constituted by a text or as the specification of rules for constituting a display. When Ono showed a material display of the work, she did not follow her own instructions: she lit the canvas with a candle, not a cigarette, perhaps signaling that the instructions are not to be taken too literally. Ono's *Smoke Painting* thus has a dual life as an instruction for constituting a display and as a text-based work in its own right, and this very ambiguity is central to the artistic project of the work. Whereas Felix Gonzalez-Torres's instructions to create piles of candy that audience members can consume are clearly rules for constituting a display and not a text to be displayed or contemplated in its own right, Ono's instructions can legitimately be treated either as the primary object of appreciation or as rules for constituting a display; and when they serve the latter function, they do not simply recede into the background, allowing the material painting to be the sole object of attention. The text remains present as an entity for direct encounter. The dual role of the text is an artistically distinctive element of Ono's project.

Just as an artist may play with ambiguities in the very ontological nature of the work, an artist may play with the variable trajectories along which a work may evolve. Tino Sehgal's artistic practice virtually guarantees that the initial instructions for displaying his works will morph and erode over time. Sehgal's "constructed situations," several of which have now entered museum collections, are works for which the institution must hire and train performers to carry out Sehgal's instructions. As described in Chapter 7, the rub is that when the institution acquires the work, Sehgal provides instructions only in the form of person-to-person verbal transmission and demonstration. No written documents or recordings are provided, and no such documents may be created for the institution's official archive. While museum staff members may jot down notes for their own use, these may not be filed or shared; when they wish to transfer information to other staff members or to performers, they must use the same person-to-person transmission method that Sehgal himself used. Some of the works involve singing, and the lyrics and melody must be maintained primarily in memory (Laurenson and van Saaze 2014; van Saaze 2015).

Through the meta-rules he has sanctioned for institutional engagement with his work, Sehgal has interfered with the typical process of constituting the archive, ensuring that microarchives will never be integrated into the official archive and that memory and tacit knowledge will indefinitely play a central role in grounding his works. This highlights Sterrett's point that regular display of the work and engagement with the archive promotes the survival of works constituted of rules: if Sehgal's work spends long periods in "dark storage" without institutional engagement, many details are likely to be lost (Gale, Lake, and Sterrett 2009, n.p.).

I participated in a workshop with Seghal at Tate Modern in 2012, and the process of loss was actively apparent. One of the workshop activities was to learn to perform Sehgal's 2012 work *These Associations*, which involves singing or chanting a passage derived from Hannah Arendt's *The Human Condition*. (See Paramana 2014 for a first-person description of the work by someone who has participated in performing it.) Some of the other participants in the workshop had previously performed *These Associations*, and disagreements between Sehgal and the performers emerged about how many times some elements of the text should be repeated, with a consensus among the performers that differed from the instruction that Sehgal was giving to the workshop participants. Although Sehgal seemed to accept that the workshop members' memories were accurate, he continued, seemingly by accident, to instruct us to diverge from the instructions that he had previously articulated for the work.

If disputes arise among those who have engaged deeply with the work and even the artist cannot keep track of the performance protocol, it is predictable that the work will evolve rapidly: person-to-person transmission of the work, especially with temporal gaps during which instructions are preserved in memory, is bound to produce loss of information.

This leaves us with a dilemma. Should we see the work as grounded in the rules as initially sanctioned, such that shifts over time produced through miscommunication and forgetting constitute damage and inauthenticity? Or should we, instead, see the work as a structure that is intentionally designed by the artist to evolve? If we adopt the latter approach, the states of the work that reflect this evolution are seen not as compromised, inauthentic, or damaged, but simply as authentic states of the work as it exists at a given moment in its lifespan.

Sehgal's practice seems designed both to shed light on the bureaucratization of art—the endless reams of acquisition and loan contracts, printed out emails, and meticulously annotated conservation reports that fill file folders in most museums—and to de-bureaucratize his own works, reconnecting them to the kinds of oral traditions through which non-material artworks were transmitted over most of human history. Given that Sehgal made this choice quite consciously, in a way that contravenes practices of acquisition, documentation, and conservation that are deeply embedded in museums, we should see him as having created a structure that is designed to evolve. Though for some works, evolution along a trajectory that diverges too much from the artist's initial communications involves inauthenticity or damage, Sehgal's work embraces evolution so as to render many forms of change consistent with full authenticity. This doesn't mean the work couldn't suffer damage such as an intentional violation or dramatic discontinuity; but it does mean that gradual, extensive change that might compromise another work leaves this one intact. Ironically—or not, if we see the evolution of the work as analogous to natural evolution—Sehgal enhances the survival prospects of his work through the same mechanism that increases the likelihood of change over time.

Conclusion

Artworks are subject to various forms of evolution to which many individuals contribute. Artworks with essential material components evolve as conservators make choices about restoration. But because the evolution of works constituted by rules is not concretized in the state of a specific material object, there is more latitude for evolution to follow a variety of trajectories and, in some instances, to backtrack and proceed in a different direction. Nonetheless, the artist's initial creative activity is the touchstone guiding evolution of the work, and the artist also has a significant degree of control over the extent to which such evolution occurs: artists who choose to specify their works in greater detail can secure those works against more radical forms of evolution—or, as in the case of Sehgal, an artist can secure their works against damage precisely by embracing evolution as a process internal to the work. These choices are, in themselves, an aspect of the artist's expressive activity in creating the work.

The upshot is that there is no simple answer to the question of which rules constitute the work. When the work is not yet in a collection, it may be constituted by the rules the artist has in mind, even if these are never perfectly captured in the artist's outward communications: for the rules can depend ontologically on the artist's relevant mental states. During this period, the artist is the authoritative interpreter who gets to specify the content of the rules. But once the work has entered the institution, it depends ontologically on an archive that consists both of concretely expressed communications by the artist and other parties and of tacit knowledge and memory; and reconstructing the rules based on the archive is an interpretive project. There may be mistakes and false starts in interpretation of the archive, with the result that the work sometimes exists in a state that is less than fully authentic. But something similar may happen with a work of painting or sculpture: if the object has been damaged or poorly conserved, there will be moments where the work persists, but the authentic state is to some extent compromised. If the change that has led to the inauthentic state is reversible, it may be possible to get things back on track; if not, the work may persist in a partially authentic state or may eventually, through further compromising and irreversible change, be destroyed. The greatest difference between rules and physical states may be that inauthentic constructions of the rules—that is, constructions that do not appropriately embody the artist's statements, values, and artistic project as reflected in the archive—are more likely to be reversible, as long as no critical information has been lost; whereas when objects have been conserved in ways that compromise their material authenticity, the reversibility of these changes is contingent on matters of chemistry, not rectifiable through reinterpretation.

To say that contemporary artworks are constituted partly of rules is not, then, to say that the structure and content of these rules is fixed for all time: just as a game can evolve as changes are made to its rules, an artwork can evolve as rules are reconstructed through interpretation of the archive. There are better and worse ways of undertaking this project, and so a work may sometimes persist in a damaged or compromised state. And the trajectory of evolution is affected by contingent matters not under the artist's control. But ultimately, as long as the work has the right sort of genealogical connection to the artist's original creative act, it remains the artist's work.

9

Rule Violations and Authenticity

I've argued that most contemporary artworks are material-rule hybrids, and that rules serve as part of the medium of contemporary art: they are central expressive resources for many works, and they affect both audience experience and the work's meanings.

But it is a familiar fact for anyone who has worked in a museum exhibiting such works that many displays don't perfectly follow the rules sanctioned by the artist. This can happen for a wide variety of reasons, including theft of components, vandalism, accidental damage, mistakes in installation, changes in gallery space, and safety considerations. Can a display that fails to comply fully with the rules actually be a display of the work? Can there ever be good reasons to mount an intentionally non-compliant display? This chapter will address these questions, answering "yes" to both. We'll consider examples both of mistakes and of intentional rule violations. We'll also examine the effects on the work's authenticity when an institution codifies a set of rules that conflicts with those sanctioned by the artist.

Mistakes

When the rules sanctioned by the artist are complex and have been expressed at various moments over an extended period, it is not surprising that institutions sometimes make mistakes.

Brad Tucker, *Drum Solos*

The first example involves a minor mistake. Brad Tucker's (2001) *Drum Solos*, briefly discussed in Chapter 8, is an installation artwork consisting of custom-made records along with a turntable connected to three speakers (Figure 9.1). The work is visually interesting, but sound is also a fundamental component: the artist custom cast two records for this work, which can be played on the turntable. In a series of communications with the museum, Tucker offered extensive instructions for constructing the display. According to the installation instructions that are in the object file for the work, "The record cover of the currently used record should be placed on the floor, leaning up against the wall. The record cover of the unused

Figure 9.1 Brad Tucker, *Drum Solos*, 2001. Polyester, denim, Lycra, Spandex, painted wood, plastic, turntable, speakers, electrical components, guitar cables, and drum leg. Dimensions vary.

Dallas Museum of Art, Texas Artists Fund 2003.17.A
© Brad Tucker
Courtesy of the artist and the Dallas Museum of Art

record should be place[d] on the floor in front of the other cover, top edge flush against the leaning record cover. The unused record should be taken out to lie on its cover."[1] These instructions are important: as Tucker says, the visual elements of the work "act like paintings by butting against a wall or flattening themselves out on the floor."[2]

Because the records are brightly colored—one pink, one yellow—having them visible outside of their jackets is visually striking. Leaning the jacket of the record that is currently on the turntable up against the wall provides information about that record. Also, Tucker sanctioned a rule for participation: namely, that viewers should be permitted to play the records, though no signage should indicate this. Having both records out of their jackets and available may contribute to the sense that playing the records is invited.

The file photo of the installation, however, shows an incorrect display, as an assistant registrar at the DMA noticed in 2004. In the photo, both record jackets are leaning against the wall, and the yellow record, which is not currently on the turntable, has not been removed from its jacket for display. As the registrar notes, "Maybe, though (since there seems to have been a lot of correspondence with Brad

---

[1] Installation instructions, T42956, Brad Tucker, *Drum Solos*, 2001, undated.
[2] Dallas Museum of Art website, https://collections.dma.org/artwork/5325565.

Tucker), there are subsequent instructions."[3] Although another assistant registrar checked the instructions, confirmed that the display was incorrect, and added Polaroid images of a correct installation to the file,[4] the incorrect photograph continues, as of this writing, to represent the work on the Dallas Museum of Art's website.[5] The reasons for this are likely practical: photographing this relatively large installation artwork anew would involve removing it from storage, installing it, and scheduling a photo shoot, a significant investment of time and energy, given competing demands and priorities, to correct a relatively minor error.

Tucker's work illustrates the risks that arise when the rules for display must be reconstructed from a complex archive: there are risks that details will be missed, that confusion will arise from communication happening at different moments, and that material added to the archive based on a mistaken display may contribute to future incorrect displays. I have suggested that artworks like Tucker's consist of a combination of physical stuff and rules about what we should do with that stuff. If that's true, then what should we say when a display of the work violates the rules? Does this mean that, in fact, the work wasn't on display at all? Before answering this question, let's look at another, more serious case of mistaken display.

Glenn Ligon, *Notes on the Margin of the Black Book*

Robert Mapplethorpe was a well-known American artist working in black and white photography.[6] A significant part of his body of work consisted of homoerotic photographs of men, sometimes involved in BDSM practices. In 1986, Mapplethorpe, who was white and gay, made *The Black Book*, a book of photos of Black men, many of which are sexualized or homoerotic. American artist Glenn Ligon, who is Black and gay, had a complex reaction on seeing Mapplethorpe's work:

> I asked myself if those photographs were racist. I realized then that the question was too limiting, that it was more complicated. Can we say that Mapplethorpe's work is documentary or fetishistic? Maybe, but at the same time he put black men into a tradition of portraiture to which they've never had access before.
>
> (Ligon 2011)

Ligon ultimately responded with a work of his own, *Notes on the Margin of the Black Book* (1991–3). *Notes on the Margin*, in the collection of the Solomon

---

[3] Email from Sarah Evans to Elayne Rush, January 12, 2004.
[4] Email from Elayne Rush to Sarah Evans, August 2, 2004.
[5] https://collections.dma.org/artwork/5325565.
[6] This section is an expanded version of a discussion found in Irvin 2019.

R. Guggenheim Museum, involves ninety-one image panels appropriated by disassembling copies of Mapplethorpe's *Black Book* and seventy-eight unique text panels of quotations from various sources.[7] As Ligon says, his aim was to

> [p]ut the work in the context of all these debates around black male representation, gay sexuality, censorship, AIDS, personal desire. Put all of that next to the work and let the viewers sort it out. And they can choose. They can not read the text and look at the photos or read the text and sort through those issues in the same kind of process that I went through when thinking about that work. It's just a way to open up that work to a sort of larger context.   (N. Gale 2013)

He thus included quotations from well-known authors, cultural theorists, art historians, and artists—including, notably, Mapplethorpe himself. Some remark directly on Mapplethorpe's work, while others comment more generally on matters of race and representation. A few of the quotes are drawn from conversations Ligon had with friends and acquaintances.

The work is installed in four long horizontal rows. The image panels, which are larger, are installed on the top and bottom rows, and the smaller text panels are installed in two rows in between them. There are more image panels than text panels, so the positioning of the text panels does not make them appear to be commentaries on particular images: they sit alongside the images but also have a clear degree of independence.

The text panels have a prescribed order, and the juxtapositions of text are often striking. Consider, for instance, these texts, which are to be arranged one above the other:[8]

> Mapplethorpe appropriates the conventions of porn's racialized codes of representation, and by abstracting its stereotypes into "art," he makes racism's phantasms of desire respectable. The use of glossy photographic textures and surfaces serves to highlight the visible difference of black skin: Coupled with the use of porn conventions in body posture, framing devices like cropping, and the fragmentation of bodies into details, his work reveals an underlying fetishism.
>
> —Isaac Julien and Kobena Mercer

It is not that Mapplethorpe is unaware of the political implications of a white man shooting physically magnificent black men, and such implicit tensions lend

---

[7] https://www.guggenheim.org/artwork/10382.

[8] All six of the quotations to follow were included as text panels in Ligon's *Notes on the Margin of the Black Book*. Some were taken from published sources; others were previously unpublished, sometimes drawn from Ligon's conversations about Mapplethorpe's work (Schjeldahl 2011). This information is confirmed in an undated wall label found in the Solomon R. Guggenheim Museum's object file for *Notes on the Margin of the Black Book* (2001.180). The Julien and Mercer quotes are from Julien and Mercer 1991; the Hollinghurst quote is from Hollinghurst 1983; the Mapplethorpe quote is from Kardon 1989.

a piquancy to these pictures. But the stereotypes are transcended by a potent mood of celebration and sex, in which the artist reacts towards his subject with as much feeling as the camera allows.   —Alan Hollinghurst

One of the functions of the panels is to create a dialogue among perspectives on the work that are in tension with each other: Hollinghurst acknowledges the formal and stereotypic features to which Julien and Mercer point, while suggesting that Mapplethorpe's images nonetheless have the ability to "transcend" the connections to porn and fetishization. Texts in the series offer various positions on this debate, while raising a wide variety of other issues as well.

The following two pairs of texts are installed right next to each other:

The whole notion that these men are in control of their representations is tired. We know what Mapplethorpe got out of it—the photographs. What did these men get?   —Lyle Ashton Harris

While we recognize the oppressive dimension of these images of black men as Other, we are also attracted: *We want to look but don't always find the images we want to see.*   —Isaac Julien and Kobena Mercer

They were taken because I hadn't seen pictures like that before. That's why one makes what one makes, because you want to see something you haven't seen before; it was a subject that nobody had used because it was loaded.
                                                                    —Robert Mapplethorpe

It didn't even occur to me that I might be attractive, or that I might be something that somebody would want to look at, or would want to photograph. And so when it happened, I thought, "Well, gee, isn't this a good way for me to at least get to see what I look like."   —Ken Moody

The series of texts gets at complex issues of exploitation and control over representation. It is inherent in the photographic project that the artist has control over how subjects are represented. Artists have occasionally pushed back against this by giving their subjects more control over the content or execution of the photograph—as, for instance, when Gillian Wearing did the project *Signs that say what you want them to say and not Signs that say what someone else wants you to say* (1992–3), in which she invited her subjects to write a message on a sign and then be photographed holding it. This sort of democratization, however, is anathema to Mapplethorpe's intensely formalist project, in which he exerts control over all visible aspects of the image.

The potential for exploitation in photography with human subjects has been much discussed (e.g., Sontag 1977). And, of course, the potential for exploitation is multiplied when a racial dynamic involving a white photographer shooting exclusively Black subjects is introduced. Yet, as Julien and Mercer (a Black male artist and a Black male art historian, respectively) acknowledge, they are attracted to these images even as the presentation of Black men as an exotic, sexualized Other troubles them. Mapplethorpe, while acknowledging that the subject matter is "loaded," says he is drawn to create the pictures in part because of historic underrepresentation: Black men have been depicted extensively—and in quite problematic ways—in porn, but formally sophisticated artistic celebrations of the Black male form have been rare in European and American art. This observation prepares us for the quote from Ken Moody, who featured in many of Mapplethorpe's photographs: "It didn't even occur to me that I might be attractive, or that I might be something that somebody would want to look at, or would want to photograph." The choice to make the photographs, then, served—among other things—as an affirmation that the Black male body is a subject worth representing. And this provides something of an answer, even if not a completely satisfying one, to the question posed by the Black artist Lyle Ashton Harris in the first quotation above: "What did these men get?"

Clearly, then, the order of the text panels is extremely important: it has been carefully designed to allow specific ideas to create context for each other, and to position speakers from different perspectives in dialogue. The fact that Moody's words offer something of a response to Harris's question, with intervening thoughts by Julien and Mercer and by Mapplethorpe to complicate the question in ways relevant to Moody's answer, is no accident.

Ligon is clear about the importance of the order of elements. "The Mapplethorpe pages," he says,

> have an order from the page numbers the photos appear on. The quotes have a more elusive narrative, but one that roughly follows the evolution of my thoughts about Mapplethorpe's work and a gradual acknowledgement [of] my own investments in and ambivalence about the critique of the photos. The quotes don't form captions to individual photographs, but run as a separate but related narrative to the narrative logic of [the] *Black Book*.[9]

The observation that the text panels make up a carefully constructed narrative prepares us to understand the significance of a mistaken display. When *Notes on the Margin of the Black Book* was lent by the Guggenheim to another institution, the text panels were not installed according to Ligon's most recent instructions for the work; Ligon found the order of text panels to be severely mistaken and noticed instances of duplication. This occurred despite the fact that the borrowing institution was very diligent about many details of the display, corresponding with

---

[9] E-mail from Glenn Ligon to Nancy Spector, May 7, 2002. Quoted with the permission of Ligon and Spector.

the Guggenheim and with Ligon about physical spacing of the image and text panels.[10]

Such an error can occur for a wide variety of reasons, and reflects the complexity and still-evolving nature of the acquisition and documentation process for contemporary artworks. Because the procedures are not standardized across institutions, processes that work well within one institution may fail when a work is loaned to another. In addition, Ligon's work was acquired as part of a gift of 275 works from the Bohen Foundation in 2001.[11] The gift included a number of large, intricate installation works, such as Nam June Paik's *TV Garden*, an extremely complicated work that has been the subject of a case study by the Variable Media Network (Hanhardt 2003). The Guggenheim was thus faced with the influx of many objects and documents at once, and the aggregation and standardization of this material into a set of workable exhibition and conservation instructions for each of the 275 works is a demanding task that, in the context of other projects, would take years to complete.

In addition, Ligon's *Notes on the Margin* has undergone change over time that may have contributed to the error. Correspondence in the object file for the work indicates that some of the text panels had numbering on the back that does not match the prescribed order. When Ligon first displayed the work at the 1993 Whitney Biennial, he prepared a larger number of text panels, but removed some of them in the course of the installation. Correspondence in 2002 indicates that the Guggenheim has ninety-six text panels; thus, perhaps some duplicates or panels that are no longer part of the display were transferred to the Guggenheim along with other elements of the work. The additional panels may have been crated and shipped to the borrowing institution along with the rest. Different parts of the instructions had been conveyed at different times and through different means, including fax and email. Somehow, the final list indicating the proper order of the text panels did not come to the attention of the other institution as the display was being prepared.

Following the mistaken display, a team at the Guggenheim met with Ligon to ensure that the rules he sanctioned for display were clearly recorded in the file for future use. The object file now contains a clear and detailed set of installation instructions in which information from a variety of sources, including an interview with the artist, is aggregated in one place.

The point of this discussion is not to place blame on any of the parties involved; incorrect artwork displays are quite common for a variety of reasons. But what should we say about the displays of Tucker's and Ligon's works? Are these, in fact, displays of the artists' works at all? If so, how can we reconcile the fact that the

---

[10] Evidence for these claims is found in the Solomon R. Guggenheim Museum's object file for *Notes on the Margin of the Black Book* (2001.180).

[11] https://www.guggenheim.org/artwork/special_collection/the-bohen-foundation-gift.

work consists partly of rules with the fact that a display of the work can violate those rules?

The mistaken display of Tucker's work contains some missing and incorrect information—the visual appearance should not include both album covers leaning against the wall, and the record that is not currently playing should be visible outside its jacket. But this situation is not so severe as to prevent the audience member from having a good sense of the work's central qualities: the overall visual effect of the round speakers and turntable juxtaposed with the square album covers still comes through, and the sonic element of the work remains available when the record is played. There is no information to suggest that, in asking that the unplayed album be displayed on the jacket flat on the floor, Tucker is introducing a key element that is essential to encountering and appreciating the work. Thus, although the appearance is misleading, it doesn't seem to be so serious as to undermine the display's ability to make the work experientially available to the audience.

In the case of Ligon's *Notes on the Margin*, the mistake bears much more strongly on the work's central point and purpose. *Notes on the Margin* functions by removing the images from the private interior space of Mapplethorpe's book, placing them on public display, and juxtaposing them with a series of text panels whose order weaves a critical narrative that reflects a process of thinking through the images' significance given ongoing racialized power dynamics and the history of fetishization and erasure of Black male bodies, as it occurs through the presence of some kinds of representations and the absence of others.

The fact that the images are displayed correctly, then, is far from sufficient for the display to get Ligon's point across; for his point is not to create a graphic effect. The images and their order are simply appropriated from Mapplethorpe's book. The narrative created by the text panels is essential, and given a dramatic misordering of the text panels, that narrative is absent. Ligon's work is not aleatory, any more than Mapplethorpe's is: both of them exert careful control over all elements of their work's design so as to make specific points and create specific effects.

An artist *could* have created a work with all the same elements as Ligon's, but in which the text panels are to be reshuffled each time the work is exhibited. Such a work would function quite differently from Ligon's: the texts would still provide context for the work, but there would be no specific narrative unfolding across a prescribed sequence. Each ordering of texts might be experienced by viewers as constructing some sort of narrative or dialogue, but the fact that the text order is determined by a rule for reshuffling rather than a rule for a specific sequence would reveal this narrative as merely contingent, always subject to being replaced by some other. The ordering of texts might also resist narrative, creating a more fragmentary effect.

When audience members encounter such a seriously mistaken display, then, they are deeply misled about the work's nature and central point. They lack access to a central element of the work Ligon sanctioned, an ordering of texts that makes available a specific narrative. I conclude that this mistake is so serious as to make it reasonable to conclude that the mistaken display was not, in fact, a display of Ligon's work at all, though it used elements that Ligon created and did so in a way that complied with some of the rules he sanctioned for *Notes on the Margin*.

There is no bright line separating displays that still count as displays of the underlying work, however flawed, and displays that are so badly distorted that they no longer count. Musical performances offer an instructive analogy here. We typically think that a performance with a few wrong notes still counts as a performance of the underlying musical composition. But it is possible to have a performance that diverges so much from the rules for performing that work—due either to the performer's incompetence or to nonstandard interpretative choices— that it no longer seems to be a performance of that work, even though it does bear a relation to it by using some of the work's resources. What we say in a particular case depends on how serious and central we understand the distortion to be, and different people may disagree on this matter. Nonetheless, at a certain level of non-compliance with the rules, what we have is no longer a display or perform- ance *of* the artist's work, but instead some other kind of thing that uses some of the work's material as a resource.

Intentional Rule Violations

The examples above involve mistakes, but institutions sometimes break the rules on purpose. Often this is due to competing concerns, such as ensuring the work's long-term preservation or the audience's safety. Occasionally full compliance with the rules is so complicated or expensive that is it not feasible, and the institution is faced with a choice about whether to forgo displaying the work or to mount an imperfect display.

Since making works available to audiences is a central function of the museum, it would be undesirable to stop displaying every work for which full compliance with the rules is not feasible. We continue to show paintings and sculptures from earlier periods when they are physically damaged, if it is not possible to restore them. Though the resulting display is imperfect, it still allows the audience to go quite a distance in appreciating the work. Similar considerations guide displays of contemporary artworks: though there are limits, it is often better to show the work in an imperfect state than not. We'll look at several cases and then consider what is at stake in rule violations and how competing interests might best be balanced.

Lygia Clark, *Bichos*

The series of *Bichos* (critters) made in the 1960s by Brazilian artist Lygia Clark are sculptures made from hinged sheet metal (Figure 9.2).[12] The hinges allow the objects to take on many different configurations, and Clark designed them to be manipulated by viewers. She regarded the interactive relation as essential to the work:

> Each *Bicho* is an organic entity that fully reveals itself within its inner time of expression . . .
>
> It is a living organism, a work essentially active. A full integration, existential, is established between it and us.
>
> There is no room for passivity in the relationship that is established between the *Bichos* and us, neither from them nor from us.
>
> What happens is a body-to-body between two living entities.[13]

Figure 9.2 Lygia Clark, *Bichos*, 1960. Installation view of the exhibition Lygia Clark: A Retrospective, Itaú Cultural, São Paulo, September 1 to November 11, 2012.
Photo: Edouard Fraipont
Courtesy of The World of Lygia Clark Cultural Association

---

[12] The discussion in this section is revised from Irvin 2019.
[13] Artist's statement translated by Licia R. Olivetti and reprinted in Butler and Pérez-Oramas 2014, 160.

Throughout her career, Clark became increasingly interested in the therapeutic potential of direct interactions with objects. She designed masks and full-body costumes that were designed to alter sensory inputs and, in some cases, structure interaction with another participant. She created simple objects such as plastic bags filled with water and shells to enhance tactile awareness. For some time she ceased to call herself an artist at all and understood her practices of fabricating and manipulating objects in relation to the body of the participant as a form of therapy, though she later returned to an understanding of herself as an artist and participated in the organization of a major retrospective of her work.[14]

We see clearly from her statement about the *Bichos* that the permission for viewers to manipulate them is central to Clark's understanding of them. As critic Guy Brett says, the artist "fought a constant battle for people to be able to continue to handle and play with the sculptures after they had passed into public and private collections. They were never intended to be merely looked at" (Brett 1994, 61). However, the *Bichos* are fragile (and, at this point, extremely valuable) objects, and the institutions and private collectors who own them generally aim to preserve them. As a result, handling them during exhibition is not typically permitted.

It's important to recognize the vastness of the loss associated with this restriction. The kind of experience Clark designed for us is not available. To revisit some of her own language, we do not experience a full existential integration with the works; we are forced into passivity in our encounters with them; and a sense of the work as a living, expressive entity is not available to us. Our sensory experience of the works, when they are displayed on a pedestal or under a vitrine, is truncated: we can't feel the temperature and texture of the metal in our hands, experience the movement and flexion of the material, hear the sounds of contact between surfaces.

We can't learn about the objects' potentiality; we can't experiment with their possibilities for form and expression. We can't engage our own agency, explore our creativity and expressiveness, in our interactions with them. We can't experience what curator Luis Pérez-Oramas describes as their tendency to "question the physical certainty of the user as they are at all moments at the brink of collapsing."[15] When we look at Clark's statements about the *Bichos*, as well as the aims and priorities that are manifest throughout her work, we can recognize that a non-interactive presentation of the *Bichos* dramatically misrepresents the aesthetic experience she designed for the audience member.

---

[14] Bois 1999. For discussion of Clark's trajectory and resistance to the narrative that she abandoned art, see Brett 1994 and Butler and Pérez-Oramas 2014, especially Pérez-Oramas's own essay.

[15] Museum of Modern Art, "Lygia Clark, Bichos (as a group)," undated audio clip released in conjunction with the 2014 exhibition Lygia Clark: The Abandonment of Art, 1948–1988, https://www.moma.org/audio/playlist/181/2403.

Institutions have tried a number of strategies to restore to the viewer a sense of what it would be like to interact with the *Bichos*. The Walker Art Center has posted a short video of curator Peter Eleey discussing a 1960 *Bicho* while manipulating it, allowing us to see a few of the forms the work can take and experience the sights and sounds of the transitions between them (Figure 9.3).[16] Because Eleey is interacting with the work quite spontaneously, and begins with the *Bicho* folded down to its flattest form, some of the shapes it takes on during the very brief interaction are quite pedestrian. The video closes with a view of the work on display under a vitrine, carefully styled to show off one of the more attractive sculptural arrangements in its repertoire.

Other institutions, particularly when displaying multiple *Bichos*, have made replicas of some of the objects available for the public to manipulate. In a 2012 retrospective, the Itaú Cultural in São Paulo presented at least a dozen replicated *Bichos* for viewer manipulation, while the originals were presented on a taller pedestal just behind so that audience members could easily glance up from their play and see the objects Clark created (Figure 9.2). In 2014, the Museum of Modern Art in New York displayed three replicas along with dozens of original

Figure 9.3 Video still featuring curator Peter Eleey manipulating Lygia Clark's *Bicho*, 1960. Aluminum, 15 × 15 × 20 in. (38 × 38 × 51 cm) variable.
Collection Walker Art Center, Minneapolis, T. B. Walker Acquisition Fund, 2007
Video credit: Andy Underwood-Bultmann for Walker Art Center, 2009
Courtesy of Walker Art Center and The World of Lygia Clark Cultural Association

[16] Peter Eleey, *Bicho by Lygia Clark* (Walker Art Center, May 6, 2009), https://www.youtube.com/watch?v=7Cq2OVD7dvA.

Bichos. The original *Bichos* were grouped together on pedestals with no interaction permitted (Figure 9.4), while the manipulable replicas were displayed on low, accessible pedestals in a different gallery space. As one reviewer described it, "MoMA has appealingly recreated a number of these for us to play with, while Clark's originals wistfully look on from their sacred plinths" (Budick 2014).

To what extent do these solutions restore the viewer's ability to have an experience sufficiently close to what Clark designed for us? Simply knowing that the objects are governed by a rule for participation is a crucial first step: without such knowledge, one does not yet even understand what the works are. A video that shows someone interacting with them is a good source of information: it reveals some of the object's potential and gives a partial sense, visual and auditory, of what it would be like to manipulate them. But given Clark's understanding of the works, being able to engage one's body and agency in direct interaction is crucial. To observe someone else manipulating the objects is rather like seeing a reproduction of a painting in a catalog: it is not a sufficiently direct form of experience to give one full access to the work.

To make a few replicas available for manipulation, as the MoMA did in 2014, is helpful. Clark endorsed the display of replicas meant for manipulation alongside

Figure 9.4 Lygia Clark, *Bichos*, 1960. Installation view of the exhibition Lygia Clark: The Abandonment of Art, 1948–1988, May 10, 2014 to August 24, 2014, The Museum of Modern Art, New York.

Photographer: Thomas Griesel
Digital image © The Museum of Modern Art/Licensed by SCALA/Art Resource, NY
Courtesy of The World of Lygia Clark Cultural Association

her original objects in a 1986 retrospective of her work in Rio de Janeiro (Bois 1999). This approach allows the viewer to have the sort of experience Clark envisioned with these few objects: a body-to-body experience in which one engages one's agency, creativity, and senses and learns about the objects' expressive potential. This approach doesn't go far enough, however. It doesn't sufficiently respect the distinctiveness of the objects: it tends to suggest that three can serve as stand-ins for dozens of unique works, and that once one has experienced these, one can project oneself into experience of the others as well. But since each object has a unique profile of behaviors and potential forms, interacting with one may give us only a very vague and incomplete sense of what it would be like to interact with others.

In addition, the static displays of the original *Bichos* tend to have a triumphal quality: each has been manipulated into a dynamic, upward-reaching form that seems to have been selected on the grounds of visual appeal. But people who have manipulated these objects frequently speak of the experience in terms of collapse (as we heard from Pérez-Oramas earlier), refusal and failure:

Clunky and awkward, they refuse to lie flat but don't really stand up, either.
(Dawson 2014, n.p.)

They sort of fight back.   (Curator Connie Butler, quoted in Dawson 2014, n.p.)

The dialogue between *Bicho* and "beholder" is at times exhilarating, at times frustrating, but it always undermines the notion that one could ever be in control of the other.   (Bois 1999)

You push the *Bicho* one way and it resists, another and a whole part of the sculpture flops over, swinging around with a flap and bang.   (Randolph n.d.)[17]

[I]f one does not work with the logic of the beast's interlocking parts, it will refuse to hold the appropriate shape; indeed, more than this, it will very noisily collapse in a heap, underscoring the participant's failure to enter into a satisfactory relationship with it.   (Best 2014, 53)

When the objects are all arranged in forms that are read as sculpturally satisfying, this highlights certain aims, values, and experiences to the exclusion of others. Since only the outcomes of "successful" manipulations are shown, the fact that these configurations are the product of a challenging interaction recedes into the background. As one critic notes, "There is no hint that something surprising and lively might happen in the hand, might happen between you and the beast" (Randolph n.d.). To the extent that interaction is acknowledged at all, the displays suggest that the proper end of such interaction is to wrest from

---

[17] Randolph is speaking of an experience of manipulating replica *Bichos* in a 2014 exhibition at the Jewish Museum.

the *Bicho* the most visually appealing configuration. This kind of display implicitly reinstates the very notion of fixed form that Clark was centrally concerned to repudiate.

The Itaú Cultural's 2012 display, with a much higher ratio of replicas to originals, is more satisfying: it foregrounds the interactions, literally placing the deactivated objects in the background. This presentation suggests, correctly in my view, that Clark's *Bichos*, as artworks, are not really on display; the objects on the inaccessible pedestal are, rather, relics.

This is the crux of the matter: we are forced, I think, to conclude that a display in which one cannot interact with Clark's original *Bichos* is not, in fact, a true display of her work. Clark wanted the audience to continue to have direct access to the objects she created, not merely to copies. Thus, very few contemporary viewers have encountered true displays of Clark's work, though many more have seen the original objects and have interacted with replicas.

Is this a sign that the exhibiting institutions have done something wrong? Unless we think there is an absolute obligation to mount a true display of the work at all costs, it need not be. Many works in museum collections are rarely shown for a variety of reasons, including light sensitivity and other forms of fragility. It seems clearly better to provide the audience with some form of access to the work, even if not a full-fledged display, than to refrain from showing it altogether. Maintaining the works so that future audiences can have an experience of them, even if incomplete, seems consistent with Clark's artistic project: though she valued audience interaction with her works, she does not seem to have sanctioned the idea that the works' destruction through such interactions was welcome. A mode of exhibition that allows the viewer to imaginatively reconstruct the kind of experience that would be available from an actual display may be the best way to optimize over the competing considerations. For this reason, exhibits that allow for interaction with replicas are far better than those that simply show the original objects with no interactive component: and, as we have seen, the more replicas the better, because the individual personalities of the works are elided when a few are positioned as stand-ins for all.

In addition, greater diversity in the way the original objects are exhibited would be valuable in overcoming the tendency to default to standard visual modes of appreciating these works. Showing some of the objects flat, or in collapsed or "failed" compositions, would help audience members connect their experiences of interaction with replicas to the full range of potential of the objects.

Competing values, then, can prevent institutions from mounting true displays even of a work that it would, in principle, still be possible to display. This is an unfortunate situation, but thoughtful exhibition practices can still go a long way toward giving the public knowledge of and experiential access to such works.

Mark di Suvero, *For W. B. Yeats*

Let us now consider another sculptural work governed by a rule for participation that is not exhibited in accordance with this rule. Mark di Suvero's (1985–7) *For W. B. Yeats*, in the collection of the Nasher Sculpture Center in Dallas, is a kinetic sculpture made of Cor-Ten steel. While many of di Suvero's works are monumental in scale, this one is only about 8 feet tall. The Nasher's website mentions that the sculpture is kinetic and suggests that it "cultivates an intimacy with viewers" through its capacity for movement.[18] On the Nasher's YouTube page, there is a video of di Suvero himself activating the sculpture.[19]

When I discussed this work with Nasher curators Jed Morse and Catherine Craft, Craft mentioned that she had never seen anyone activate it. Morse replied that this was probably a good thing, since it is a massive steel sculpture and could potentially injure someone even if moving slowly. I asked them: If I activated the sculpture, would someone tell me not to? Morse replied:

> They would probably say, please don't. It's one of the tricky things about works of art when they make their way into the world, and particularly when they make their way into a museum collection. Because we're a public space, we have to be cognizant of the safety of our patrons—and also the safety of the works of art, because part of our mission is to preserve them for future generations. With works of art like that, the more they're moved around and interacted with, the quicker they deteriorate. You have to balance those competing issues.[20]

The Nasher displays the work with a placard that says, "Please do not touch the sculptures."

Clearly, given that the work is governed by a rule for participation, a display in which audience members are instructed not to touch it is non-compliant. Does this prevent it from being a true display of di Suvero's work at all, as I have argued is the case for Lygia Clark's *Bichos*? I suggest that the violation of di Suvero's rule for participation, while significant, does not play as extensive a role in undermining the viewer's grasp of the work. Certainly, to be able to set the work in motion alters one's experience quite significantly: one can feel its heft and texture, hear the sounds it makes, and have a very different kind of visual experience. The object's

---

[18] https://www.nashersculpturecenter.org/art/artists#!/artartists/f/detail/object/220/748?artist=mark-di-suvero&title=for-wb-yeats. A similar statement is made by Jan Garden Castro in an interview with the artist: "Your sculpture cultivates intimacy with the viewer through participation" (Castro 2005, 24).

[19] Nasher Sculpture Center, "Mark di Suvero Activating *For W. B. Yeats*," August 23, 2015, https://www.youtube.com/watch?v=NeKjIus0TOU.

[20] Interview with Catherine Craft and Jed Morse, Nasher Sculpture Center, July 2013.

movement, as the elements rotate around a central vertical axis and one part also swings on a horizontal axis, is surprisingly fluid, as the video mentioned above shows. Activating the sculpture can make the audience member aware of central matters that di Suvero is grappling with in the construction of his works: "I'm always conscious of balance and gravity's center point. Like a dancer or an acrobat—I'm feeling for that invisible point" (Myers 2011).

Seeing the parts continually changing in orientation relative to each other, the viewer, and the surroundings transforms the experience into one that is inherently time-based. Moreover, one is able to make choices about how one will engage with the object: Will one spin it slowly? As quickly as possible? Will one refrain from interaction, despite knowing it is permitted?

At the same time, the kinetic variability of this work is far more limited than that of the *Bichos*: it is designed to move along two axes, not to be reconfigured in a multitude of ways. In addition, while Clark's understanding of the *Bichos* and subsequent works foregrounds the event in which audience interacts with the object—and for subsequent works such as *Caminhando*, she suggests that the work just is an act by the participant and nothing more (Butler and Pérez-Oramas 2014, 25)—di Suvero's prior and subsequent production remains clearly object-based. The function of interaction, which is more predictable in the case of *For W. B. Yeats*, seems to be primarily to reveal the object's potential, not to reshape audience members' understanding of their own agency or to replace an object-centered conception of the work with an act- or event-based conception.

While a non-interactive exhibition of the original *Bichos* is not a true display of the work, then, I regard a non-interactive exhibition of *For W. B. Yeats* as a borderline case. The central experience di Suvero had in mind for us seems to be one of appreciating this specific object. We are able to do this by moving around the object, examining its forms, and, for those aware of its kinetic potential—perhaps even having seen the video of di Suvero activating it—imagining what it would be like to see it turn and swing as we encounter it. At the same time, quite significant aspects of sensory experience of the object are withheld from us, and di Suvero is fully attentive to their importance; as he notes, "there can be a kind of linked relationship of motion with a sculpture and a blossoming of the human erotic imaginative impulse" (Castro 2005).

I will not draw a conclusion about whether or not the non-interactive display is a display of di Suvero's work, but this discussion at least brings out what is at stake. Either way, we might still wonder whether the display might be made compliant. Could viewers be asked to exercise caution in activating the work, or to seek assistance from a guard if they wish to activate it? Could there be scheduled sessions of supervised interaction? Perhaps some such measure could resolve competing concerns and bring the display more fully into compliance.

Felix Gonzalez-Torres, *"Untitled"*

Felix Gonzalez-Torres's 1990 work *"Untitled"*,[21] in the collection of the Pérez Art Museum Miami, includes a stack of sheets of white paper embossed with dolphins. This work is one of Gonzalez-Torres's "stacks," which, like his candy spills, are the artist's gifts to the public: audience members are invited to remove and consume pieces of candy, or to take home sheets from the stacks. In most instances, the works are inexhaustible: staff members periodically replenish the piles of candy or stacks of prints so that audiences can continue to engage fully with the work, which thereby acquires a sort of immortality that does not consist in the conservation of a particular, precious material object.

But the stack in the Pérez collection is one of a very small number of stacks that are not replenishable. It was in a private collection, and when the collector died it was at his memorial, where people were allowed to remove sheets from the stack. But after it came to be held by the museum as a promised gift, it was presented with a vitrine, so that the stack was not physically accessible to viewers. The crucial information that the artist intended audience members to be able to take away particular sheets was presented on the wall label when the work was displayed. Two versions of the wall text describe the situation a bit differently.

> This stack piece is one of a few works in which the artist has requested that it not consist of 'endless' copies but will disappear once the individual sheets are gone.

> This stack piece is one of a very few the artist did not intend to be renewable. It consists of a finite number of sheets that cannot be replaced.[22]

The first text makes reference to the fact that the work "will disappear once the individual sheets are gone," while the second one emphasizes the fact that "the sheets...cannot be replaced," which helps to justify keeping the stack under a vitrine.

Two fundamental interests are in tension with one another: the interest in displaying the work as sanctioned by the artist and the interest in preserving the work so that future viewers will have the opportunity to engage with it. These are both, without question, very important interests. To expect that a museum would allow a work in its permanent collection simply to walk away—perhaps in the course of a few hours on a busy weekend—is to expect it to abandon a central part of its usual mission.

---

[21] I follow the artist's preference, according to the Felix Gonzalez-Torres Foundation, that "Untitled" be in quotation marks in the titles of his works.

[22] Undated documents from the object file for *"Untitled"*.

There are clear circumstances in which the museum would be obligated to do so: if Gonzalez-Torres, in selling the work directly into the museum collection, had instructed that viewers were to be permitted to take sheets from the stack unobstructed until the stack was completely depleted, and if the museum had made the acquisition in awareness of those terms, then the interest in preserving the work could not, I think, outweigh the obligation to display the work as the artist sanctioned. But in the actual case, while the artist's sanction that viewers be permitted to take sheets from the stack is clear, there was no direct negotiation with the museum; the work was previously in a private collection, and there may have been a reasonable expectation on the artist's part that in that context, the stack's depletion would take a very long time, or might never happen at all.

A display of this work involving a vitrine is clearly non-compliant. Is it a display of the work, or, instead, a presentation of an object as a relic? Let's think about what is at stake here. There are two distinct, though interrelated, clusters of questions that arise here, as in other cases of non-compliance. One cluster concerns the nature of the artwork, the nature of the display that is sanctioned by the artist, and the matter of what we should say about cases in which the display does not satisfy all of the artist's rules. Is this a case in which we should say that the artwork isn't really on display?

The second cluster concerns ethical matters. When two legitimate interests, like the interest in complying with the artist's sanction and the interest in preserving the work so that future viewers can experience it, cannot both be satisfied, what is to be done? Must the museum create a display in accordance with the artist's rules if it possibly can, even if this will result in the work's early demise? While, as I have suggested, there are some circumstances in which this is required, it is far from clear that the present case is one of those. As with Lygia Clark's *Bichos*, the art community has a strong and legitimate interest in the preservation of this work by a very important twentieth-century artist. This is particularly true because of the work's rarity: it is, as I noted earlier, one of only a very small number of non-replenishable stacks Gonzalez-Torres created. There is no obvious reason that the interest in displaying the work as the artist sanctioned should *automatically* override the interest in preserving the work so that many viewers can experience it.

Let us consider the situation now from the perspective of the viewer. The sanctioned experience is to be able to take a piece from the stack and do what one wishes with it: tape it up on one's wall, frame it, neglect it, give it away, throw it away, and so forth. This is, potentially, a pretty profound sort of experience (and would have been especially so in 1990, when Gonzalez-Torres created the work): after many visits to art museums where one is not allowed to touch anything, and where one can only marvel at objects that are far too precious for one to acquire personally, one gets to walk over to the stack, take a piece, and walk away with it. The feelings evoked by the act are complex: one feels that one is receiving a gift, but also that one is transgressing an important boundary. This may change the way one looks at other artworks as well: Is there really any reason why they must be so very precious? Must they, and the institutions that house them, withhold themselves to such a very great extent?

This sort of experience is not available to a viewer who encounters Gonzalez-Torres's stack enclosed in a vitrine. But viewers who know what the artist sanctioned can nonetheless reconstruct this experience to a great degree. Such reconstruction requires both cognition and emotionally sensitive imagination: What might I do if I were able to take a sheet from the stack, particularly in the knowledge that the sheet would never be replaced, and that I would be hastening the demise of the stack? What would I do with the sheet? How might this experience have transformed my engagement with other artworks? If I have the information about what the artist sanctioned, I am in a position to know what the work is, and also in a position to reflect plausibly—if I choose to engage in some imaginative labor—on how the work would affect me if I were able to experience a display that satisfied the artist's sanction.

Now we can return to the questions from the first cluster I mentioned: What is the work? And should we say that when the stack is presented in the vitrine the work isn't really on display? Gonzalez-Torres said of his stacks, "Without the public these works are nothing. I need the public to complete the work" (Spector 1995, 57). Of course, this statement applies most obviously to the stacks designed for endless replenishment, but it remains true that when the public is excluded from any interaction, the work cannot exhibit its characteristic behavior and is deactivated. The information that the stack is not a static object permits the viewer to imaginatively reconstruct the experience of interacting with the work. But imaginative reconstruction is not what the work was designed to produce. Thus, there are some compelling reasons to think the work is not genuinely on display: the display that has been constructed is simply too distant from the kind of display Gonzalez-Torres sanctioned.

However, as with the *Bichos*, this does not show that the museum has acted in error. There are legitimate and compelling reasons to prevent the work's rapid depletion, and the vitrine is in some ways an elegant solution. The work was made in honor of Gonzalez-Torres's lover Ross Laycock, who was dying of AIDS. It contrasts with another work made for Ross, *"Untitled" (Portrait of Ross in L.A.)*, a candy spill discussed at length in Chapter 1. While the candy spill, which is indefinitely replenishable, can be seen as emphasizing the way Ross, like all of us, lives on even after death through the effects he had on others, the work in the Pérez collection is quite different: it emphasizes the finitude of human existence, the fact that Ross himself is gone and cannot be replaced. The placement of the stack in a vitrine highlights the poignancy of this. To see the work under a vitrine is a bit like visiting a gravesite; and the resonance of this is compatible with the underlying meaning of the work.

But as with di Suvero's work, we may consider whether a more fully compliant display might be mounted, at least intermittently. Might it be possible to remove the vitrine briefly, from time to time, and allow an occasional viewer to take a sheet from the stack? This would allow some viewers to have the full experience sanctioned by the artist, and would allow others to see the effects of the gradual depletion as the stack grows smaller. The decision might be made to cease this practice when only a small number of sheets remain; and viewers seeing the work at that point would be forced to confront the issues of morality and finitude in an especially vivid way—much as mortality is more vivid in the minds of the aged than in the minds of the young, who see such a long future stretched out before them that it appears inexhaustible.

A few principles emerge from this discussion. Ideally, an institution will mount a fully compliant display. But compliance with the artist's sanction is not always the most compelling consideration: protection of the audience and safeguarding the physical integrity of the artwork's components are among the legitimate interests that might make full compliance impossible. When competing considerations arise, the institution should exercise ingenuity to mount a display that comes as close as possible to full compliance while respecting these considerations. Where the display falls short of full compliance, viewers should be informed of this so that they can imaginatively reconstruct the experience of a fully compliant display. Finally, even a display that is so far from compliant that it may not be or is not truly a display of the work can be valuable, and can realize the aim of giving viewers an experience that helps them appreciate the artist's work.

Jamelie Hassan, *Los Desaparecidos*

Jamelie Hassan's 1981 work *Los Desaparecidos* is made up of seventy-four porcelain pieces that are displayed on the floor, along with a photocopied dossier containing information about missing Argentineans believed to have been murdered by the military junta in power from 1976 to 1983 (Figure 9.5).[23] The porcelain pieces allude to white scarves, bearing the names of disappeared family members, worn on the heads of demonstrators protesting the regime (Gagnon 2000, 157).

After the National Gallery of Canada acquired and exhibited the work, the artist wrote to a curator to supply instructions for installation, since she had found the initial installation to be "somewhat cramped."[24] The new instructions sent by the artist included both text and a drawing; in particular, she indicated that the pieces of porcelain should be placed to allow "enough room to move around and

[23] The discussion in this section is revised from Irvin 2006.
[24] Jamelie Hassan, letter to Jessica Bradley, October 19, 1983.

Figure 9.5 Jamelie Hassan, *Los Desaparecidos*, 1981. Ceramic with dossier of photocopied texts, various sizes.
National Gallery of Canada, Ottawa, purchased 1983
Photo: NGC
© Jamelie Hassan

throughout the pieces. As a guide to measure ... distance from the adjacent walls and between each piece a foot step between is appropriate ... Positioning the piece in this way allows for physical accessibility into the work."[25] In the drawing, she has placed arrows between some of the porcelain pieces, presumably illustrating her instruction that enough space should be left for the viewer to step between them (Figure 9.6). Her drawing also shows the dossier placed very close to the porcelain pieces; since the dossier is to be handled by the viewer, this placement might well encourage people to move through the piece. Hassan even suggests, "Perhaps a note of explanation that the dossier can be handled and read would help in breaking down the intimidation set up by the 'do not touch' approach of an institution."[26]

Based in part on the drawing and instructions supplied by the artist, conservator Richard Gagnier of the National Gallery of Canada generated a new drawing

[25] Jamelie Hassan, "Desaparecidos: Instructions for installation," memo dated October, 1983.
[26] Ibid.

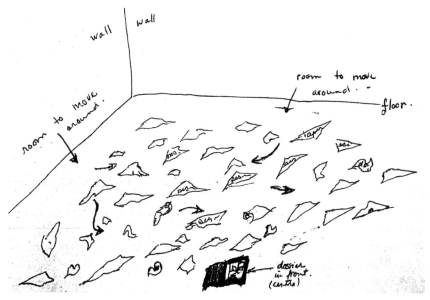

Figure 9.6 Jamelie Hassan, instructions for installing *Los Desaparecidos*, 1981.
© Jamelie Hassan
Courtesy of the artist

and set of installation instructions for a particular exhibition of the work. These instructions include the following:

> A walk way is provided all around the work by allowing about 80 cm in between the wall and the pieces... Distance in between the pieces within the triangle is about 15 to 20 cm, providing a fair amount of space in between them yet not enough to encourage [the] viewer to walk within the grouping for protection of the porcelain objects.

The conservator adds:

> When selecting the porcelain pieces for the side edges, try to choose the ones that [offer] a more flat or compact appearance leaving the ones with raised floating fold corner[s] for the interior arrangement as they are prone to multiple breaks if hurt by [the] viewer by accident.[27]

The National Gallery of Canada's object file for this work also contains photographic documentation of such breakage. Finally, in the conservator's drawing,

---

[27] Richard Gagnier, "Installation notes—Survey Results show," undated memo.

unlike the artist's, very little space seems to be allowed between the porcelain pieces, but considerable space is left between the dossier and the pieces (Figure 9.7). This has two effects: it cleanly and aesthetically frames the dossier rather than integrating it with the other elements, and it discourages viewers from believing that their access to the dossier should be translated into access to the porcelain pieces themselves.

The conservator's installation instructions depart from the artist's sanction in at least two ways. First, the conservator adds an element on which the artist is silent: he advocates placing the flatter porcelain pieces around the perimeter of the installation, whereas the artist's drawing seems to indicate a more random array, with both flat and curved pieces interspersed. Second, he is explicit in allowing less space between the pieces precisely to discourage viewer access to the interior of the work. It is clear that the work installed in accordance with the conservator's instructions will be aesthetically different from the work installed in accordance with the artist's instructions and diagram. The work will look different: with less space between the pieces, the installation will be more compact; and with the dossier framed by empty space, it will be neater.

Moreover, these differences will, as the conservator predicts, influence viewers' relationship to the work. The artist proposes the assembly of objects as something in which viewers can immerse themselves, and with which they can interact intimately. By walking among the pieces, a viewer is surrounded by them and experiences their fragility, as well as the viewer's own power to damage them and responsibility not to. Because they are still very much present in the field of vision of viewers consulting the dossier, the elements of fragmentation and fragility are

Figure 9.7 Richard Gagnier, instructions for installing Jamelie Hassan's *Los Desaparecidos*, 1981.
Courtesy of Richard Gagnier

perhaps more present to viewers' thoughts as they look over the pictures and notes in Spanish about those who have disappeared.

The experience available from an installation in accordance with the conservator's instructions is rather different. Viewers experience themselves as distanced from the piece rather than immersed in it. The piece does not invite them to enter and immerse themselves within it; instead, its very configuration becomes a subtle expression of the institutional conventions that serve to control viewers by creating a buffer zone that discourages contact. The piece thus becomes part of an institutional framework in which viewers are seen as posing a threat to artworks, which must be protected from them. Hassan's awareness of the danger that viewers will feel distanced and controlled in the museum context is indicated by her suggestion to include a note that says the dossier may be handled to "help in breaking down the intimidation set up by the 'do not touch' approach of an institution."

The factor of institutional intimidation and exclusion is crucially important here, since the piece is all about intimidation and control of a population by its government. When the viewer's experience of the piece is, even subconsciously, one of being controlled and excluded, this becomes interpretatively relevant; the artwork, rather than seeming to be a vulnerable individual response to a situation of intimidation and coercion, which the viewer is invited to share in, becomes the expression of an institutional agenda which, while comparatively benign, is still one in relation to which individuals are largely powerless.

The artist has clearly sanctioned certain aspects of the installation of the piece, and an installation in accordance with the conservator's instructions will violate that sanction in certain respects. This means that the display is not fully compliant: it will not possess the attributes that the artist sanctioned for it, and thus viewers will be misled, to some degree, about the work's nature. This, in turn, is likely to lead to misinterpretation unless the institution does something to inform viewers about the ways in which the display fails to duplicate that sanctioned by the artist.

But should we condemn the institution for failing to present the work in accordance with the artist's sanction, or the conservator for generating instructions that conflict, in some ways, with those supplied by the artist? To answer this question, it is important to note that the generation of explicit instructions is not the only mechanism for sanctioning features of the work. Selling the work into the collection of a major museum, with its established policies and conventions, is itself an act of presentation which affects what the artist has sanctioned. When Hassan sold her work to the National Gallery of Canada, she relinquished it to an institution with a clear mandate to maintain the physical integrity of the artifacts under its care. She thus implicitly sanctioned that the porcelain objects should be maintained in an unbroken state (and that measures should be taken so to maintain them) (Irvin 2005b).

Thus, we have an explicit sanction that viewers be permitted to walk among the pieces and an implicit sanction that the physical integrity of the pieces be maintained. There is nothing internally contradictory or incoherent about this pair of sanctions; if viewers could be counted on to be very careful, it would be possible to respect the two sanctions simultaneously. Given the real-world situation of a public museum, however, in which audiences and objects often literally collide, it is unreasonable to expect that the pieces will be maintained unbroken in a situation where viewers are allowed to circulate within the work: as mentioned earlier, instances of damage to the porcelain pieces due to viewer contact have already been documented.

The museum, then, is faced with a decision about how to preserve the work's material integrity while complying to the extent possible with the artist's explicit sanction. At first glance, it might seem clear that when tension arises between them, the artist's explicit sanction should take precedence over the implicit sanction, and so viewers should be allowed to circulate among the porcelain pieces regardless of the consequences. However, if Hassan had regarded the integrity of the porcelain pieces as unimportant, or had thought of them as replaceable, it was open to her to communicate this to the National Gallery of Canada, and perhaps to supply a set of replacement objects, instructions for the fabrication of replacement objects, or even a rule that breakage is integral to the work, not to be repaired. In the absence of such an action, conventional practices remain intact: practices that, in this context, imply that the appearance and integrity of the objects created by the artist are important and to be preserved in the long term, for future generations of viewers. The best way for the museum to discharge its obligation with respect to the integrity of the work may be to take special measures to prevent damage to the porcelain pieces, even if this involves less than full compliance with the artist's explicit sanction.

Thus we should not hold that the museum has an absolute obligation to exhibit the work in a way that accords with the explicit artist's sanction: if doing so results in damage which the artist has not explicitly sanctioned, future viewers may lose the possibility of encountering the work at all, or their experience of it may be even further from that sanctioned by the artist. The conservator's decision to formalize a set of rules distinct from those sanctioned by the artist is reasonable given the competing concerns at play. But it leaves the work with artificial components: just as a broken sculpture might be restored through the introduction of artificial material parts, this work's conservation has involved the introduction of artificial rules.

Here as elsewhere in art conservation, artificiality is best avoided when possible. In traditional conservation, the aim is generally to preserve the work's original materials, as fabricated by the artist. When the artist is involved in conservation decisions and endorses the replacement of material elements, the new elements are not artificial, but genuine. The same is true of changes in the rules: if the artist makes or accepts changes to the rules, the new rules are now integrated into the work. But where changes to the rules for display or conservation are made without the artist's involvement, the resulting rules are artificial to the extent that they diverge from what the artist originally specified. Artificial rules don't have the same standing as rules sanctioned by the artist when it comes to our understanding of the work: we shouldn't start to assign new meanings to it in light of rules that have been imposed by the institution. In the same way, if a sculpture is damaged and a new part is inserted whose surface is visibly distinct from the rest, we do not now understand the artwork as having meanings that derive from this discontinuity: and to the extent that it alters our experience, we attempt to bracket this effect and appreciate the work as we know it would have appeared prior to the damage.

Here is the upshot: the museum may decide, for good reason, to violate the rules sanctioned by the artist. This may even involve putting in place new rules that will be used to generate future displays, changing what the viewer experiences. But the museum does not have the authorial status to generate a new version of the work. If the artist is involved in fabricating new objects or sanctioning new rules, on the other hand, the situation is no longer one of artificiality: the artist has the authority to integrate new or altered parts into the work, generating a new version if the changes are extensive enough.

When violating some aspect of the artist's sanction is necessary, either in a specific display or in an ongoing situation where rules with an artificial element have been formalized, the institution should present the work so as to provide the viewer with an experience that is as close as possible to that designed by the artist through the sanctioning of rules. Where these experiences diverge, audience members should be made aware of this and, where possible, given the information they need to imaginatively reconstruct the experience of the work as sanctioned by the artist. In the case of *Los Desaparecidos*, the institution might fulfill this obligation by providing a wall text indicating that the artist meant for audience members to be able to circulate among the porcelain pieces. Perhaps even a video presentation of the work as seen from the point of view of a spectator walking among the pieces would be helpful. Of course, the experience of reading a wall text or viewing a video is not that of walking among the pieces. And inevitably, some of viewers' attention will be drawn to the fact that the museum is precluding them from having a full experience of the work as sanctioned by the artist. But at least, given these remedies, viewers will be able to construct a better understanding of the work, as they recognize that it is not entirely aligned with the agenda of the institution that houses it.

My aim here is not to offer a definitive solution for this work, but to outline the considerations that should come into play when there are tensions between the artist's sanction and the institution's central aims. Challenges include how to convey the relevant information about the artist's sanction without being too heavy-handed, and how to encourage viewers to imaginatively reconstruct the experience of the work as sanctioned by the artist without leading them to jeopardize the objects by physically pursuing that experience. Museum curators and conservators who routinely deal with these issues are probably in the best position to strike a balance among the various competing considerations.

Conclusion

These examples suggest that a non-compliant display may still be a display of the artwork, just as a musical performance containing a few wrong notes is still a performance of the underlying composition. Moreover, there is a threshold beyond which non-compliance may undermine the claim that the work is truly on display. It is not for me, as a philosopher, to pronounce on the specific location of this threshold, but I have made some suggestions about displays lying on both sides of the threshold and about the considerations that might lead us to think that, for instance, Mark di Suvero's *For W. B. Yeats* is on display while Lygia Clark's *Bichos* are not, even though in both cases the rule for participation sanctioned by the artist is violated.

We have also seen that the institution does not have an absolute obligation to mount a display that is maximally compliant with the artist's explicit sanctions. Both the artist's implicit sanction (when the artist was directly involved in the work's acquisition by an institution) and the institution's underlying mission to preserve artworks for future viewers can lead to legitimate choices to mount a non-compliant display, even a display that (as in the case of Clark's *Bichos*) is not an authentic display of the artwork. Providing an experience of interaction with replicas that allows that audience to reconstruct what it would have been like to interact with the original objects, while also making the originals available to view without touching, may be the optimal solution given competing claims.

When the institution systematically adopts a rule for display, conservation, or participation that conflicts with the rules the artist has sanctioned, this introduces an element of artificiality within the work, just as the introduction of an artificial material in the repair of a sculpture would do. The artificial element may help us to understand what the work was like in its original state, and it may help to preserve the work for future audiences; but audiences should be aware that it is an artificial element, not a part of the artist's communicative act that contributes to the work's expressive content.

Of course, not all viewers will read wall labels and avail themselves of supplementary information; some will simply immerse themselves in the experience of the presented display, and may draw incorrect conclusions (e.g., based on understanding the *Bichos* as static structures with a fixed configuration rather than works centrally designed for audience manipulation). There is no deep problem here: works often have the capacity to produce rewarding experiences at many different levels of engagement, and humans have a sophisticated ability to find meanings in the entities they encounter. But there is a difference between having a rewarding and meaningful experience in the presence of a display and having an experience *of the artwork* underlying the display; the former is not sufficient for the latter. Experiencing the artwork involves, among other things, a sufficient grasp, in an epistemic sense, of what the artwork in fact is. Viewers who are misled about the artwork's nature may have experiences that are well worth having. But appreciation of the work itself requires acquaintance with both its material nature and the rules shaping the display; and institutions should provide the relevant information for viewers who wish to achieve a fuller understanding of particular works.

10

Rules? Really?

Throughout this book, I've tried to build an affirmative case that many contemporary artworks are partly (or, occasionally, wholly) constituted by rules sanctioned by the artist. These rules govern matters of display, conservation, and participation. The structure of rules, much like the structure of any physical stuff that the artwork includes, may evolve, but as long as the structure at any given time has the right kind of connection to the artist's original creative activity, it still counts as an authentic state of the artwork.

I've also argued that rules are meaningful: they contribute to the expressive and thematic content of the artwork. The extent of their contribution varies: they are peripheral in some cases and central in others. Sometimes we become aware of them because they have an obvious and direct impact on our experience; other times, both we and the institution might have to do a little more work to secure our knowledge of the rules. But either way, rules, like physical objects fabricated by the artist, are among the elements that can and should contribute to our understanding and appreciation of the work. Because rules may partly or wholly constitute the work's structure and contribute to its meanings, they should be understood as an artistic medium in contemporary artworks.

But some may remain skeptical of this picture. If that's you, and you've made it this far, I salute you! This chapter is for you.

Art? Rules?

Your skepticism might come in the form of thinking that the very idea of art, especially contemporary art, being governed by rules is outrageous on its face: the whole point of art is to violate rules and explore new, ungoverned terrain. Let me first summarize the affirmative case for thinking that rules are important, and then we'll dig into some more specific skeptical worries.

1. Artists give a lot of information about rules, and museums take it seriously

Artists and art institutions treat rules as important, and this has been going on for decades. Artists see expressing rules as part of the process of creating their works, and many works come with detailed diagrams and installation instructions. Curators and conservators collect copious information about rules from artists and make decisions that are extensively shaped by what the artist has said about the rules. There is a large theoretical literature about this, developed by art critics, curators, and especially conservators.[1] The Canadian organization DOCAM, a leader in research on media artworks, says this about the process of acquiring technology-based works:

> The documentary process should include an audio or video interview with the artist to ensure that the museum has gathered the requirements regarding the eventual needs for migration support or evolving technology. It is essential that the artist provide a detailed description of the concept and meaning of his or her work, which will prove useful to avoid compromising the artist's concept or the desired behaviour of the work when having to make decisions about modifying it...[2]

Thus, we have artists supplying extensive documentation and instructions related to the display and conservation of their works, institutions placing a high priority on collecting such information, and conservators suggesting that the artists' instructions are central to the work and must be followed in order to maintain its integrity. Rules are playing a central role in the practices of creating, collecting, and displaying contemporary art.

2. Sometimes, the rules are all there is

Some works are reduced to rules, with scarcely a material component to be found. As we saw in Chapter 3, this is true of Lawrence Weiner's 2008 *A WALL BUILT TO FACE THE LAND & FACE THE WATER, AT THE LEVEL OF THE SEA*: installing the work is simply a matter of displaying some inscription of the words constituting the title, even "in lipstick on a sidewalk."[3] Artists like Weiner, Jan Dibbets, Felix Gonzalez-Torres, Sol LeWitt, Tino Sehgal, and Jana Sterbak all create works whose structure consists of rules for creating displays. Consider these remarks by Roy A. Perry, then Head of Conservation at Tate:

---

[1] See, e.g., Buskirk 2003, chapter 1; Corzo 1999; Scholte and Wharton 2011; and the work of organizations including Matters in Media Art, DOCAM, INCCA, PRACTICs, and Forging the Future (formerly the Variable Media Network). See Dekker 2013 for discussion of several projects focused on media art.

[2] Madeleine Lafaille, "Introduction" to the *Cataloguing Guide*, DOCAM, http://www.docam.ca/en/introduction.html.

[3] July 1, 2009, email from Associate Curator René Morales to Senior Curator Peter Boswell regarding a telephone discussion between Morales and Andrew Richards of Marian Goodman Gallery, which represents Weiner.

A Sol LeWitt wall drawing is re-created with new material each time it is exhibited. Each version is a unique "performance" of the work that will vary from showing to showing within the parameters set by the artist. The materials may be unique, variable, or replaceable, but in all cases [of physically ephemeral works] it is the artist's instructions that are the constant, conservable core of the work.   (Perry 1999, 44)

3. Rules affect experience

The rules expressed by the artist typically relate to matters that affect the viewer's experience, sometimes quite significantly. The rules expressed by Felix Gonzalez-Torres allow us to take and consume the candies in a display of his work. The rules expressed by Weiner have the result that displays of *A WALL BUILT* may be vastly different from one another. As we saw in Chapter 2, the rules expressed by María Fernanda Cardoso prescribe that displays of *Cemetery—Vertical Garden* will have very specific aesthetic features related to the arrangement of the artificial flowers, and that they will closely resemble each other. The fact that these rules originate with the artist and shape the viewer's experience is another strong reason to think that they are of importance in our understanding of the work.

4. We need to know about the rules to grasp their import

Seeing a display of Weiner's *A WALL BUILT* doesn't give me enough information about what the artist created. Suppose I see the words painted on the gallery wall. Is that specific appearance, with letters in that size, color, and typeface, what Weiner prescribed? Does the display have to be in paint, in which case I may want to consider Weiner's work in relation to the history of painting? The display alone can't tell me. Likewise, a display of Cardoso's work can't tell me whether the perfect fluffing of the artificial flowers is a product of her creative activity or of an installer's care and aesthetic sensibility. A display of El Anatsui's *Dusasa II* can't tell me whether Anatsui himself carefully arranged each fold and drape, or whether these were the product of others' choices. Since, as we saw in Chapter 2, allowing others to make independent choices about display is central to Anatsui's artistic project, we need to know about this rule to understand what he has done.

Seeing more displays isn't enough. Suppose that we see two or three displays of *Dusasa II* that are different from one another. There are several possible explanations:

(a). The installers screwed up. Recall, from Chapter 2, the irate viewer who wrote to the Solomon R. Guggenheim Museum to complain that installers had botched the display of Eva Hesse's *Expanded Expansion*, a conclusion he drew because the display didn't match a photograph he had seen.

(b). The artist was directly involved in configuring each display, and the only permissible displays are ones he has approved.

(c). The artist has expressed parameters that give the installers some latitude.

(d). The artist has left it completely open to others to make a wide array of choices about display, including which side is up and which side is the front.

Any collection of displays underdetermines the rules that were used to generate those displays. Each new display eliminates some possibilities for what the rules might be, but the options remain expansive. (If you want to get technical about it, there are indefinitely many possible sets of rules that could have generated any given collection of displays, no matter how large or variable. To see why, consider a collection of displays we'll call A, B, C, and D. These displays could have been generated by rules that allow only displays just like A, B, C, and D. Or they could have been generated by rules that allow A, B, C, D, and E. Or A, B, C, D, E, and F ... The possibilities are, literally, endless.)

And we can't forget the possibility that some displays are wrong due to installer error or some other condition, as discussed in Chapter 9. In these cases, the display may actively mislead us about the rules. (Displays A, B, C, and D may have been generated by rules that actually allow only A, B, and C. Or A, B, C, and E. Or ...)

If we see enough displays, we may be able to make reasonable inferences about what the rules are. But direct information about the rules is the most reliable way of knowing what they are. And if we don't know, our ability to grasp what the artist actually did in creating the work is limited. For some works, without direct knowledge of the rules we may not have a handle on what the work is at all.

5. Rules are meaningful

As we have seen throughout the book, rules, just like physical features, are a resource artists use to shape the meanings of their work in ways large and small. When Zoe Leonard refused aggressive conservation for the fruit peels in her work *Strange Fruit*, that gave her work special expressive power in relation to themes of decay and grief. If we contemplate swapping out the actual rules of a work for a different set—as we did for Felix Gonzalez-Torres's *"Untitled" (Portrait of Ross in L.A.)* in Chapter 1—we end up with a different work and a different set of possible meanings. The rule that we can eat the candies of Gonzalez-Torres's actual work is essential to what the work is at the deepest level.

6. Rules lead to better experience. (Usually. Or often. Well, at least sometimes)

Artists can screw up with rules just like they can screw up with objects. The fact that an artist sanctions custom rules does not guarantee that the work is a good work. (More on this in the next section, 'Rules Suck'.) But generally speaking, where an artist has sanctioned custom rules for their work, taking those rules into account tends to yield a richer and more satisfying experience. Considered simply as a pile of candy on the floor of a gallery, Gonzalez-Torres's *"Untitled" (Portrait of Ross in L.A.)* is inert. The thoughts it is most likely to give rise to are thoughts about the bankruptcy of contemporary art. Is the artist, and indeed the whole art world, making fun of us by dumping an ordinary pile of candy on the floor, claiming that it is art, and telling us we can't have any? But when we consider that the artist specified that we may eat the candy, this changes the terms of our engagement with the artwork and the institution, and it sheds light on the usual distance between artwork and audience, and the institution's typical role in protecting artworks from us, treating the audience as a danger rather than a collaborator. Even before we consider meanings related to the loss of Gonzalez-Torres's lover Ross to AIDS, the rules specified by the artist can be evocative and thought provoking.

7. Rules are unavoidable

The case of Gonzalez-Torres's *"Untitled" Portrait of Ross in L.A.* reveals that we can't escape from the rules in any event. To disregard the rule that the candy may be eaten is to treat the work as subject to a rule of non-participation. If María Fernanda Cardoso hadn't specified that the artificial flowers in *Cemetery* should be carefully arranged, this would mean the rules for displaying her work are different, not that there aren't any rules.

8. Rules are not new

Rules are also relevant to works from earlier historical eras. This just wasn't as obvious until artists in the twentieth century started pushing certain limits. There are rules for display, conservation, and (non-)participation for pre-twentieth-century paintings: a particular object must be displayed; it has a correct orientation with a front, back, top, and bottom; it is to be maintained, to the extent feasible, in the state it was in when it left the artist's studio; and audience members should leave it alone. Historically, these rules were largely a matter of convention, and it was straightforward to infer the rules from the work's physical features: the picture should be right side up and should face away from the wall. In the last several decades, artists have created avenues to intervene and sanction rules that subvert these conventions. But rules were there all along, even if it wasn't obvious: if you find yourself scrutinizing the lovely oil stains on the back of the canvas rather than looking at the picture, something has gone wrong (Binkley 1977).

Rules Suck

You might nonetheless think that this whole movement toward custom rules is artistically bankrupt, generating works that are boring or ugly and rewarding artists for being one-trick ponies with a mediocre trick. Working with rules gives cover to artists who don't really know how to make things, and the rules themselves often aren't that interesting either. Art made out of rules is just bad art.

I'll get my least satisfying reply out of the way first. My central point—that artists are using custom rules as an expressive resource in contemporary art, and that these rules are part of the structure of the work—doesn't depend on thinking that these are good developments or that the resulting works are good. I have tried to show that this movement toward custom rules raises interesting philosophical issues and also gives us plenty to appreciate artistically. If you disagree, this may be reason to regret the movement, but not to deny its existence.

This move toward rules sometimes brings out the worst in artists. I won't mention any names, but in museum files I have occasionally glimpsed correspondence from artists who are making rather unreasonable demands, sometimes with regard to a work that was made decades earlier. Hey, museum: now that you own my work, you must refabricate the object—originally made from styrofoam—in bronze! Otherwise I won't let you exhibit it. (This is a real case, but the materials have been changed to protect the guilty.)

Artists working with rules don't always make magnificent objects. Gerald Ferguson's *Maintenance Paintings*, as we first saw in the introduction, are "a series of paintings in a variety of sizes and colors, on standard supports, using latex paint, installed in a reasonable manner and whose reinstallation and maintenance (re-painting) is at the discretion of the end user."[4] They are not the most visually striking works: some would say they're really asking to be painted over. Ferguson wasn't trying to impress us with his painting skills. (At least, let's hope he wasn't.)

---

[4] This wording is from the label affixed to the back of each *Maintenance Painting*.

You might think that's the problem: artists should be making things that the rest of us couldn't make. But the whole point of Ferguson's project (and the projects of many other conceptual artists) is to suggest that it's equally the business of artists to think thoughts the rest of us would never have thought. Some people say that art that deals more in thoughts than in objects is bad art or isn't art at all. I won't rehash this old discussion here. I'll simply note that these developments have occurred squarely within the practices and institutions of art; that this isn't the first time in history that people have gotten mad at artists for dramatically changing how they approach art; and that it's not surprising that these developments are intriguing for some people and annoying to others.[5]

Art made from rules can be deeply repetitive in ways that some will find irritating or even anathema to the idea of art. For decades, Lawrence Weiner has made works whose medium is listed as "language + the materials referred to," and for which his main creative activity is to specify a sequence of words that is to be inscribed on a surface. When he created *A STAKE SET* in 1969, this was an expression of his new realization that the underlying concept, not the fabrication of an object, was his central concern. But one might think that by 2008, when he made *A WALL BUILT TO FACE THE LAND & FACE THE WATER, AT THE LEVEL OF THE SEA*, the point had been made, and the project of generating word sequences for display was a bit tired. Indeed, some aspects of Weiner's project evolved in a way that might be thought to acknowledge this: while he gave the institution carte blanche to inscribe the work however they wished, his own displays of his works had evolved to include striking elements of color, typeface, and design.

But, of course, art made from rules is not uniquely susceptible to repetition, as decades' worth of white paintings by Robert Ryman and date paintings by On Kawara remind us. Moreover, these projects seem designed to make the case that there is nothing inherently wrong with repetition, recalling Heraclitus's observation that you can never step into the same river twice: every white painting is a different white painting with infinite variability of hues and structural details, and every day is a different day—sometimes in its finest details, like how I saw the breeze playing on the leaves outside my window, and sometimes in its major events. If we criticize Weiner for continuing to specify strings of words, will we also dismiss poetry as a bankrupt art form?

So there is no argument here that art made from rules is invariably brilliant, or that everyone is duty-bound to enjoy the particular works or the movement they belong to. Art constituted of rules, just like any other kind of art, can be boring, clumsy, or gimmicky. But sometimes, magnificent objects come together with rules to make for a significant artistic project. I would say that this is the case for

---

[5] For discussion of related issues, see Goldie and Schellekens 2007 and 2009.

Anatsui's works governed by the nomadic aesthetic. And at other times, while the object may be perfunctory—a mere pile of candy, in the case of Gonzalez-Torres—the rules for what to do with it provide a fresh and inviting experience, support the work's expressive content, and reframe the relationship between museums and their visitors. At their best, artworks made from rules—again, just like any other kind of art—can give us new kinds of experiences and stimulate new understandings of what art is and can be.

Who Needs Rules?

I've claimed that rules are relevant both for institutions and for us: institutions should follow them, and we need to know about them. A skeptic might accept that rules are binding on professionals (who are required to treat the work correctly) but hold that audience members should just pay attention to what's in front of them: the rules are background information and not the viewer's business. After all, we often aren't given information about these rules. The wall label for a display of Anatsui's works may not mention how displays are generated; and even if it does, who wants to go around reading labels?

Many works made partly from rules, including Anatsui's, offer a lot to appreciate even if you know nothing about the rules. You're not completely missing Anatsui's point if you admire the inventive use of ordinary materials, the repetition and variability of elements, the compositional aspects of color and form. Major aspects of his project can be grasped by attending carefully to a particular display, and even more will be apparent to a viewer who notes the variability among different displays. But until you know that the variability is due to his giving control over the display to others, part of his artistic project is unavailable to you. If you're trying to recognize what the artist has done in making the work, it's important to be aware of the rule that installers can display the object however they wish.

In some cases, there is no acquaintance with the work at all if you don't know about the rules. If you don't know you're allowed to eat the candies of Gonzalez-Torres's *"Untitled" (Portrait of Ross in L.A.)*, you aren't in touch with the work, even if you have seen the pile of candies sitting there in the corner. And you can stare at one of Ferguson's *Maintenance Paintings* all day, but until you know about the rule that it can be repainted, you'll be missing the main thing Ferguson did in creating the work. There are a number of ways we might understand Ferguson's move: as a demystification of the artist and a democratization of art; as a slackerish refusal to bother making a surface that is worth preserving; as an ironic sendup of such refusals made by others;[6] as an exploration of the limits of interactivity in art; or as an invitation to loosen our grip on the idea that artmaking is principally about fabrication of objects. But we can't get in touch with any of these possibilities if we don't know about the rule for repainting.

We may disagree about the value of Ferguson's maneuver: some may think it is a clever probing of the artist's role, occurring around the time that appropriation artists like Sherrie Levine and Richard Prince were borrowing images created by others and presenting them as their own work, testing the limits of what one must do to count as an artist. Others may see the permission to repaint the work as a cheap gimmick or a thin attempt at retrieving mediocre paintings. But none of these thoughts are available to a viewer who disregards the rule: all that viewer can do is ask how satisfying a body of monochrome and neo-Expressionist paintings is in the art historical context of the early 1980s. This surely is *one* thing we should consider in assessing Ferguson's works, but we hamstring ourselves in considering their significance if we ignore the fact that, in addition to painting surfaces, Ferguson has enjoined us not to treat these surfaces as sacred.

Sometimes the role of rules is more subtle. Sigalit Landau's *Barbed Salt Lamps* can be enjoyed from a formal, visual perspective, and noting that the medium is "barbed wire and Dead Sea salt" triggers contemplation of the political import of the objects. But when the artist says that the museum should not reattach the salt if it falls off, as we saw in Chapter 1, she embraces erosion of the objects as part of the expected trajectory, and this has clear implications for interpretation. This rule alters the significance of the artist's actions in making and displaying those particular objects, and it does so in a way that contributes to the work's meaning. The institution should give us this information so we can fully grasp and appreciate the work.

Zoe Leonard acknowledges a similar effect of rules when she prescribes that the objects of *Strange Fruit* should be allowed to deteriorate: especially given the work's connection to mortality and grief, either actively embracing or actively rejecting change in the objects over time is a meaningful element of the artist's creative activity. The rules enrich our understanding of what the artist was up to and inform the meanings it makes sense to attribute to the works.

---

[6] Ferguson considered a subset of the *Maintenance Paintings* created for a 1982 exhibition "to be 'bad' painting" whose "appearance reawakens in the viewer responses conditioned by the emotionally charged Abstract Expressionism of the 50s, and, by extension, much of the Neo-expressionist activity in vogue today." Press release for the exhibition Gerald Ferguson *Maintenance Paintings*, May 18–June 5, 1982, Mercer Union: A Centre for Contemporary Art.

You Can't Make Me

Sure, maybe artists want audience members to think about and sometimes follow their rules. But why think that I, as an audience member, have any real obligation to do it? When I go into a museum or gallery, I just want to immerse myself in what's there in front of me. I don't want to read wall labels, I'm not interested in contemplating abstract structures of rules, and I should be able to find meaning and value in the display (or not) in any way I see fit. You're trying to tell me how I should experience the work, but you can't make me.

This variety of skepticism fits with the observation that from a long historical perspective, artworks are fluid: they change physically, societies adapt them to their own cultural purposes, and they have different resonance for audiences at different times. Audience members, like whole societies, may respond to works on the basis of particular encounters and idiosyncratic tendencies. Each audience member has different knowledge, tastes, background experiences, and inclinations. We encounter the display as it is and as we are, and this may involve particular desires, blind spots, preoccupations, and goals. We address the artwork in whatever way provides the most satisfying experience for us. There is no need for "shoulds" in this process.

If that's your view, you have a point. Neither I nor the artist can make you follow or pay attention to the rules. The museum might be able to make you follow some of them, but only because it has security. Fundamentally, it's up to you whether you find the rules interesting and rewarding enough to bother with. My point is that if you want to be fully in touch with what the artist has done in creating the work, you need to attend to rules and not just displays. This will matter more for some works than others. For many works, the rules remain straightforward: display this object in this orientation and then leave it alone. Viewers won't miss anything if they don't pay any special attention to the rules for works like this. But for others, custom rules are central to the artistic project.

There is a difference between appreciation of an artwork, as such, and appreciation of the affordances of life in general. It makes sense for people to seek out whatever kind of experience will satisfy them and fulfill their needs. But if I decide to watch a 3D movie without the special glasses because I enjoy the blurry overlapping images, my experience is not altogether an experience *of that movie*. If I ignore the rule of participation for Ferguson's *Maintenance Paintings* because I just like to look at objects without considering supplementary information, I will not have had a full encounter with the *Maintenance Paintings*, as the particular works Ferguson created. Now, there is no inherent human obligation to appreciate an artwork as the kind of thing that it is. But if I neglect rules that are central to the artist's project, I won't understand the work fully or be able to make well-founded claims about some aspects of it.

Even for works that make serious use of rules, the display alone may offer a great deal to appreciate. Any given hanging of Anatsui's *Dusasa II* gives us a magnificent object to enjoy. But an added layer of meaning is available if we consider Anatsui's nomadic aesthetic, which is intertwined with the rule that installers get to decide how to install the work in ways that fit their space and their aesthetic sensibilities. Do you *have* to think about this? No. But you'll understand more of what Anatsui did in making the work if you do.

Most rules in life are conditional imperatives: they only apply if you're already committed to a certain project or activity. I only have to follow the rules of basketball if I want to play basketball. The fact that I'm carrying a basketball doesn't obligate me to follow the rules of basketball; I can use the basketball to play other kinds of games or just to mess around in a way that isn't rule-bound at all. The rules of art are similar: we only have to attend to them if we're committed to the project of grasping the artist's creative activity and product. This project is not the only game in town, and if you prefer just to encounter displays as intriguing physical structures, there is no god's eye view from which I can say you're doing it wrong. To misquote Bonnie Raitt, I can't make you love rules if you don't.

In a sense, appreciation of contemporary art is a kind of cultural game. The rules can change over time, and the nature of the rules may be under debate at a particular moment. But they are ultimately a product of the social practices in which this game is embedded. Given the current state of the social practices that shape the nature of the game, rules sanctioned by the artist are the sort of thing that viewers do and should consider in their encounters with contemporary artworks.

No one is obligated to play this game: and it's fine if people want to use the objects of contemporary art to play different games, just as someone might use chess pieces to play checkers. The point of this book is, in a sense, to offer a picture of what the game is now, of what kinds of things contemporary artworks must be given their role in the game, and of moves that it makes sense for institutions and viewers to make.

I bet you do care about some kinds of rules, though. I bet you wouldn't deface the painting even if there were no guard around to stop you. And I bet you'd be irritated if it were hung upside down.

Rules? What Rules?

I've admitted that you don't have to follow or pay attention to the rules if you don't want to. But you might think that they aren't really rules at all. We saw in Chapter 9 that people violate them all the time, and that some violations are inevitable. I even admitted that sometimes it's justified for an institution to violate them. If that's true, are these really rules? Don't rules have to have some kind of force to count as rules rather than empty words?

As we saw in Chapter 7, no one has fully taken Gerald Ferguson up on his invitation to repaint his *Maintenance Paintings*, and this might make us skeptical that it is really a rule at all. The owners of the *Maintenance Paintings*, and even their creator, have treated them as precious surfaces whose allure (and perhaps monetary value) would be destroyed by an intervention on their surfaces by someone other than the artist. And this shows that simply by expressing a rule, an artist can't imbue it with full normative and motivational force. Custom rules arrive in a landscape of longstanding conventions that condition our understanding and treatment of art.

But I suggest that this is precisely what's interesting in artists' activity of expressing custom rules. By intervening in conventions and practices that have been in place for long periods, artists shed light on them and prompt our reflections on their significance. Institutions and audiences may be reluctant to give things up: the psychological and institutional force of conventions for preserving and revering material art objects is significant and not easily suspended. And that is part of what the back and forth between custom rules and longstanding conventions reveals. But frequently, a negotiation over time between these elements results in a reduction in force of conventions and a broader landscape of options that artists can pursue without resistance. As we saw in Chapter 2, early displays of Anatsui's wall-hung sculptural works often either copied previous displays or involved the objects being hung flat like traditional tapestries. It took time for institutions to acknowledge and embrace the freedom to make significant choices not traceable to Anatsui's own aesthetic preferences.

Different institutions engage with custom rules in different ways. Some institutions are more bound to conventional practices, while others are willing to enter uncharted territories. The Philadelphia Museum of Art acquired Zoe Leonard's 1992–1997 *Strange Fruit* even though there was no established plan to preserve a set of objects potentially subject to rapid deterioration, and Leonard ultimately rejected conservation measures that would have kept them suitable for display over a long period. The departure of the specific curator who had a strong commitment to the work seems to have shaped its evolution, resulting in a long period when it was not displayed. Tate acquired Tino Sehgal's 2002 work *This Is Propaganda* although Sehgal insisted that instructions for presenting the work can only be transmitted through direct person-to-person interaction, and not officially documented in any way. The Walker Art Center acquired Danh Vo's 2010 work *Tombstone for Phùng Vo* despite the fact that when Phùng Vo dies, the object will leave the Walker's grounds for a Denmark cemetery, never to return. The Kröller-Müller Museum was able to acquire Jan Dibbets's 1969 work *All shadows...* because when the work was first displayed, it was assumed that a work requiring a team of people to mount a time- and context-sensitive variable display could not be integrated into a museum collection (Stigter 2015, 106). But by 2007, the context had shifted such that the acquisition of the work into a permanent collection could be envisioned, and the Kröller-Müller had the capacity to work with the artist to define the rules constituting the work to ensure its persistence.

When artists express custom rules that get to the heart of established conventions, then, their rules may not receive immediate uptake. But over time, institutional practices may shift to accommodate them, and the associated conventions may be destabilized. Whereas preservation of objects fabricated by the artist was a well-established default practice a few decades ago, institutions are now much more likely to ask the artist which forms of intervention are permissible and whether elements of the work may be replaced. Where a work has a component that degrades more rapidly than traditional art materials, there is no longer a clear presumption that this element must be preserved rather than replaced.

Custom rules, when they are operating in resistance to longstanding conventions, have an aspirational element. Whether or not the resistance succeeds teaches us something about the institutions and context in which the artistic project is undertaken. For this reason, disregarding the rules will impoverish our encounters with many works, even if the rules don't receive—or, at least, haven't yet received—full uptake.

To return to the question of whether the rules are really for audience members or only for institutions, we can see that there is instability in the position that the rules are irrelevant for viewers while binding on those mounting displays. Some questions we ask in appreciation, such as questions about why the display is as it is, can be answered only by appealing to the rules. Suppose someone encounters a group of the *Maintenance Paintings*, including some that were painted gray on their edges by John Murchie and others that were not maintained in this way. Viewers, seeing the objects, will apply the conventional assumption that their appearance is the product of the artist's choices and direct activity. They may wonder: why did the artist choose to paint the edges of some of these works and not the others? What effect was he trying to achieve? What is the point of drawing attention to the narrow surface, perpendicular to the front of the canvas and to the wall, that we typically ignore? These are the sorts of questions that we ask in appreciating art, questions that are geared to understanding what the artist was up to. But in relation to the *Maintenance Paintings*, these questions can be answered only by recognizing that the appearances of some of the objects may be the product of Ferguson's choice to transfer his authority to others. If we ignore this fact, our theories about why the works differ in appearance will be spurious.

Is It Really the Artist's Work?

We need to attend to the rules to be in touch with the artist's work: if we don't know about Ferguson's rule allowing repainting, we've missed his whole point. But we've seen that the process of sanctioning custom rules is deeply susceptible to others' influence: curators and conservators ask questions, request details, and sometimes even push back against rules the artist is trying to establish. As we saw in Chapter 8, quite often the rules are not clearly and straightforwardly laid out in a communication by the artist: rules may need to be reconstructed based on a complex archive containing information amassed over time from a variety of sources, including but not limited to the artist. As the archive changes over time, the rational reconstruction of the rules may change as well.

We have, then, two interconnected concerns: the rules may be influenced by people other than the artist, calling into question the idea that they are genuinely outgrowths of the artist's creative activity; and they may change over time in ways that seem incompatible with saying that the work is the product of the artist's creative activity.

In Chapter 3, we discussed an interview with artist Sarah Sze by conservator Carol Mancusi-Ungaro, in which Mancusi-Ungaro asked Sze a number of questions about the conservation of her work *Migrateurs*. Interviews like this don't simply capture or secure a work as it already existed: they bring about change in the rules, and thus change in the work. When Sze offers new instructions about which elements of *Migrateurs* should be replaced and under what circumstances, this changes the rules she has sanctioned—often by making them more precise— and thus changes the work itself.

For this reason, participating in interviews and filling out questionnaires about the rules for conservation should be understood as aspects of the artist's creative activity: like object fabrication, these are parts of the process by which the work is refined and articulated. The stage of creative activity for a work with custom rules sometimes extends well into the work's life in the institution, as it typically does not for object-based works that don't employ custom rules. As van de Vall et al. (2011) note, there are several stages in the life of a complex contemporary artwork during which change is especially likely to occur. These include the first time the work is shown, the moment when it is acquired by a museum, and also moments when it is subsequently re-exhibited. This list is not exhaustive: change can happen any time the artist is invited to weigh in. Joanna Phillips, describing a new model for the documentation of time-based media art, suggests that the conception of the work's identity may need to be updated whenever there is a new installation, which may involve change in the components and parameters constituting the work (Phillips 2015, 171). The same is true of many installation artworks that don't involve time-based media (van Saaze 2013).

Should we be concerned about the influence of museum professionals on this process? Mancusi-Ungaro clearly brings specific interests and concerns derived from professional conservation to her interview with Sze. She encourages Sze to reflect on issues with materials that may arise far in the future, the prospects for display in a wide variety of potential locations, and other matters implicated in the work's longevity. The interview ranges over practical matters including cost, storage, the permissibility of replacing organic elements with artificial replicas less subject to deterioration, and the availability of staff to maintain elements of the display. Such matters may or may not have been at the forefront of the artist's thinking prior to the interview. The interviewer's questions and ideas will certainly affect what the artist says and may affect her artistic practice in the future.[7]

In my view, there is no fundamental problem here. When artists make works, their choices and actions are affected by a wide range of considerations and constraints. What techniques has the artist mastered? What kinds of paint can she afford? How large is the display space for the object? How much time does she have to complete the fabrication? Will the object be exposed to bright light or fluctuations of temperature and humidity? Successful artistic creation is, standardly, a matter of problem-solving about how to express one's artistic vision in the face of practical constraints. The artist may be influenced by others at any stage: she may engage in dialogue with other artists, teachers, curators, and critics, not to mention with her accountant. These individuals may encourage her to further articulate her own creative vision, or they may cajole her toward taking seriously artistic or practical matters she hadn't previously thought much about. None of this undermines the status of the final product: regardless of the reasons and causes that led to her putting those brushstrokes on the canvas in that way, she made the work with those features, and it is hers.

As Sze discusses in the interview, the process of making the sculptural object of *Migrateurs* was deeply affected by practical matters. She had a very short time to prepare the exhibition at the Musée d'Art moderne de la Ville de Paris, and as a result the piece has a "frenetic, desperate quality" and "slight patheticism" that Sze regards as part of its expressive import (Sze 2008). In fabricating the object, then, Sze integrated both practical and artistic interests. The object has some of its expressive content precisely because it shows signs of having been created quickly. Of course, not every artist will grapple so successfully with practical constraints like lack of time; the result might, instead, be an object that simply looks shoddy, and not in a way that we read as contributing to some valuable meaning or theme. But even where we find the work not to be successful, it is nonetheless the artist's work unless the artist renounces it.[8] The rules an artist expresses in response to a conservator's questions may be more or less successful at grappling with practical constraints and artistic considerations. But, like elements that have been

---

[7] Sanneke Stigter describes a colleague's joking concern that a question Stigter's team asked Jan Dibbets affected how the artist expressed the rules for the artwork (Stigter 2015, 112), and Stigter notes in another instance that she "might have lured the artist to setting a rule" (Stigter 2014, her translation). Matthew Gale remarks, similarly, that when you ask questions about things the artist has not previously considered, "that may affect his or her practice from then on" (M. Gale, Lake, and Sterrett 2009).

[8] As K. E. Gover (2011, 2012a) discusses, in 2006 artist Christoph Büchel walked away dissatisfied from an enormous work in progress at the Massachusetts Museum of Contemporary Art (MASS MoCA), renouncing the assemblage as his work and forbidding the museum to exhibit it.

physically fabricated, the fact that they may not be perfectly successful does not exclude them from the work. They remain expressions of the artist's creative process.

This is not to say that anything goes in interviewing, from an ethical perspective. An approach to interviewing can be manipulative, ignoring the artist's creative vision and attempting to impose a set of aesthetic and/or practical concerns that, from the artist's perspective, are alien. Especially where there is a significant power differential of the institution over the artist, interviewing can be coercive, leading the artist to make choices that depart from the goals and values she would prefer to pursue through the work. The same is true of commissions: especially for an early-career artist, the preferences of a buyer may influence the creation of the work in directions the artist would not otherwise have pursued. But the mere possibility of manipulation or coercion does not poison the fundamental processes of interviewing or commissioning. A successful interview like Mancusi-Ungaro's is designed to identify the artistic vision expressed through the work and draw out its future implications for practical matters of conservation and display. Change in the work that happens during such an interview typically brings the work further into line with the artist's vision and aims. When artists are invited to reflect on these matters, this affords an opportunity for them to offer the sort of "second-order endorsement" of their earlier creativity that Karen Gover argues is central to full artistic authorship (Gover 2018, 161).

It's only after ten minutes of asking questions about which elements of *Migrateurs* Sze would wish to restore and why that Mancusi-Ungaro begins to articulate principles that seem to be guiding Sze's decisions: she suggests that Sze is comfortable with some material elements showing signs of aging while others are replaced to look new, and that "there's nothing sentimental about the materials." Each of these proposals follows rather directly from what Sze has already said, and in articulating them Mancusi-Ungaro gives Sze the opportunity to respond by agreeing, modifying, or further elaborating. In relation to the point about sentimentality, Sze responds by saying that in securing materials for her work, "I wanted to get objects that actually had very little value. And the way I was defining value was, they had no romance to them. They had no memory. They had no history." As a result, "when you went to a work, you really felt like the value came from a kind of touch, and a kind of location, a kind of juxtaposition." Sze remarks that the interview is helpful in "clarifying [her] own process." A well-conducted interview, far from being manipulative, can help to ensure that the artist's vision and values are fully articulated to inform the long-term disposition of the work.

There is nothing inherently troubling, then, about the fact that rules for conservation may change over time and this change may be influenced by practical factors and institutional interests. But I would like to acknowledge one more pressing worry that Mancusi-Ungaro raises: when the artist is consulted on conservation of a work that was made long before, "The risk is that the artist reworks it." Of all the discussions about rules, conservation discussions are perhaps most likely to be far separated in time from the original stage of creation of the work. What if the artist attempts to impose a new artistic vision, one that doesn't coincide with the original impetus for the making of the work? Sze is sensitive to this issue. She notes, "The marks in [*Migrateurs*] and the decisions are dated for me . . . My touch has changed." She recognizes that *Migrateurs* belongs to a particular historical moment, and she is motivated to preserve the work as the product of that moment. But on a different occasion, an artist might bring an anachronistic perspective to the situation; indeed, this is something institutions periodically struggle with.[9]

Some rule changes may amount to the artist initiating new versions of the work, much as there may be multiple versions of a poem, novel, or musical work. There is no hard and fast way to distinguish alterations to a single version from changes that are sufficient to generate a new version; it's a matter of judgment. But it is legitimate for a collector or institution to resist the transformation of a collected work into a different version, just as one might resist the artist's desire to repaint a canvas already in the collection. Artists have authority to sanction the rules associated with their works during the process of creation, which may extend well beyond the moment of acquisition. But this does not imply that the artist has the indefinite authority to make changes of any nature or magnitude.

There is, then, nothing pernicious about the fact that the sanctioning of custom rules may occur over time or may be influenced by others. As Martha Buskirk notes, "authorship is based on a whole series of specific, separable, and sometimes even negotiated decisions" (Buskirk 2003, 5). But what of the fact that long after the creation of the work and without the involvement of the artist, institutions may have to make decisions about conservation and display in relation to matters that the artist could not have predicted and did not pronounce on, resulting in evolution of the work in directions the artist never intended, as we discussed at length in Chapter 8? This concern is not unique to works involving custom rules: even object-based works can develop unexpected conservation problems that require the institution to make decisions about the work's material substance that affect the nature of the work going forward. Notoriously, the plastics used by Naum Gabo in many of his sculptures in the 1920s are unstable, a fact that Gabo denied and blamed on mistreatment of the objects by their owners (Lodder 2007). During his lifetime, Gabo repaired some damaged sculptures and replicated others, offering the replications as authentic works; however, "he certainly did

---

[9] In Irvin 2006, I discuss a case in which Jana Sterbak attempted, a decade after the work's creation, to change the rules for display of her 1984–5 work *I Want You to Feel the Way I Do ... (The Dress)*, in the collection of the National Gallery of Canada. The institution pushed back on the grounds that the change undermined the original character and aesthetic quality of the work they acquired.

not allow replicas or reconstructions by others except under exceptional circum-stances" (Lodder 2007, n.p.). As a result, institutions are now faced with complex decisions about whether and how to replace or repair decayed original materials, or whether, in cases of severe deterioration, to produce careful replicas that document the original works and allow audiences to have the kind of experience Gabo originally designed (Heuman and Morgan 2007).

Over the centuries, a fabricated object may undergo extensive change as conservators work to preserve and repair it. The prospect for evolution of rules over time is similar. This process is inherent to cultural enterprises that involve attempts to preserve creative products over time: many forces affect the persist-ence of physical and informational structures. Our practices of identifying works over time already allow that an artist's work can survive a significant amount of physical evolution; evolution of rules occurs for similar reasons and can be similarly consistent with the work's persistence and attribution to the artist.

Unruly Works

What about the many works that don't involve custom rules? Even today, most new works are straightforwardly object-based, and the artist's primary creative activity is in the fabrication of the object. Most artists don't conceive their work for audience interaction, complicated variable displays, performative activity, or specialized conservation interventions. Does my account have anything to say about these works? Does the decision to focus elsewhere imply that these works are less interesting or less valuable?

Artistic practices involving object fabrication independent of rules continue to have profound importance. Created objects address us both as embodied creatures through mechanisms of perception and embodied cognition, and as thinking creatures through the vast array of narratives, emotions, and conceptual reflection that they are able to evoke. Some contemporary artworks have distinctive expres-sive potential by virtue of their inclusion of non-standard materials and non-art objects (Irvin 2020). But artworks using traditional techniques and art-making materials, and not deploying custom rules, remain powerful in their ability to engage us as thinking, feeling, sensing agents. In my choice to focus on custom rules, there is no suggestion that primarily object-based works are less interesting or less valuable.

The movement toward custom rules has a number of implications for such works. First, the choice *not* to sanction rules for one's work now has stylistic significance in a way that it did not before the turn toward custom rules. As Frank Boardman (2015) discusses in an elaboration of a position first offered by Arthur Danto (1964), as new stylistic options become available, this alters the landscape within which artists make their creative choices. Boardman lays out the case with regard to representation and abstraction: the advent of abstraction makes subsequent choices to create representational art into stylistic choices in a way that, previously, they were not.

> Leonardo did not—because he could not—make a stylistic decision when he decided to paint a representational painting that ended up the *Mona Lisa*. He could not, in fact, have consciously set out to paint a representational painting at all, in the sense that there was a choice to paint representationally separate from the choice to paint a painting.   (Boardman 2015, 444)

Representation was not a stylistic property in the sixteenth century, Boardman suggests, because "[i]f a given artistic property does not provide us with meaningful and useful distinctions among artworks, it is not stylistic and cannot help us characterize a particular style" (2015, 444).

But once abstraction in painting developed, representation became a stylistic property; and this shifts, if subtly, how we should understand subsequent representational works. An artist who makes representational paintings now is making that choice against a background of dramatically expanded options; the choice to make representational paintings manifests a certain kind of traditionalism that it would not have prior to the movement of representation into the space of stylistic properties. Representation was once perfunctory—to use Kendall Walton's (1970) terminology, it was a standard feature of paintings in Euro-American contexts, and thus was not expressive. When representation became a variable property exhibited by some paintings and not others, the very fact of being representational gained new expressive import as the product of a choice made in a context where other options were available.

Similarly, the choice to make works that are governed by longstanding conventions of display, conservation, and participation is now a substantive choice made against the background of a practice of articulating custom rules. Moreover, those conventions have lost some of their normative force: while they still serve as defaults, there is no longer such a strong presumption that works will have fixed displays, that material elements of a work will be preserved, or that audience members are precluded from participation. When these conventions were at their height, they served as part of the foundation for artistic practices, whereas now the relationship is arguably reversed: artists who make works in accordance with those conventions may be thought of as shoring up conventions whose security has been shaken.

Kara Walker's 2014 work *A Subtlety*, discussed in Chapters 4 and 7, illustrates the way that the context of custom rules has expressive import even for works not deploying such rules. Walker conceived this work, involving alluring objects made using various forms of sugar, with the conventional rule of non-participation: signs instructed audience members not to touch the objects. But she also understood that a variety of factors, including the expansion of participatory art practices that invite direct audience engagement, were likely to invite violations of the rule. The nature of these violations was of specific interest to her, and she documented them in her 2014 work *An Audience*. Creating this work with a rule of non-participation, in a historical context where the rule is no longer conventionally in force for all works, was an expressive act that contributed to thematic content having to do with race- and gender-based exploitation and with care and reverence.

Considering custom rules reveals that virtually all artworks have a degree of normativity baked into their structure. Once we note that some contemporary artworks involve custom rules for display, we are in a better position to recognize that there are rules for display of traditional representational paintings as well: they are to be hung with their representational content right side up and facing away from the wall. And one result of the advent of custom rules is that when artists engage with institutions, they are asked questions about display and conservation that prompt explicit reflection and decision about how works should be treated. Even artists who make object-based works not involving custom rules, then, are operating within the expanded landscape of options that has been generated by this movement.

Not all artists have full access to artistic practices that involve the sanctioning of custom rules. Conceiving a work that involves custom rules may require some degree of engagement with institutions and some level of power in relation to those institutions. Most people who view and purchase art are not in a position to mount variable displays, host participatory situations, or engage in complex conservation practices. They do not maintain an archive that will accompany the work and guarantee its persistence when it changes hands. Most art collectors seek out stable objects that will maintain their material integrity so that they can be engaged with and enjoyed over an extended period. Only artists who have access to institutional structures or to collectors with uncommon resources are in a position to articulate complex or demanding rules with any expectation that they will have normative force.

Even when engaging with institutions, artists may need a degree of power and institutional influence to receive uptake for works that involve the sanctioning of custom rules. As we saw in Chapter 2, it took some time for El Anatsui's custom rule that installers may exercise creative agency in displays of his works to receive full uptake. While Brad Tucker conceived his work *Drum Solos* for audience participation to play the sound component of the work, as we saw in Chapter 8, the collecting institution engaged in a negotiation that resulted in Tucker's declaring the participatory aspect optional and the institution's displaying the work without the sound component. When an artist whose work is collected by a major comprehensive art museum receives pushback in his attempt to sanction custom rules for his work, this reveals a politics of the situation that extends far beyond the artist's original creative activity.

That being said, even artists who are working outside of institutional structures may conceive of their works in ways that involve the expression of custom rules. My father, Ken Irvin, makes welded sculptures from a wide array of materials including horseshoes, railroad spikes, rebar, and parts from found objects such as old bicycle frames, engines, chainsaws, and washing machines. The works often include mechanical elements with movable parts, and he encourages those who engage with the works to pull out the oil dipstick or play with the rotor. He values the accumulation of rust patina on his works, so he displays them outdoors and encourages others to do the same.

My father is not a contemporary art consumer, and to my knowledge he has never considered the display of his works in galleries or museums. But it is a natural outgrowth of his art practice to specify that people are welcome to engage physically with his works and to specify a preferred practice related to conservation and display. The practice of articulating rules related to display, conservation, and participation, then, is not inherently embedded within institutions or restricted to artists engaging with institutions. However, institutions are a natural home for this practice and a straightforward place to study it, and they have the resources to follow rules that are more complex and demanding than those sanctioned by my father in relation to his works.

The context in which custom rules are a possibility, then, shapes the expressive import of the choices of all artists. Artists now make their creative choices in a landscape where many other artists are articulating custom rules. They are still free to decline the option of engaging with new rule-oriented practices: but this is an act of declining, not a simple background condition of their very participation in artmaking.

Conclusion

Most contemporary artworks are not immaterial, and many are extravagantly material. However, an immaterial structure of custom rules, grounded in the artist's creative activity and guaranteed by the archive, is part of the inherent nature of many contemporary artworks. The possibility of sanctioning custom rules emerged over a period of several decades as artists resisted conventional expectations, practices, and norms, and it is now a well-established strategy that artists routinely use to achieve their expressive ends. Artists and institutions discuss custom rules as inherent in the nature of artworks and recognize their expressive import as well as the need to inform audiences about them.

Not all artists use this strategy well; as with any aspect of creative activity, the sanctioning of custom rules can be done well or poorly. The ability to deploy the strategy may be affected by power relations: artists with less social or institutional power may have less leverage to sanction custom rules, which often impose a burden for collectors and institutions. And some audience members find the movement toward custom rules a pernicious departure from practices of object fabrication that they feel should be central to art.

But many artists make successful expressive use of custom rules, sometimes in concert with the fabrication of evocative material objects. When custom rules and fabricated materials are deployed together and well, the resulting works can be distinctively powerful both in their effects on us and in conveying specific themes and meanings. Attending to custom rules provides us with greater understanding of contemporary art practices and promises rewarding experiences as we access elements of the artistic project and its expressive content that would otherwise be unavailable.

Bibliography

ahtone, heather. 2019. "Considering Indigenous Aesthetics: A Non-Western Paradigm." *American Society for Aesthetics Newsletter* 39 (3): 3–5.

Antoni, Janine. 2013. "Janine Antoni in Conversation with Klaus Ottmann." Interview by Klaus Ottman. Annual Distinguished Artists' Interviews 2013, College Art Association Annual Conference, February 15, 2013. Video, 46:03. https://www.youtube.com/watch?v=MUoAO9C2yxQ.

Appiah, Kwame Anthony. 2010. "Discovering El Anatsui." In *El Anatsui: When I Last Wrote to You about Africa*, edited by Lisa Binder. 63–74. New York: Museum for African Art.

Bacharach, Sondra. 2015. "Street Art and Consent." *The British Journal of Aesthetics* 55 (4): 481–95.

Barnett, Caroline. 2015. "Purposeful Impermanence: Biodegradable Art and Its Challenge to Conservation." *Interventions* 4 (1): n.p. https://interventionsjournal.wordpress.com/2015/01/21/purposeful-impermanence-biodegradable-art-and-its-challenge-to-conservation/.

Barone, Joshua. 2016. "An Artist's Eye to the Sky, Transformed at MoMA PS1." *New York Times*, October 5. https://www.nytimes.com/2016/10/06/arts/design/james-turrell-skyspace-an-artists-eye-to-the-sky-transformed-at-moma-ps1.html.

Bass Museum of Art. 2014. "Gravity and Grace: Monumental Works by El Anatsui." https://www.bassmuseum.org/art/gravity-and-grace-monumental-works-by-el-anatsui/.

Bass, Chloë. 2014. "Adrian Piper Binds Us with Impossible Trust." *Hyperallergic*, May 21, 2014. https://hyperallergic.com/127622/adrian-piper-binds-us-with-impossible-trust/.

Baxandall, Michael. 1985. *Patterns of Intention: On the Historical Explanation of Pictures*. New Haven, CT: Yale University Press.

Becker, Carol. 2012. "Microutopias: Public Practice in the Private Sphere." In *Living as Form: Socially Engaged Art from 1991–2011*, edited by Nato Thompson. 64–71. New York: Creative Time and Cambridge, MA: The MIT Press.

Beerkens, Lydia, Paulien 't Hoen, IJsbrand Hummelen, Vivian van Saaze, Tatja Scholte, and Sanneke Stigter, eds. 2012. *The Artist Interview for Conservation and Presentation of Contemporary Art: Guidelines and Practice*. Heijningen: Jap Sam Books.

Berger, Christian, and Jessica Santone. 2016. "Documentation as Art Practice in the 1960s." *Visual Resources* 32 (3–4): 201–9.

Best, Susan. 2014. *Visualizing Feeling: Affect and the Feminine Avant-Garde*. London: I. B. Tauris & Co. Ltd.

Bicchieri, Cristina. 2005. *The Grammar of Society: The Nature and Dynamics of Social Norms*. Cambridge: Cambridge University Press.

Binder, Lisa M., ed. 2010. *El Anatsui: When I Last Wrote to You about Africa*. New York: Museum for African Art.

Binkley, Timothy. 1977. "Piece: Contra Aesthetics." *The Journal of Aesthetics and Art Criticism* 35 (3): 265–77.

Bishop, Claire. 2012. "Delegated Performance: Outsourcing Authenticity." *October* 140: 91–112.

Boardman, Frank. 2015. "Back in Style: A New Interpretation of Danto's Style Matrix." *The Journal of Aesthetics and Art Criticism* 73 (4): 441–8.

Bois, Yve-Alain. 1999. "Lygia Clark, Palais des Beaux-Arts, Paris." *Artforum* 37 (5): 116–17, 134.

Bourriaud, Nicolas. 2002. *Relational Aesthetics*, translated by Simon Pleasance and Fronza Woods with the participation of Mathieu Copeland. Dijon: Les presses du réel.

Brett, Guy. 1994. "Lygia Clark: In Search of the Body." *Art in America* 82, July: 56–63, 108.

Buchloh, Benjamin. 2016. "Surplus Sculpture." In Okwui Enwezor, Benjamin H. D. Buchloh, and Laura Hoptman, *Sarah Sze*. 39–91. London: Phaidon.

Budick, Ariella. 2014. "Lygia Clark, Museum of Modern Art, New York." *Financial Times*, May 13. https://www.ft.com/content/c1eea3c8-d6cc-11e3-b95e-00144feabdc0.

Buist, Kevin. 2011. "Art, Design, and Clocks." *Art21 Magazine*, February 1. http://magazine.art21.org/2011/02/01/art-design-and-clocks/.

Buskirk, Martha. 2003. *The Contingent Object of Contemporary Art*. Cambridge, MA: MIT Press.

Butler, Cornelia H., and Luis Pérez-Oramas. 2014. *Lygia Clark: The Abandonment of Art, 1948–1988*. New York: Museum of Modern Art.

Cabañas, Kaira. 1999. "Ana Mendieta: 'Pain of Cuba, Body I Am.'" *Woman's Art Journal* 20: 12–17.

Caldarola, Elisa. 2020. "Methodology in the Ontology of Artworks: Exploring Hermeneutic Fictionalism." In *Abstract Objects: For and Against*, edited by Concha Martínez-Vidal and José L. Falguera. 319–37. Dordrecht: Springer.

Carpio, Glenda R. 2017. "On the Whiteness of Kara Walker's *Marvelous Sugar Baby*." *ASAP/Journal* 2 (3): 551–78.

Carroll, Noël. 1992. "Art, Intention, and Conversation." In *Intention and Interpretation*, edited by Gary Iseminger. 97–131. Philadelphia, PA: Temple University Press.

Carroll, Noël. 2003. "Forget the Medium!" In *Engaging the Moving Image*. 1–9. New Haven, CT: Yale University Press.

Carroll, Noël. 2008. "Medium Specificity." In *The Philosophy of Motion Pictures*. 35–52. Malden, MA: Blackwell.

Carvajal, Doreen. 2014. "A Town, if Not a Painting, Is Restored." *New York Times*, December 15. http://www.nytimes.com/2014/12/15/world/a-town-if-not-a-painting-is-restored.html.

Castro, Jan Garden. 2005. "To Make Meanings Real: A Conversation with Mark di Suvero." *Sculpture* 24 (5). https://sculpturemagazine.art/to-make-meanings-real-a-conversation-with-mark-di-suvero/.

Cembalest, Robin. 2013. "Self-Portrait of the Artist as a Self-Destructing Chocolate Head." *ARTnews*, February 21. http://www.artnews.com/2013/02/21/chocolate-self-portraits-by-janine-antoni-and-dieter-rot/.

Chackal, Tony. 2016. "Of Materiality and Meaning: The Illegality Condition in Street Art." *The Journal of Aesthetics and Art Criticism* 74 (4): 359–70.

Chen, Adrian. 2010. "Vomit! Nudity! Litter! Marina Abramovic's Marathon Performance Ends in Chaos." *Gawker*, May 31. https://gawker.com/5551849/vomit-nudity-litter-marina-abramovics-marathon-performance-piece-ends-in-chaos.

Cooke, Lynne. n.d. "7000 Oaks." New York: Dia Art Foundation. http://web.mit.edu/allanmc/www/cookebeuys.pdf.

Corzo, Miguel Angel, ed. 1999. *Mortality, Immortality? The Legacy of 20th Century Art*. Los Angeles: The Getty Conservation Institute.

Cotter, Holland. 2010. "700-Hour Silent Opera Reaches Finale at MoMA." *The New York Times*, May 30. https://www.nytimes.com/2010/05/31/arts/design/31diva.html.

Couture, Francine. 2013. *Variations et pérennité des œuvres contemporaines?* Québec: Éditions MultiMondes, Cahiers de l'Institut du patrimoine de l'UQAM.

Cross, Susan. 2011. "Revolutionary Gardens." *American Art* 25 (2): 30–3.

D'Agostino, Fred. 1981. "The Ethos of Games." *Journal of the Philosophy of Sport* 8 (1): 7–18.

Danto, Arthur. 1964. "The Artworld." *The Journal of Philosophy* 61 (19): 571–84.

Danto, Arthur C. 2000. "Life in Fluxus." *The Nation*, December 18: 34–6. https://www.thenation.com/article/life-fluxus/.

Darley, John M., and Bibb Latané. 1968. "Bystander Intervention in Emergencies: Diffusion of Responsibility." *Journal of Personality and Social Psychology* 8 (4): 377–83.

Davidson, Maria del Guadalupe. 2016. "Black Silhouettes on White Walls: Kara Walker's Magic Lantern." In *Body Aesthetics*, edited by Sherri Irvin. 15–36. Oxford: Oxford University Press.

Davies, David. 2004. *Art as Performance*. Malden, MA: Blackwell.

Davies, David. 2005. "Medium in Art." In *The Oxford Handbook of Aesthetics*, edited by Jerrold Levinson. 181–91. Oxford: Oxford University Press.

Davies, David. 2009a. "On the Very Idea of 'Outsider Art.'" *The British Journal of Aesthetics* 49 (1): 25–41.

Davies, David. 2009b. "Rehearsal and Hamilton's 'Ingredients Model' of Theatrical Performance." *The Journal of Aesthetic Education* 43 (3): 23–36.

Davies, David. 2009c. "The Primacy of Practice in the Ontology of Art." *The Journal of Aesthetics and Art Criticism* 67 (2): 159–71.

Davies, Stephen. 1982. "The Aesthetic Relevance of Authors' and Painters' Intentions." *The Journal of Aesthetics and Art Criticism* 41 (1): 65–76.

Davies, Stephen. 2001. *Musical Works and Performances: A Philosophical Exploration*. Oxford: Oxford University Press.

Davis, Angela Y. 1981. *Women, Race and Class*. New York: Vintage.

Davis, Angela Y. 1990. *Women, Culture and Politics*. New York: Vintage.

Davis, Dána-Ain. 2014. "june 6, 2014 waiting to see a subtlety by kara walker," *Anthropology Now*, July 24, 2014. http://anthronow.com/reach/reflections-on-kara-walkers-a-subtlety-or-the-marvelous-sugar-baby.

Dawson, Jessica. 2014. "Hands-On Art at the MoMA: Please Touch the Replicas of Lygia Clark's Work." *Wall Street Journal*, May 8. https://www.wsj.com/articles/hands-on-art-at-the-moma-1399598061.

Dekker, Annet. 2013. "Enjoying the Gap: Comparing Contemporary Documentation Strategies." In *Preserving and Exhibiting Media Art: Challenges and Perspectives*, edited by Julia Noordegraf et al. 149–69. Amsterdam: Amsterdam University Press.

Dilworth, John. 2005a. "A Double Content Theory of Artistic Representation." *The Journal of Aesthetics and Art Criticism* 63 (3): 249–60.

Dilworth, John. 2005b. *The Double Content of Art*. Amherst, NY: Prometheus Books.

Dyck, John. 2014. "Perfect Compliance in Musical History and Musical Ontology." *The British Journal of Aesthetics* 54 (1): 31–47.

Eaton, A. W. 2003. "Where Ethics and Aesthetics Meet: Titian's *Rape of Europa*." *Hypatia* 18 (4): 159–88.

Elgin, Catherine Z. 1993. "Understanding: Art and Science." *Synthese* 95 (1): 13–28.

Elgin, Catherine Z. 2011. "Making Manifest: The Role of Exemplification in the Sciences and the Arts." *Principia: An International Journal of Epistemology* 15 (3): 399–413.

Enwezor, Okwui. 2011. "Cartographies of Uneven Exchange: The Fluidity of Sculptural Form: El Anatsui in Conversation with Okwui Enwezor." *Nka: Journal of Contemporary African Art* 28: 96–105.

Enwezor, Okwui. 2016. Interview with Sarah Sze. In Okwui Enwezor, Benjamin H. D. Buchloh, and Laura Hoptman, *Sarah Sze*. 7–36. London: Phaidon.

Evnine, Simon. 2016. *Making Objects and Events: A Hylomorphic Theory of Artifacts, Actions, and Organisms.* Oxford: Oxford University Press.

Evnine, Simon. 2018. "The Anonymity of a Murmur: Internet Memes." *The British Journal of Aesthetics* 58 (3): 303–18.

Feinstein, Rachel A. 2018. *When Rape Was Legal: The Untold History of Sexual Violence during Slavery.* New York: Routledge, Taylor and Francis Group.

Finkelpearl, Tom. 2013. "The Art of Social Cooperation: An American Framework." In *What We Made: Conversations on Art and Social Cooperation*, edited by Tom Finkelpearl. 1–50. Durham, NC: Duke University Press.

Fischer, Peter, Joachim I. Krueger, Tobias Greitemeyer, Claudia Vogrincic, Andreas Kastenmüller, Dieter Frey, Moritz Heene, Magdalena Wicher, and Martina Kainbacher. 2011. "The Bystander-Effect: A Meta-Analytic Review on Bystander Intervention in Dangerous and Non-Dangerous Emergencies." *Psychological Bulletin* 137 (4): 517–37.

Fraleigh, Warren P. 2003. "Intentional Rules Violations—One More Time." *Journal of the Philosophy of Sport* 30 (2): 166–76.

Frasco, Lizzie. 2009. "The Contingency of Conservation: Changing Methodology and Theoretical Issues in Conserving Ephemeral Contemporary Artworks with Special Reference to Installation Art." Undergraduate thesis, University of Pennsylvania. https://repository.upenn.edu/cgi/viewcontent.cgi?article=1004&context=uhf_2009.

Freedman, Estelle B. 2013. *Redefining Rape: Sexual Violence in the Era of Suffrage and Segregation.* Cambridge, MA: Harvard University Press.

Gagnon, Monika K. 2000. "The Possibilities of Knowledge: Jamelie Hassan." In *Other Conundrums: Race, Culture, and Canadian Art*. 157–63. Vancouver and Kamloops: Arsenal Pulp Press, Artspeak Gallery, Kamloops Art Gallery.

Gale, Matthew, Susan Lake, and Jill Sterrett. 2009. "Competing Commitments: A Discussion about Ethical Dilemmas in the Conservation of Modern and Contemporary Art." *Getty Conservation Institute Newsletter* 24 (2): n.p. http://www.getty.edu/conservation/publications_resources/newsletters/24_2/dialogue.html.

Gale, Nikita. 2013. "Q&A: Glenn Ligon Explores Sources, Influences, Racial Politics of His Text-Based Abstractions." *ArtsATL*, January 7. https://www.artsatl.org/qa/.

Gaut, Berys. 2010. *A Philosophy of Cinematic Art.* Cambridge: Cambridge University Press.

Gogarty, Larne Abse. 2014. "Art and Gentrification." *Art Monthly* 373: 7–10.

Goldie, Peter, and Elisabeth Schellekens. 2009. *Who's Afraid of Conceptual Art?* New York: Routledge.

Goldie, Peter, and Elisabeth Schellekens, eds. 2007. *Philosophy and Conceptual Art.* Oxford: Oxford University Press.

Gonzalez-Torres, Felix. 1988. Letter to Ross Laycock. In *Felix Gonzalez-Torres*, edited by Julie Ault. 155. Göttingen: Steidl Publishers, 2006.

Goodman, Nelson. 1976. *Languages of Art: An Approach to a Theory of Symbols.* Indianapolis, IN: Hackett Publishing.

Gover, K. E. 2011. "Artistic Freedom and Moral Rights in Contemporary Art: The Mass MoCA Controversy." *The Journal of Aesthetics and Art Criticism* 69 (4): 355–65.

Gover, K. E. 2012a. "Christoph Büchel v. Mass MoCA: A *Tilted Arc* for the Twenty-First Century." *The Journal of Aesthetic Education* 46 (1): 46–58.

Gover, K. E. 2012b. "What Is Humpty-Dumptyism in Contemporary Visual Art? A Reply to Maes." *The British Journal of Aesthetics* 52 (2): 169–81.

Gover, K. E. 2018. *Art and Authority: Moral Rights and Meaning in Contemporary Visual Art*. Oxford: Oxford University Press.

Grigsby, Darcy Grimaldo. 1991. "Dilemmas of Visibility: Contemporary Women Artists' Representations of Female Bodies." In *The Female Body: Figures, Styles, Speculations*, edited by Laurence Goldstein. 83–100. Ann Arbor, MI: University of Michigan Press.

Gupta, Anika. 2015. "The Art of Chocolate (and Soap)." *Smithsonian Magazine*, February 10. https://www.smithsonianmag.com/smithsonian-institution/art-chocolate-and-soap-180954180/.

Haeg, Fritz. 2008. *Edible Estates: Attack on the Front Lawn*. New York: Metropolis Books.

Haney, Craig, Curtis Banks, and Philip Zimbardo. 1973. "Interpersonal Dynamics in a Simulated Prison." *International Journal of Criminology and Penology* 1: 69–97.

Hanhardt, John G. 2003. Introduction to case study of Nam June Paik's *TV Garden*. In *Permanence through Change: The Variable Media Approach*, edited by Alain Depocas, Jon Ippolito, and Caitlin Jones. 70–7. New York: Guggenheim Museum Publications and Montreal: Daniel Langlois Foundation for Art, Science, and Technology.

Haslanger, Sally. 2003. "Persistence through Time." In *The Oxford Handbook of Metaphysics*, edited by Michael J. Loux and Dean W. Zimmerman. 315–54. Oxford: Oxford University Press.

Heuman, Jackie, and Lyndsey Morgan. 2007. "Tate Sculpture Replica Project." *Tate Papers* 8: n.p. https://www.tate.org.uk/research/publications/tate-papers/08/tate-sculpture-replica-project.

Higgins, Hannah. 2002. *Fluxus Experience*. Berkeley, CA: University of California Press.

Hölling, Hanna B. 2017. *Paik's Virtual Archive: Time, Change, and Materiality in Media Art*. Oakland, CA: University of California Press.

Hollinghurst, Alan. 1983. "Robert Mapplethorpe." In *Robert Mapplethorpe 1970–1983*. 8–17. London: Institute of Contemporary Arts.

Horodner, Stuart. 1999. Interview with Janine Antoni. *Bomb Magazine*, January 1. https://bombmagazine.org/articles/janine-antoni/.

Howarth, Sophie. 2010. "Piero Manzoni, Artist's Shit, 1961." https://www.tate.org.uk/art/artworks/manzoni-artists-shit-t07667.

Huyssen, Andreas. 1984. "Mapping the Postmodern." *New German Critique* 33: 5–52.

Hylton, Will. 2013. "How James Turrell Knocked the Art World off Its Feet." *New York Times*, June 13. http://www.nytimes.com/2013/06/16/magazine/how-james-turrell-knocked-the-art-world-off-its-feet.html.

Ippolito, Jon. 2003. "Accommodating the Unpredictable: The Variable Media Questionnaire." In *Permanence through Change: The Variable Media Approach*, edited by Alain Depocas, Jon Ippolito, and Caitlin Jones. 47–53. New York: Guggenheim Museum Publications and Montreal: Daniel Langlois Foundation for Art, Science, and Technology.

Irvin, Sherri. 2005a. "Appropriation and Authorship in Contemporary Art." *The British Journal of Aesthetics* 45 (2): 123–37.

Irvin, Sherri. 2005b. "The Artist's Sanction in Contemporary Art." *The Journal of Aesthetics and Art Criticism* 63 (4): 315–26.

Irvin, Sherri. 2006. "Museums and the Shaping of Contemporary Artworks." *Museum Management and Curatorship* 21 (2): 143–56.

Irvin, Sherri. 2008. "The Ontological Diversity of Visual Artworks." In *New Waves in Aesthetics*, edited by Kathleen Stock and Katherine Thomson-Jones. 1–19. New York: Palgrave Macmillan.

Irvin, Sherri. 2013a. "Installation Art and Performance: A Shared Ontology." In *Art and Abstract Objects*, edited by Christy Mag Uidhir. 242–62. Oxford and New York: Oxford University Press.

Irvin, Sherri. 2013b. "Sculpture." In *The Routledge Companion to Aesthetics*, 3rd ed., edited by Berys Gaut and Dominic McIver Lopes. 606–15. London: Routledge.

Irvin, Sherri. 2019. "Authenticity, Misunderstanding, and Institutional Responsibility in Contemporary Art." *The British Journal of Aesthetics* 59 (3): 273–88.

Irvin, Sherri. 2020. "Materials and Meaning in Contemporary Sculpture." In *Philosophy of Sculpture: Historical Problems, Contemporary Approaches*, edited by Kristin Gjesdal, Fred Rush, and Ingvild Torsen. 165–86. New York: Routledge.

Joyce, Erin. 2013. "Walk into a Painting's Colorscape." *Hyperallergic*, July 29. https://hyperallergic.com/74845/walk-into-a-paintings-colorscape/.

Julien, Isaac, and Kobena Mercer. 1991. "True Confessions: A Discourse on Images of Black Male Sexuality." In *Brother to Brother: New Writings by Black Gay Men*, edited by Essex Hemphill. 167–73. Washington, DC: RedBone Press.

Kania, Andrew. 2008. "The Methodology of Musical Ontology: Descriptivism and Its Implications." *The British Journal of Aesthetics* 48 (4): 426–44.

Kant, Immanuel. 1790/1987. *Critique of Judgment*. Translated by Werner S. Pluhar. Indianapolis, IN: Hackett.

Kardon, Janet. 1989. "Robert Mapplethorpe Interview." In *Robert Mapplethorpe: The Perfect Moment*. 23–29. Philadelphia, PA: Institute of Contemporary Art.

Kawaguchi, Yukiya. 2011. "A Fateful Journey: A Curator's Perspective." *Nka: Journal of Contemporary African Art* 28: 106–12.

Kennedy, Garry Neill. 2000. *Garry Neill Kennedy: Work of Four Decades = Quarante Ans de Création*. Halifax: Art Gallery of Nova Scotia.

Kester, Grant. 2004. *Conversation Pieces: Community and Communication in Modern Art*. Berkeley, CA: University of California Press.

Kosuth, Joseph. 1991. *Art After Philosophy and After: Collected Writings, 1966–1990*. Cambridge, MA: MIT Press.

Krauss, Rosalind E. 1999. "Reinventing the Medium." *Critical Inquiry* 25 (2): 289–305.

Krauss, Rosalind E. 2000. *"A Voyage on the North Sea": Art in the Age of the Post-Medium Condition*. London: Thames & Hudson.

Krauss, Rosalind E. 2006. "Two Moments from the Post-Medium Condition." *October* 116: 55–62.

Laurenson, Pip. 2004. "The Management of Display Equipment in Time-Based Media Installations." *Studies in Conservation* 49 (sup. 2): 49–53.

Laurenson, Pip. 2006. "Authenticity, Change and Loss in the Conservation of Time-Based Media Installations." *Tate Papers* 6. https://www.tate.org.uk/research/publications/tate-papers/06/authenticity-change-and-loss-conservation-of-time-based-media-installations.

Laurenson, Pip, and Vivian van Saaze. 2014. "Collecting Performance-Based Art: New Challenges and Shifting Perspectives." In *Performativity in the Gallery: Staging Interactive Encounters*, edited by Outi Remes, Laura MacCulloch, and Marika Leino. 27–41. Bern: Peter Lang.

Lebowitz, Cathy. 2009. "Propaganda in the Garden." *Art in America* 97 (9): 100–6.
Lessing, Gotthold. 1766/1984. *Laocoön*. Translated by Edward A. McCormick. Baltimore, MA: Johns Hopkins University Press.
Letts, Philip. 2015. "Against Kania's Fictionalism about Musical Works." *The British Journal of Aesthetics* 55 (2): 209–24.
Levinson, Jerrold. 1980. "What a Musical Work Is." *The Journal of Philosophy* 77 (1): 5–28.
Lewis, David. 1969. *Convention: A Philosophical Study*. Cambridge, MA: Harvard University Press.
Lewis, Richard, and Susan I. Lewis. 2013. *The Power of Art*, 3rd ed. Belmont, CA: Wadsworth.
LeWitt, Sol. 1967. "Paragraphs on Conceptual Art." *Artforum* 5 (10): 79–83.
Ligon, Glenn. 2011. "Get the Picture: An Interview with Marie de Brugerolle (1995)." In *Yourself in the World: Selected Writings and Interviews*, edited by Scott Rothkopf. 78–86. New Haven, CT: Yale University Press, in association with Whitney Museum of American Art.
Lippard, Lucy. 1973. *Six Years: The Dematerialization of the Art Object from 1966 to 1972*. Berkeley, CA: University of California Press.
Lippard, Lucy, and Adrian Piper. 1972. "Catalysis: An Interview with Adrian Piper." *The Drama Review: TDR* 16: 76–8.
Lodder, Christina. 2007. "Naum Gabo and the Quandaries of the Replica." *Tate Papers* 8: n.p. https://www.tate.org.uk/research/publications/tate-papers/08/naum-gabo-and-the-quandaries-of-the-replica.
Lopes, Dominic McIver. 2004. "Digital Art." In *The Blackwell Guide to the Philosophy of Computing and Information*, edited by Luciano Floridi. 106–16. Malden, MA: Blackwell.
Lopes, Dominic McIver. 2007. "Shikinen Sengu and the Ontology of Architecture in Japan." *The Journal of Aesthetics and Art Criticism* 65 (1): 77–84.
Lowe, Rick. 2013. "Rick Lowe: Project Row Houses at 20." *Creative Time Reports*, October 7. https://creativetimereports.org/2013/10/07/rick-lowe-project-row-houses/.
Lubow, Arthur. 2010. "Making Art out of an Encounter." *New York Times*, January 15. https://www.nytimes.com/2010/01/17/magazine/17seghal-t.html.
Mack, Abigail, Friederike Steckling, and Sara Levin. 2018. "Considering the Continuum of Care for Outdoor Kinetic Sculpture." In *Keep It Moving? Conserving Kinetic Art*, edited by Rachel Rivenc and Reinhard Bek. 138–9. Los Angeles, CA: Getty Conservation Institute.
Maitra, Ishani. 2011. "Assertion, Norms, and Games." In *Assertion: New Philosophical Essays*, edited by Jessica Brown and Herman Cappelen. 277–96. Oxford: Oxford University Press.
Margolis, Joseph. 1977. "The Ontological Peculiarity of Works of Art." *Journal of Aesthetics and Art Criticism* 36 (1): 45–50.
Marmor, Andrei. 2009. *Social Conventions: From Language to Law*. Princeton, NJ: Princeton University Press.
McCrickard, Kate. 2006. Interview with El Anastui. In *El Anatsui 2006*. n.p. New York: David Krut Publishing in association with October Gallery.
McElroy, Gil. 2006. "A Moment of Our Time: The Sculpture of Micah Lexier." *Espace Sculpture* 76: 36–8.
McLendon, Matthew. 2015. Interview with Jill Sigman. In *Re:Purposed*. 112–25. New York: Scala Arts Publishers, Inc.
Michaud, Eric. 1988. "The Ends of Art According to Beuys." Translated by Rosalind Krauss. *October* 45: 36–46.

Milgram, Stanley. 1963. "Behavioral Study of Obedience." *Journal of Abnormal and Social Psychology* 67: 371–8.

Milgram, Stanley. 1974. *Obedience to Authority: An Experimental View*. New York: HarperCollins.

Miranda, Carolina. 2014. "Q&A: Kara Walker on the Bit of Sugar Sphinx She Saved, Video She's Making." *Los Angeles Times*, October 13. http://www.latimes.com/entertainment/arts/miranda/la-et-cam-kara-walker-on-her-sugar-sphinx-the-piece-she-saved-video-shes-making-20141013-column.html.

Myers, Marc. 2011. "America's Great Man of Steel." *Wall Street Journal*, August 25. http://www.wsj.com/articles/SB10001424053111904006104576500170627655498.

Nguyen, C. Thi. 2017. "Philosophy of Games." *Philosophy Compass* 12 (8): e12426. https://doi.org/10.1111/phc3.12426.

Nguyen, C. Thi. 2019a. "Games and the Art of Agency." *Philosophical Review* 128 (4): 423–62.

Nguyen, C. Thi. 2019b. "The Right Way to Play a Game." *Game Studies* 19 (1): n.p. http://gamestudies.org/1901/articles/nguyen.

Nguyen, C. Thi. 2020. *Games: Agency as Art*. Oxford: Oxford University Press.

Nisbett, Richard E., and Timothy D. Wilson. 1977. "Telling More than We Can Know: Verbal Reports on Mental Processes." *Psychological Review* 84 (3): 231–59.

Norden, Linda. 2007. "Show and Hide: Reading Sarah Sze." In Arthur C. Danto and Linda Norden, *Sarah Sze*. 8–13. New York: Abrams.

Nussbaum, Martha C. 1992. *Love's Knowledge: Essays on Philosophy and Literature*. Oxford: Oxford University Press.

Nyman, Michael. 1999. *Experimental Music: Cage and Beyond*. Cambridge: Cambridge University Press.

Ono, Yoko. 2000. *Grapefruit: A Book of Instructions and Drawings by Yoko Ono*. New York: Simon and Schuster.

Ono, Yoko, and Hans Ulrich Obrist. 2009. "Mix a Building and the Wind: New York, November 2001." In *Yoko Ono/Hans Ulrich Obrist: The Conversation Series*. 7–31. New York: Distributed Art Publishers.

Paramana, Katerina. 2014. "On Resistance through Ruptures and the Rupture of Resistances in Tino Sehgal's These Associations." *A Journal of the Performing Arts* 19 (6): 81–9. https://www.tandfonline.com/doi/abs/10.1080/13528165.2014.985112.

Perry, Roy A. 1999. "Present and Future: Caring for Contemporary Art at the Tate Gallery." In *Mortality Immortality? The Legacy of 20th-Century Art*, edited by Miguel Angel Corzo. 41–4. Los Angeles, CA: Getty Conservation Institute.

Phillips, Joanna. 2015. "Reporting Iterations: A Documentation Model for Time-Based Media Art." In *Revista de História da Arte—Série W* 4: 168–79 http://revistaharte.fcsh.unl.pt/rhaw4/RHAw4.pdf.

Piper, Adrian. 1996. *Out of Order, Out of Sight: Selected Writings in Meta-Art 1968–1992*. Cambridge, MA: MIT Press.

Piper, Adrian. 2013. "The Humming Room." In *Do It: The Compendium*, edited by Hans Ulrich Obrist. 309. New York: Distributed Art Publishers, Inc.

Quabeck, Nina. 2019. "Intent in the Making: The Life of Zoe Leonard's 'Strange Fruit.'" *Burlington Contemporary* 1 (May): n.p. https://contemporary.burlington.org.uk/journal/journal/intent-in-the-making-the-life-of-zoe-leonards-strange-fruit.

Randolph, Sal. n.d. "The Uses of Art: Little Beasts." *The American Reader*. http://theamericanreader.com/the-uses-of-art-little-beasts/.

Reiland, Indrek. 2020. "Constitutive Rules: Games, Language, and Assertion." *Philosophy and Phenomenological Research* 100 (1): 136–59.

Riggle, Nicholas A. 2010. "Street Art: The Transfiguration of the Commonplaces." *The Journal of Aesthetics and Art Criticism* 68 (3): 243–57.

Rinehart, Richard. 2003. "Berkeley Art Museum/Pacific Film Archive." In *Permanence through Change: The Variable Media Approach*, edited by Alain Depocas, Jon Ippolito, and Caitlin Jones. 25–7. New York: Guggenheim Museum Publications and Montreal: Daniel Langlois Foundation for Art, Science, and Technology.

Rinehart, Richard. 2007. "The Media Art Notation System: Documenting and Preserving Digital/Media Art." *Leonardo* 40 (2): 181–7.

Rivenc, Rachel, and Reinhard Bek, eds. 2018. *Keep It Moving? Conserving Kinetic Art.* Los Angeles, CA: Getty Conservation Institute.

Roberts, Veronica. 2012. "'Like a musical score': Variability and Multiplicity in Sol LeWitt's 1970s Wall Drawings." *Master Drawings* 50 (2): 193–210.

Rohrbaugh, Guy. 2003. "Artworks as Historical Individuals." *European Journal of Philosophy* 11 (2): 177–205.

Rohrbaugh, Guy. 2012. "Must Ontological Pragmatism Be Self-Defeating?" In *Art and Abstract Objects*, edited by Christy Mag Uidhir. 29–48. Oxford: Oxford University Press.

Ryan, Bartholomew. 2012. "Tombstone for Phùng Vo." *Walker Art*, January 4. https://walkerart.org/magazine/tombstone-for-phung-vo.

Ryan, Gwynne. 2011. "Variable Materials, Variable Roles: The Shifting Skills Required in Contemporary Art Conservation." *AIC Objects Specialty Group Postprints* 18: 105–12.

Ryan, Gwynne. 2016. "Considerations in the Acquisition of Contemporary Art: Refabrication as a Preservation Strategy." *Studies in Conservation* 61 (sup. 2): 198–202.

Sandals, Leah. 2016. "Scream into My Sculptures, Please: Babak Golkar and the Art of Frustration." *Canadian Art*, October 5. https://canadianart.ca/interviews/babak-golkar/.

Sautman, Anne. 2003. *Self-Guide: Modern and Contemporary Art at the Art Institute.* Chicago, IL: Art Institute of Chicago.

Schefer, Jean Louis. 2000. "Art as a Tightrope Act." In Jérôme Sans and Jean Louis Schefer, *Sarah Sze.* 20–6. London: Thames & Hudson.

Scheidemann, Christian. 2010. "Is the Artist Always Right? New Approaches in the Collaboration between Artist and Conservator." Filmed June 2010 at International Symposium, Contemporary Art: Who Cares? Research and Practices in Contemporary Art Conversation, Contemporary Conservation Ltd., New York. Video, 26:16. http://vimeo.com/14603693.

Schimmel, Paul. 1999. "Intentionality and Performance Based Art." In *Mortality Immortality? The Legacy of 20th-Century Art*, edited by Miguel Angel Corzo. 135–40. Los Angeles, CA: Getty Conservation Institute.

Schjeldahl, Peter. 2011. "Unhidden Identities." *New Yorker*, March 21. https://www.newyorker.com/magazine/2011/03/21/unhidden-identities.

Scholl, Brian. 2007. "Object Persistence in Philosophy and Psychology." *Mind & Language* 22 (5): 563–91.

Scholte, Tatja, and Glenn Wharton, eds. 2011. *Inside Installations: Theory and Practice in the Care of Complex Artworks.* Amsterdam: Amsterdam University Press–RCE Publications.

Scott, Andrea. 2012. "A Million Easy Pieces." *New Yorker*, May 14. http://www.newyorker.com/magazine/2012/05/14/a-million-little-pieces.

Searle, John. 1995. *The Construction of Social Reality.* New York: Simon & Schuster.

Searle, John. 2010. *Making the Social World: The Structure of Human Civilization*. Oxford: Oxford University Press.

Shaked, Nizan. 2017. *The Synthetic Proposition: Conceptualism and the Political Referent in Contemporary Art*. Oxford: Oxford University Press.

Shenk, David. 2006. *The Immortal Game: A History of Chess*. New York: Doubleday.

Sigman, Jill. 2016. "Live, Body-Based Performance: An Account from the Field." In *Body Aesthetics*, edited by Sherri Irvin. 153–79. Oxford: Oxford University Press.

Sigman, Jill. 2017. *Ten Huts*. Middletown, CT: Wesleyan University Press.

Smith, Barry. 2003. "The Ontology of Social Reality." *American Journal of Economics and Sociology* 62 (2): 285–99.

Smith, Barry. 2008. "Searle and De Soto: The New Ontology of the Social World." In *The Mystery of Capital and the Construction of Social Reality*, edited by Barry Smith, David Mark, and Isaac Ehrlich. 35–51. Chicago, IL: Open Court.

Smith, Barry. 2012. "How to Do Things with Documents." *Rivista di Estetica* 50: 179–98.

Smith, Barry. 2014. "Document Acts." In *Institutions, Emotions, and Group Agents: Contributions to Social Ontology*, edited by Anita Konzelmann Ziv and Hans Bernhard Schmid. 19–31. Dordrecht: Springer.

Smith, Barry, and John Searle. 2003. "The Construction of Social Reality: An Exchange." *The American Journal of Economics and Sociology* 62 (1): 285–309.

Smith, Murray. 2006. "My Dinner with Noël; or, Can We Forget the Medium?" *Film Studies* 8: 140–8.

Sontag, Susan. 1977. *On Photography*. New York: Farrar, Straus and Giroux.

Spector, Nancy. 1995. *Felix Gonzalez-Torres*. New York: Guggenheim Museum.

Spring, Christopher. 2009. *African Art in Detail*. London: British Museum.

Stecker, Robert. 2003. *Interpretation and Construction: Art, Speech, and the Law*. Malden, MA: Blackwell.

Steinhauer, Jillian. 2018. "Nicholas Galanin Remixes Native American Identity at Phoenix's Heard Museum." *The Art Newspaper*, August 6. https://www.theartnewspaper.com/review/nicholas-galanin-remixes-native-american-identity-at-phoenix-s-heard-museum.

Stigh, Daniela. 2010. "Marina Abramović: The Artist Speaks." *INSIDE/OUT*, June 3. https://www.moma.org/explore/inside_out/2010/06/03/marina-abramovic-the-artist-speaks/.

Stigter, Sanneke. 2011. "How Material Is Conceptual Art? From Certificate to Materialization: Installation Practices of Joseph Kosuth's *Glass (one and three)*." In *Inside Installations: Theory and Practice in the Care of Complex Artworks*, edited by Tatja Scholte and Glenn Wharton. 69–80. Amsterdam: Amsterdam University Press–RCE Publications.

Stigter, Sanneke. 2014. "Co-produrre arte concettuale: della conservazione di un'installazione variabile di Jan Dibbets." In *Tra memoria e oblio: Percorsi nella conservazione dell'arte contemporanea*, edited by Paolo Martore. 118–41. Rome: Castelvecchi.

Stigter, Sanneke. 2015. "Co-Producing Conceptual Art: A Conservator's Testimony." *Revista de História da Arte—Série W* 4: 103–14. http://revistaharte.fcsh.unl.pt/rhaw4/RHAw4.pdf.

Stigter, Sanneke. 2016a. "Autoethnography as a New Approach in Conservation." *Studies in Conservation* 61 (sup. 2): 227–32.

Stigter, Sanneke. 2016b. *Between Concept and Material. Working with Conceptual Art: A Conservator's Testimony*. PhD diss., University of Amsterdam. https://hdl.handle.net/11245/1.535063.

Stigter, Sanneke. 2017. "A Behaviour Index for Complex Artworks: A Conceptual Tool for Contemporary Art Conservation." In *ICOM-CC 18th Triennial Conference Preprints, Copenhagen, 4–8 September 2017*, edited by J. Bridgland, art. 0910. Paris: International Council of Museums. https://www.icom-cc-publications-online.org/1744/A-behaviour-index-for-complex-artworks–A-conceptual-tool-for-contemporary-art-conservation.

Stringari, Carol. 1999. "Installations and Problems of Preservation." In *Modern Art: Who Cares?*, edited by IJsbrand Hummelen and Dionne Sillé. 272–81. Amsterdam: Foundation for the Conservation of Modern Art/Netherlands Institute for Cultural Heritage.

Stringari, Carol. 2003. "Beyond 'Conservative': The Conservator's Role in Variable Media Preservation." In *Permanence through Change: The Variable Media Approach*, edited by Alain Depocas, Jon Ippolito, and Caitlin Jones. 55–9. New York: Guggenheim Museum Publications and Montreal: Daniel Langlois Foundation for Art, Science, and Technology.

Suits, Bernard. 2014. *The Grasshopper: Games, Life and Utopia*, 3rd ed. Peterborough, Ontario: Broadview Press.

Swenson, Gene R. 1961. "Yoko Ono." *ARTnews*. September. Reprinted in "Before the Museum of Modern (F)art: On Yoko Ono's First New York Show, in 1961." *ARTnews*, June 8, 2015. http://www.artnews.com/2015/06/08/before-the-museum-of-modern-fart-on-yoko-onos-first-new-york-show-in-1961/.

Sze, Sarah. 2008. Interview with Carol Mancusi-Ungaro. Artists Documentation Program, June 30. http://adp.menil.org/?page_id=67.

Sze, Sarah. 2010. "Clarice Smith Distinguished Lecture." Smithsonian American Art Museum, November 16. https://americanart.si.edu/videos/clarice-smith-distinguished-lecture-artist-sarah-sze-154334.

Temkin, Ann. 1999. "*Strange Fruit.*" In *Mortality, Immortality? The Legacy of 20th Century Art*, edited by Miguel Angel Corzo. 45–50. Los Angeles, CA: The Getty Conservation Institute.

Thomasson, Amie L. 1999. *Fiction and Metaphysics*. Cambridge: Cambridge University Press.

Thomasson, Amie L. 2003. "Realism and Human Kinds." *Philosophy and Phenomenological Research* 67 (3): 580–609.

Thomasson, Amie L. 2006. "Debates about the Ontology of Art: What Are We Doing Here?" *Philosophy Compass* 1 (3): 245–55.

Thomasson, Amie L. 2010. "Ontological Innovation in Art." *The Journal of Aesthetics and Art Criticism* 68 (2): 119–30.

Thomasson, Amie L. 2014. *Ontology Made Easy*. Oxford: Oxford University Press.

Thompson, Nato, ed. 2012. *Living as Form: Socially Engaged Art from 1991–2011*. New York: Creative Time and Cambridge, MA: The MIT Press.

Thurman, Judith. 2010. "Walking through Walls: Marina Abramović's Performance Art." *The New Yorker*, February 28. https://www.newyorker.com/magazine/2010/03/08/walking-through-walls.

Thurman, Judith. 2012. "Marina Abramovic: The Artist Is Once Again Present." *The New Yorker*, June 18. https://www.newyorker.com/culture/culture-desk/marina-abramovic-the-artist-is-once-again-present.

Tsosie, Rebecca. 2010. "Who Controls Native Cultural Heritage? 'Art,' 'Artifacts,' and the Right to Cultural Survival." In *Cultural Heritage Issues: The Legacy of Conquest, Colonization and Commerce*, edited by James A. R. Nafziger and Ann M. Nicgorski. 1–36. Leiden: Brill Nijhoff.

Tsosie, Rebecca. 2015. "Just Governance or Just War: Native Artists, Cultural Production, and the Challenge of Super-Diversity." *Cybaris, An Intellectual Property Law Review* 6 (2): 56–106.

van de Vall, Renée. 2015. "Documenting Dilemmas: On the Relevance of Ethically Ambiguous Cases." *Revista de História da Arte—Série W* 4: 7–17. http://revistaharte.fcsh.unl.pt/rhaw4/RHAw4.pdf.

van de Vall, Renée, Hanna Hölling, Tatja Scholte, and Sanneke Stigter. 2011. "Reflections on a Biographical Approach to Contemporary Art Conservation." In *ICOM Committee for Conservation, 16th Triennial Conference, Lisbon Preprints*. 1–8. Almada: Critério-Produção Grafica, Lda.

van Ryzin, Jeanne Claire. 2017. "Paul Ramírez Jonas Asks What Constitutes a Public." *Hyperallergic*, June 29. https://hyperallergic.com/387731/paul-ramirez-jonas-asks-what-constitutes-a-public/.

van Saaze, Vivian. 2011. "Going Public: Conservation of Contemporary Artworks: Between Backstage and Frontstage in Contemporary Art Museums." *Revista de História da Arte* 8: 234–49. https://run.unl.pt/handle/10362/16705.

van Saaze, Vivian. 2013. *Installation Art and the Museum: Presentation and Conservation of Changing Artworks*. Amsterdam: Amsterdam University Press.

van Saaze, Vivian. 2015. "In the Absence of Documentation: Remembering Tino Sehgal's Constructed Situations." *Revista de História da Arte—Série W* 4: 55–63. http://revista-harte.fcsh.unl.pt/rhaw4/RHAw4.pdf.

Vogel, Susan M. 2012. *El Anatsui: Art and Life*. Munich: Prestel Publishing.

Walton, Kendall L. 1970. "Categories of Art." *The Philosophical Review* 79 (3): 334–67.

Weichbrodt, Elissa Yukiko. 2013. "Through the Body: Corporeality, Subjectivity, and Empathy in Contemporary American Art." PhD diss., Washington University of St. Louis. https://openscholarship.wustl.edu/etd/1049.

West, Carolyn M., and Kalimah Johnson. 2013. "Sexual Violence in the Lives of African American Women." VAWnet.org. National Online Resource Center on Violence Against Women, March 2013. https://vawnet.org/sites/default/files/materials/files/2016-09/AR_SVAAWomenRevised.pdf.

Wharton, Glenn. 2015. "Public Access in the Age of Documented Art." *Revista de História da Arte—Série W* 4: 180–91. http://revistaharte.fcsh.unl.pt/rhaw4/RHAw4.pdf.

Wharton, Glenn. 2016. "Reconfiguring Contemporary Art in the Museum." In *Authenticity in Transition: Changing Practices in Art Making and Conservation*, edited by Erma Hermens. 27–36. London: Archetype Publications.

Wharton, Glenn, Sharon Blank, and Claire Dean. 1995. "Sweetness and Blight: The Conservation of Chocolate Works of Art." In *From Marble to Chocolate: The Conservation of Modern Sculpture*, edited by Jackie Heuman. 162–70. London: Archetype.

Williamson, Timothy. 1996. "Knowing and Asserting." *The Philosophical Review* 105 (4): 489–523.

Wilson, Michael. 2011. "Paul Ramírez Jonas." *Artforum*, March 8. https://www.artforum.com/picks/paul-ramirez-jonas-27724.

Wollheim, Richard. 1980. *Art and Its Objects*, 2nd ed. Cambridge: Cambridge University Press.

Wolterstorff, Nicholas. 1975. "Toward an Ontology of Art Works." *Noûs* 9 (2): 115–42.

Zabunyan, Elvan. 2015. "Did You Hear What They Said? Historicity and the Present in the Works by Adrian Piper and Renée Green." Translated from the original French by Olga Grlic. *Perspective: actualité en histoire de l'art* 2015 (2): 1–8. https://journals.openedition.org/perspective/6012.

Index

262 INDEX

  compromised authenticity 184
  connection to artwork identity 25–6, 185
  historical authenticity 180
  impact of damage on 194–5
  material authenticity 70, 75–6, 146, 196
  original creative act and 34
  rule violations and 197

backstage practices 64, 142
Bag of Donuts (Gober) 142, 144
Banner, Fiona 2, 3*f*, 4, 6, 174
Barbed Hula (Landau) 16
Barbed Salt Lamps (Landau) 15–17, 15*f*, 18, 21,
  125, 234
barbed wire 15–17, 15*f*
Baselitz, Georg 2, 2*f*, 4, 18, 33, 38
Bass Museum of Art 48, 50
Becker, Carol 87
behaviors of artwork 67, 176–7
Behind the Gare St. Lazare (Cartier-Bresson) 130
Berndes, Christiane 158
Bettison, James 166
Beuys, Joseph 163
Bichos (Clark) 206–13, 206*f*, 208*f*, 209*f*
Binkley, Timothy 129
The Black Book (Mapplethorpe) 199–201
Black men, exploitation of 201–2
Black Spot (Kandinsky) 130–1
Black women, exploitation of 100–2, 148
The Bluest Eye (Morrison) 123
Boardman, Frank 243–4
body in art 10, 11, 78, 81–7, 82*f*, 85*f*, 95–102, 96*f*,
  97*f*, 100*f*, 136–7, 137*f*, 160, 161–2, 174–5,
  199–205, 206, 207
body-to-body experiences 206, 210
Bohen Foundation 203
Bourriaud, Nicolas 157
Breakfast in Bed (Cassatt) 138–9
Brett, Guy 207
British Museum 46
Brooklyn Museum 45
Büchel, Christoph 240n8
Buchloh, Benjamin 73
Buist, Kevin 153–4
Burden, Chris 83, 107, 108
Buskirk, Martha 8, 242

Campbell, Bruce 155, 155n4
candy spill artworks 10–15, 11*f*, 144–5,
  156–7, 230
Canopus (Paik) 180
(the capacity of absorption) (Hamilton)
  40–3, 42*f*

Cardoso, María Fernanda 38–9, 40*f*, 41*f*, 42–3,
  51, 228
Carroll, Noël 147–8, 172n1
Cassatt, Mary 138–9
Catalysis series of performances (Piper) 78
*Cemetery—Vertical Garden/Cementerio—jardín
  vertical* (Cardoso) 39, 40*f*, 41*f*, 42–3, 228
change in artworks over time 63, 68–75. *See also*
  damage to artwork; decay/degradation of
  objects
chaturanga game 119
chess game 119, 124
chocolate 61, 95–9, 96*f*, 97*f*
choreographic and performance huts 84–7,
  85*f*, 86*f*
Clark, Lygia 206–13, 206*f*, 208*f*, 209*f*
Coleman, James 129
Collecting Piece (Ono) 193
The Commons (Ramírez Jonas) 87–90, 88*f*
communities and status functions 22–3
community development and art 162–9
compromised authenticity 184
conceptual art 7, 7n2, 9, 54–5, 136, 192–3
Conduit (Antoni) 136–7, 137*f*, 139
configuration of artwork by installers 38–43
conservation rules
  aesthetics and 60, 74, 220
  *All shadows that occurred to me in . . . .
    . . . are marked with tape* (Dibbets) 114
  change in artworks over time 63, 68–75
  destruction of artworks 59, 66–8
  essential role of 27–8
  expression and 150–5
  instructions from 181–2
  introduction to 1, 21, 28, 59–61
  relationship of objects to artwork 75–6
  resisting conservation 61–5
  rules as medium 150–5
  sanctions/sanctioning and 65, 221–2
  scientific conservation 60
constitutive rules 29–33, 29n11, 117–22, 171–6,
  184–5
constrained variability 30, 52–4
constraints
  on artistic creation 44, 58, 140–1
  on display rules 31, 34, 52, 124, 130
  on materials/medium 140–1, 143, 240
  pragmatic constraint 24, 27
  structural constraints 115
contemporary, defined 7
contemporary art rules
  artistic authorship 238–43
  artistic choice/control 34, 115, 121, 170,
    191–4, 226–7